The Horse Traders

Also by Steven Crist

OFFTRACK

The Horse Traders

STEVEN CRIST

W · W · NORTON & COMPANY
New York   London

The text of this book is composed in Janson, with
display type set in Caslon 471 Italic. Composition and
manufacturing by The Haddon Craftsmen, Inc.
Book design by Jacques Chazaud.

First Edition

Library of Congress Cataloging-in-Publication Data
Crist, Steven
    The horse traders.
    1. Race horses. 2. Race horses—Breeding.
3. Race horses as an investment. I. Title.
SF338.C49   1986   338.4'779843'0973   86–5345

ISBN 0-393-02300-1

W. W. Norton & Company, Inc.
500 Fifth Avenue, New York, N. Y. 10110
W. W. Norton & Company Ltd.
37 Great Russell Street, London WC1B 3NU

1 2 3 4 5 6 7 8 9 0

Contents

List of Illustrations

Acknowledgments

This book would not have been possible without the collaboration of Robin Foster, who provided much of the research, conducted numerous interviews, and offered creative and editorial assistance at every stage of the manuscript.

I also am deeply indebted to Hilary Hinzmann, who initiated this book and was its caring and dedicated editor.

Bill Nack's definitive book on Secretariat, *Big Red of Meadow Stable*, was a valuable source. Finally, most of the photographs herein appear through the courtesy of *The Thoroughbred Record* and its editor, Timothy T. Capps.

The Horse Traders

You've Got to Spend a Buck

At 9:30 A.M. on the hot and dusty morning of June 17, 1981, a two-stall horse trailer pulled into the main driveway of Greentree Stud, one of a score of private commercial horse farms that line Paris Pike, a two-lane artery jutting seventeen miles northeast from Lexington, Kentucky. Travelers passing through Lexington take the pike to hook up with I–64 to Louisville and points west or I–75 to Cincinnati and points north, but vans like the one that pulled into Greentree travel it heavily from February to June each year to engage in the commerce that is the region's most glamorous industry. Their cargo is thoroughbred brood mares, making their annual visits to the stallions who reside in splendor at these stud farms. The result of these matings, and sixty thousand others like them at ten thousand farms from southern Florida to northern British Columbia, is the next year's crop of thoroughbred race horses.

This particular van carried Belle de Jour, an eight-year-old bay mare no better or worse than most of the eighty thousand or more brood mares in North America. As a racehorse, she was a disappointment, running just ten times and winning but once in a 1976 claiming race at Keystone Race Track near Philadelphia, a rock-bottom event in which every starter ran with a

$5,000 price tag on its head. Having cost $9,000 as a yearling and requiring at least $12,000 in annual upkeep, she lost money for everyone associated with her, earning just $3,163 in her career. Her pedigree, the blood of more successful forebears that runs through her, says she should have done better.

That is why she was being given a second career as a brood mare by Harry Love, a small-scale Maryland breeder who bought her, in foal, for $32,000. She was sired by Speak John, a moderately successful son of the high-class stallion Prince John. It was too early to tell if she would produce good runners. This was the fifth year that Belle de Jour had been bred, and her first foal, a three-year-old colt, was just starting to race.

When the van eased to a stop, she was backed down an unloading ramp and led about fifty yards into Greentree's breeding barn, a forty-by-fifty-foot shed. In more prosperous days, two Kentucky Derby winners and five of Greentree's seven other champions had been conceived at the farm. Greentree once was one of the most powerful and successful stables in the sport; its fortunes paralleled those of the Whitney family that owned and operated it.

The dynasty had begun with William Collins Whitney, the Yale-educated lawyer who built a fortune in transportation, tobacco, and mining. He was also connected to the Standard Oil millions through his marriage in 1869 to Flora Payne, whose brother Oliver was one of the founders of that company. Toward the end of his life, bored with his competition on Wall Street, Whitney turned to a different arena and began buying top race horses. When he died in 1904, he left half of his estate to his older son, Harry Payne Whitney.

Harry would go on to be a dominant owner in the early years of the twentieth century, campaigning such horses as Regret, the first filly to win the Kentucky Derby, in 1915, and Upset, the only horse ever to beat Man o' War. Harry also merged his own family fortune with another dynasty when he married Gertrude Vanderbilt. Their son, Cornelius Vanderbilt

Whitney, would go on to race a prominent stable for half a century in the famous Whitney silks of Eton blue and brown.

Harry's brother, Payne Whitney, had gotten only one-tenth of the William C. Whitney estate. Son had alienated father when he opposed William C.'s remarriage three and a half years after Flora Payne Whitney's death. That loyalty to his mother cost him a great deal of money, but it was handsomely rewarded by Flora's brother, Oliver Payne, who left his nephew nearly $50 million. Payne Whitney married Helen Hay, whose father, John Hay, had served as secretary of state to Presidents McKinley and Roosevelt. Helen Hay's interest in racing exceeded her husband's. She started a family racing stable, and named it Greentree after their Long Island estate. She began the farm in Red Bank, New Jersey, but in 1927 moved it to Lexington, on Paris Pike.

After Helen Hay Whitney's death in 1944, Greentree continued to thrive under the enthusiastic stewardship of her two children, John Hay "Jock" Whitney, publisher of the *New York Herald-Tribune*, and Mrs. Charles Shipman Payson, who would be the first owner of baseball's New York Mets. Such champions as Capot, Stage Door Johnny, and Late Bloomer were the sons and daughters of other Greentree horses. Each year, a new crop of homebreds would take to the racetracks, carrying Greentree's watermelon-pink and black silks and its pedigrees to further triumphs.

Now, though, the dynasty seemed slightly faded, still prominent but no longer a powerhouse, and the strength of the equine bloodlines appeared to be waning as well. Typical of the current fortunes was Buckaroo, the stallion who now was being slowly led from his stall in the stallion barn for a rendezvous in the breeding shed with Belle de Jour.

Buckaroo's pedigree reached back to the glory of Greentree. His paternal grandsire, Tom Fool, was perhaps the farm's finest horse, undefeated in ten starts during a brilliant 1953 campaign after which he was voted Horse of the Year. Buckaroo's sire, Buckpasser, was Tom Fool's best son and the Horse of the Year in 1966. On the maternal side, Buckaroo's grand-dam, Bebop II, had produced a filly named Bebopper who would give birth to the colts Stop the Music and Hatchet Man, both current Greentree stallions. Another of Bebop's daughters was Stepping High, who had produced Buckaroo.

As a racehorse, Buckaroo had been a slight but crucial cut below the best of his generation. He was a three-year-old in 1978, the same year that two brilliant colts named Affirmed and Alydar made history by dueling through the Triple Crown, and other races, far in front of their contemporaries. Buckaroo was kept away from them as much as possible. He won two moderately important races in their absence, the Saranac and the Peter Pan at Belmont Park in New York, but could get no closer to Alydar than ten lengths behind in the Whitney Stakes at Saratoga, a race named for William C. Whitney. Winless in five starts as a four-year-old, Buckaroo was retired to Greentree as a stallion.

In 1981, stud fees across the country ranged from $500 to $150,000. Affirmed cost a mare's owner $100,000, Alydar $50,000. Buckaroo commanded just $5,000, which Harry Love would pay by September 1 if Belle de Jour were successfully impregnated.

The range of stud fees reflected the hierarchy of the nation's stallions, according to their success and their fashionability. It also spoke to the range of expectations among the nation's horse breeders, from grinding out a living to hitting the jackpot by selling for millions at auction or raising a champion race horse.

At the very least, breeders hope their foals can earn, either in the sales ring or on the race track, more money than it cost to breed and raise them. In the early 1980's, a time of booming inflation at the upper reaches of the sales market, it was almost impossible to lose money breeding mares to the very top stallions. Northern Dancer's 1981 stud fee was $150,000; his foals went through American auction rings as yearlings two years later for no less than $410,000 and as much as $10.2 million.

The vast majority of American breeders, however, play with bankrolls more like Harry Love's, for which Buckaroo's 1981 stud fee of $5,000 was affordable. At this level, profits were neither guaranteed nor as potentially lucrative. Two years later, Buckaroo's yearlings would be auctioned for between $1,400 and $32,000, with more than half bringing $5,000 or less.

The difference between the high and low prices for any stallion's progeny is to some extent a function of the appearance of the foal, and the mood and luck of the auction ring on any given night. Most important, though, is the choice of the mare.

Matchmaking stallions and mares can be the result of hundreds of hours of genetic research or a simple case of a mare's owner taking whatever he can get with a limited budget. Harry Love's decision to breed Belle de Jour to Buckaroo fell somewhere in between. He liked Buckaroo's bloodlines, figured they would mesh pretty well with the mare's, and thought the price was right.

Belle de Jour was led into the breeding shed as Ken Walling, the Greentree groom who cared for Buckaroo, walked the bay horse over from his home in the stallion barn just 50 yards away. Orchestrating a mating between thousand-pound animals with flailing hooves and fiery temperaments is a delicate business. Mares have been killed in the process, and handlers have suffered disabling kicks and blows. Some horses are reluctant breeders and have to be coaxed and tricked like the famous pandas in the National Zoo. Though his owners will not admit it, farmworkers say that one famous stallion, perhaps a romantic at heart, only gets in the mood when he hears the sound of rain on the roof, so handlers train a hose on the shingles when he enters the shed. Another needs a virtual harem to get aroused, so a bevy of mares is lined up in front of him before he is led to the intended partner.

"Buckaroo was a little awkward at first," Ken Walling remembers. "When we first started with him, when he went up on a mare he would slap her around with his front feet pretty good, but once we bred him a few times he stopped that and went about his business."

Belle de Jour had been a bit of a problem as a breeder herself, having failed in her previous mating with Buckaroo to "catch," or get pregnant, on the first cover. This delay made her a "late breeder." The first try had taken place on May 29, just nineteen days before, and this was the tail end of the breeding season.

This mating was without incident. Belle de Jour was led into the breeding shed, her head facing the wall. A leather strap wrapped around her left front ankle bent the leg up, leaving her balanced on three legs and preventing her from kicking out with a back leg. A twitch, a loop of rope on the end of a pole, was twisted around her upper lip to help the groom control her. Her tail was wrapped in a bandage so that another groom could hold it up and out of the way.

Ken Walling led Buckaroo over to Belle de Jour. Another groom stood by to help steady the stallion if he started to lose his balance after mounting the mare. Buckaroo calmly stepped up to do his job. He mounted Belle de Jour, whose front leg was let down to help her support the stallion's weight. Buckaroo thrust somewhat awkwardly, and the mating was over in under three minutes. Buckaroo was romping in his paddock within five minutes. Belle de Jour was led back to the van and headed home to nearby Forest Retreat Farm, where Harry Love boarded his mares during the breeding season.

The Greentree crew may repeat this process six to ten times a day during the busiest parts of the breeding season, which runs from February through June. Breeders want foals to be born as soon as possible after January 1, because that is the official birthdate for all horses in the Northern Hemisphere regardless of their actual date of birth. A horse born in the latter part of the year would be at a disadvantage as a two-year-old and three-year-old, racing against horses six months older or more. Each stallion usually works just once a day. Buckaroo would be bred to about 35 mares over four and a half months and then take the rest of the year off.

The scene was repeated about sixty thousand times across the country in the late winter and spring months of 1981. Some of the mares had to be covered a second or third time to get in foal, and some of them were barren after repeated attempts. Some aborted their foals, others delivered stillborns or deformed offspring that did not survive more than a few days or weeks.

Eleven months after the matings, in the winter and spring of 1982, the foals were born, and by the following fall 38,523 of them were registered with The Jockey Club as thoroughbreds, the newest entries in a stud book that goes back to eighteenth-century England, and farther yet to three Arabian stallions the British had imported to the Isles and bred to their own sturdy mares. Every thoroughbred born in North America must be registered with The Jockey Club, which oversees breeding and racing in this country, or it is considered a non-horse, a non-thoroughbred, and it may not race or be bred.

Of the 38,523 foals of 1982, 8,705 were sold at public auction as yearlings, 87 of them for $500 or less and one for $10.2 million. Some of them were sent overseas to race, some were injured before they ever saw a racetrack, and almost half will never win a race. About 90 percent of them will end up costing their owners more money than they ever recover.

For most of the twenty thousand farm owners, horse owners, and professional breeders who orchestrated the matings, there was one glittering dream behind it all, a dream that would come true for only thirteen of the 38,523—thus overcoming odds of almost 3,000 to 1. They are the thirteen semifinalists in a pageant of speed and luck that will crown one of them, quite possibly making him worth literally more than his thousand-pound weight in gold.

♦   ♦   ♦

For those foals of 1982, that moment arrives at 5:30 P.M. on May 4, 1985, at Churchill Downs in Louisville, Kentucky. Most days, the spire-topped racetrack attracts no more than eight thousand people. But on the first Saturday in May, National Guardsmen line the inside rail of the track, and fifty thousand fans have been waiting in the infield all day. Another fifty thousand watch from the stands. The University of Louisville Marching Band plays "My Old Kentucky Home," and the few who are not already on their feet rise to join the song.

This is the day of the Kentucky Derby, the one horse race of which everyone in the country has heard, the only race that interests people who are not racing fans, and the race that everyone in the industry wants to win more than any other. Its attraction rests on tradition, not logic. In fact, almost everything is wrong with the race.

The first problem is location. Louisville, while only seventy-five miles from Lexington, center of the breeding industry, otherwise has no importance in the sport. No prominent owners or breeders live there, and the town is the site of no significant racing outside of the Derby and its sister race for fillies a day earlier, the Oaks. The sport, as conducted at Churchill Downs the rest of the year, is second rate and of no consequence to anyone but the participants and bettors. Kentucky itself, while the cradle of most of the Derby horses, is an inconvenient place for them to contest the most important race of their careers. Most Derby horses have to be flown or vanned from New York, California, or Florida, where the nation's important racing, and most prep races for the Derby, are conducted.

Churchill Downs itself is no jewel of a racetrack; it is simply very big, with massive stands and facilities to accommodate the once-a-year crowd. Its cramped paddock, where the horses are saddled up and mounted by jockeys before going to the track, often unsettles horses and many top colts have lost the race in nervous sweat before they reached the starting gate. Even the racing surface itself, rolled to an unusually hard consistency that makes for fast times but can be tough on horses, is unpopular with many trainers.

The conditions of the race, 1¼ miles for three-year-olds carrying 126 pounds on the first Saturday in May, are peculiar. The distance and date roughly imitate England's older Epsom Derby, but over there horses are trained slower to race longer. In this country, none of the horses has raced as far as the Derby distance before and few have carried the weight.

Despite it all, the Derby is America's race, thanks to the relentless promotional tactics of one Kentuckian, Matt Winn. As a boy in 1875, Winn stood on the seat of his father's flatbed grocery truck and watched Aristides win the first Derby. Twenty-seven years later, Winn, by then a successful merchant tailor, was part of a group of local businessmen who bought Churchill Downs for $40,000. The Derby was a mediocre race attracting local horses, and Winn, who was now the track's general manager, wanted to make it into an American spectacle. He did it by wooing the powerful eastern stables and sportswriters from New York, the power base of the racing world, with free travel and accommodations. In 1915, the eastern racing gentry and press were on hand to see Harry Payne Whitney's Regret become the first filly ever to win the race.

"I do not care if she never wins another race or if she never starts in another race," said an instantly converted Whitney. "She has won the greatest race in America and I am satisfied."

Winn credited Regret's victory with making the Derby a classic, saying, "It was Harry Payne Whitney, not I, who put the Kentucky Derby on the map."

The Derby quickly began to attract better horses, and its place was secured in 1930 when a colt named Gallant Fox won the Derby, the Preakness Stakes at Pimlico Race Course, and the Belmont Stakes at Belmont Park on Long Island in New

York. Sportswriters made an ad hoc decision that Gallant Fox had won a "Triple Crown," giving him that honor and extending it retroactively to Sir Barton, who had won the same three races in 1919. It was just the kind of semiorganized championship needed by racing, which was thriving nationwide but as a scattered group of gambling arenas, not as a unified sport. Baseball had its World Series, boxing its heavyweight championship, and now racing had the Triple Crown.

After Gallant Fox, the Crown was won six times in the next eighteen years, and its winners were recognized as the sport's stars. The success of the series had made the Derby the key race of the year, for while the Crown could only be won in the Belmont, the Derby winner was the only horse who had a chance to go all the way, so all eyes were on him at least through the Preakness. The first four months of the racing year became a countdown to the Derby, and every race preceding it was a test or unofficial semifinal for a berth in the field. From the moment a foal hit the ground, his breeder could not help thinking of him as a possible Derby winner.

The hoopla of Derby Day has grown with the importance of the race, blossoming into an American institution. Packing into the Churchill Downs infield on Derby Day may be second only to crowding the beaches of Ft. Lauderdale as a collegiate rite of spring. The streets surrounding the Downs are filled with students in sleeping bags for two nights before the race, and local honky-tonks and strip joints do half their annual business during Derby Week.

The grandstand seats have become so scarce that they now are inheritable family possessions. The upper reaches of the track, the prime clubhouse seats and posh dining rooms where a table for eight fetches $10,000, are reserved for celebrities and power brokers in and outside of the sport.

The gathering for this 111th Derby in 1985 included the usual rich and famous. President Ronald Reagan had reluctantly passed it up for security reasons, but his predecessors and rivals were there en masse, not only former presidents Gerald R. Ford and Jimmy Carter, but also unsuccessful presidential candidates Walter Mondale and Gary Hart. Seven United States Senators and at least twenty House representatives completed the Washington contingent. Martha Layne Collins, Kentucky's governor, was there to present the winning trophy, along with four former Kentucky governors. The Hollywood crowd included Elizabeth Taylor and John Forsythe, and the sports world sent Stan Musial, Jim Brown, and Paul Hornung. As for the racing world, everybody who mattered or thought he did was there.

Elsewhere at the track, the other half was betting, swilling mint juleps, and occasionally climbing over one another to get a view of the track. Those in the infield could see little but cared less. They were there for the sake of being there. For many, the main event was the annual game of trying to smuggle liquor past the prying security guards at the gate. Contraband hooch was confiscated from the insides of hollowed-out hero sandwiches and spiked baby bottles.

Police would make eighty-eight arrests in the course of this day, including twenty-two for felony drug possession or selling, thirty-three for misdemeanors such as possession of marijuana and public intoxication, nineteen for ticket scalping, two for bookmaking, one for trespassing, and one for possession of stolen credit cards. Still, police would call it a preppier, better-behaved crowd than in most years. Although the tunnel to the infield was as usual lined with frat boys chanting and holding up signs exhorting women to "Show Us Your Tits," there was nothing so violent or scandalous as the 1983 storming of a women's rest room.

Now, as even many of the infielders rose to join the singing of "My Old Kentucky Home"— the anachronistic line about "the darkies are gay" has been officially sanitized to "the people are gay"—thirteen of the 38,523 foals of 1982, now three-year-olds of 1985, walked onto the track. The thought had flashed through the mind of every breeder on the night his foal was born that maybe this would be a Derby horse, but now only thirteen had made it. A horse can only run in the Derby once, when he is three.

Churchill Downs crackles with the anticipation of what will be over in a few minutes. It is not so much the prospect of a good horse race that the Derby crowd looks forward to, as that of instant history.

The horses walk onto the track in the order of post positions drawn by lot two days earlier, but most of the fans run them down from long odds to short, briefly pondering the longshots before moving on to the logical contenders and favorites. While every horse in the field had won a race of some significance in his career, many of the starters in every Derby do not belong in the race. Their owners enter them anyway, for reasons ranging from the desire for a complimentary box seat (even at the cost of the $20,000 entry fee for the race), to simple vanity or the childlike belief in storybook endings.

There have been such endings: Genuine Risk, a filly who had never beaten colts, flashed through the stretch in 1980 to join Regret as the only female Derby winners; Canonero II, a mystery horse from Venezuela, won by 3¼ lengths in 1971; Hoop Jr., the first horse bought by a fledgling owner named Fred Hooper, came through in 1945. These stories are lure and lore enough for many owners with a colt of the right age and the faintest credentials. The bettors, though, studying the past performances in the *Daily Racing Form*, know to ignore these horses. In any other race during the year, it is rare for more than one horse to go off at 50–1 or higher. In this Derby, five of the thirteen runners are 90–1 or more.

This baker's dozen of Derby horses represents almost as many different ways of getting to the starting gate of the Kentucky Derby. Of the thirteen, six are racing for their breeders and seven have been purchased, either privately or at public auction, at prices ranging from $12,500 to $625,000.

Floating Reserve, the longest of the longshots at 134–1, had already been beaten soundly by several of the horses he was in against today. But owner Robert Hibbert and trainer Joe Manzi felt they had a Derby start and maybe a victory owed them. Two years earlier their colt Roving Boy, the best two-year-old in the country in 1982, was injured in a training accident four months before Derby Day. When he healed up and returned in the fall, he won a moderate stakes race but then freakishly broke both hind legs a stride past the wire and had to be given a lethal injection as he lay on the track. Floating Reserve, like Roving Boy, had been born at Hibbert's leased 100-acre farm in Lexington. Hibbert, a retired oil producer from Houston who got into racing in the mid-1950s, had gotten both colts by sending mares he owned to Olden Times, a stallion who had never sired a star but was known for getting consistent and useful runners.

Encolure, going to the post at 103–1, is a son of Riva Ridge, the 1972 Derby winner. Encolure is one of five colts in this field to have been sired by a stallion standing at Claiborne Farm, the lush nursery in Paris, Kentucky, at the end of Paris Pike, that houses more of the sport's glamorous stallions than any other spread. Claiborne, presided over by 35-year-old Seth Hancock, had not thought highly of Encolure; the farm sold him as a yearling for $25,000 to W.E. Trotter II, an investor who resold him at a sale of two-year-olds in Louisiana for $65,000 to Fred Porter, a rancher and plumber. Porter died in May of 1984 without seeing his new purchase race, and the colt was now going to the post in the name of his widow, Margaret.

I Am The Game, the first Derby starter for King T. Leatherbury, one of the sport's most successful owner-trainers, is going off at 101–1. Leatherbury is the perennial king of the Maryland circuit, most of his success coming from buying problem horses from other owners, and winning races by dropping them in class. Few horsemen resemble accountants as much as Leatherbury, who runs his stable on paper from an office in the barn and leaves the actual care and training of the animals to his assistants. The operation does not lend itself to the careful development of a Derby colt, but Leatherbury's success in racing's trenches had given him the money and freedom to shoot a little higher. I Am The Game had caught his eye in a sales ring, and Leatherbury and a partner spent $255,000 for him as a yearling.

Fast Account, by the Claiborne stallion Private Account, is racing for his breeder, W. R. Hawn, a native Texan whose involvement in the sport stretches back more than thirty years. He now bases his racing stable in California and boards his mares in Kentucky. Hawn's colt has been getting beaten pretty regularly on the west coast this year, and the crowd is dismissing him at 92–1.

Irish Fighter, 41–1 in the betting, had been purchased at a yearling auction for $60,000 by Izzy Proler, a Texas industrialist, and a partner, J. R. Straus. The latter died when Irish Fighter was a two-year-old, and Proler was watching this Derby on television from a hospital bed, recovering from surgery for a heart problem.

Skywalker is California's top hope for this Derby, but that distinction still leaves him at 17–1. At least he has the most owners rooting for him: more than twenty investors who are partners in the Oak Cliff syndicate, headed by a thirty-eight-year-old oilman named Tom Tatham. Oak Cliff had begun buying up breeding stock at auctions and dispersal sales in 1981, and one of the first horses it had bred was Skywalker.

After these six longshots come four moderately regarded runners who have decent records and some chance of beating the favorites.

Stephan's Odyssey has been sent out by the only trainer to have won the race before, Woody Stephens. The seventy-one-year-old Kentuckian won with Swale in 1984 and with Cannonade a decade earlier. In 1976, Stephens had been sought out by Henryk de Kwiatkowski, a Polish immigrant who had made a fortune selling reconstructed aircraft and wanted to put a lot of the profits into horses. The first horse he bought was a two-year-old half sister to Cannonade named Kennelot, plunking down $287,000, and one of the dozens of yearlings he later bought was a colt named Danzig for $310,000. De Kwiatkowski had purchased such well-bred stock that he now had become a breeder himself, and Stephan's Odyssey was the product of Danzig and Kennelot.

Tank's Prospect, next in the betting at 11–1, is the most expensive colt in the race, purchased for $625,000 as a yearling. The high price was largely due to the fashionability of his sire, a Claiborne stallion named Mr. Prospector. Eugene Klein, the former owner of professional football's San Diego Chargers, had purchased the colt on the advice of his trainer, D. Wayne Lukas, a spectacularly successful newcomer to the sport.

The rules of racing in most states require that two horses with common ownership run "coupled" in the betting; that is, they run as an "entry," and a bet on one horse is a bet on both. The point of the rule is to avoid the suspicion and outrage that would follow if the same owner ran a heavy favorite and a longshot in the same race and the longshot won. Most such entries in the history of the Derby were the result of a single stable having two or more Derby-quality horses, but the 1985 Derby is featuring an entry with far more complex shared ownership: Rhoman Rule, owned in name by Brownell Combs II, and Eternal Prince, who is running in the names of Brian Hurst and George Steinbrenner III. The common thread is Spendthrift Farm, Claiborne's traditional rival and the only other farm in its league, which owns a piece of both colts and will be their future home as stallions.

The more popular half of the entry is Eternal Prince, whose father, Majestic Prince, won the 1969 Derby and stood at Spendthrift until his death in 1981. Eternal Prince was born in Florida at Kinsman Stud, owned by Steinbrenner, whose involvement with thoroughbreds predated by several years his perpetually stormy reign as principal owner of the New York Yankees. Steinbrenner races half of the horses he breeds each year and sells the others at auction. Steinbrenner's advisers had rated Eternal Prince the best of the colts they put up for auction that year, and were severely disappointed when he fetched only $17,500 at an auction of two-year-olds. The buyer was Brian Hurst, a thirty-five-year-old car salesman from Norfolk, Virginia.

When Eternal Prince began to win important races a year later, Steinbrenner wanted back in as the Derby approached. Three weeks before the race, he bought back a three-eighths interest in Eternal Prince from Hurst for about $1 million— almost sixty times what he had sold the entire colt for a year earlier. This apparently cockeyed business decision began to look better when Eternal Prince ran off with the Wood Memorial, one of the most prestigious Derby preps. Just three days before the Derby, Hurst and Steinbrenner sold one quarter of the colt for $2 million to Spendthrift and one of the farm's partners, a young insurance tycoon from Dallas named John Post.

Rhoman Rule, the other half of this two-for-one betting proposition, runs in the name of Combs, then president of Spendthrift, but actually is owned by a nine-member syndicate of Combs's friends. (Two of them are named Rhoda and Manuel, thus the spelling of the colt's first name.) Rhoman Rule is the only Pennsylvania-bred in the field, that designation applying to where the foal is delivered, not where he is conceived. Mrs. Lewis Ledyard, a Pennsylvania steeplechasing enthusiast, had sent her mare Morning Bird to Stop the Music, the Greentree stallion so closely related to Buckaroo. She then sold the colt at auction for $310,000 to Combs and his partners.

The entry is 7.5–1, meaning that a winning bet would return $7.50 profit for every $1 bet, or a total return of $17 on the standard $2 bet on which payoffs are computed. The state and the track take a fixed total of 17 percent of all the bets before returning the remaining 83 percent to the winning bettors. By the time the betting machines close today, more than $26 million will have been bet legally on the race, at Churchill Downs, at off-track betting parlors in New York and Connecticut, at "horse books" in Nevada, and at thirty-one racetracks around the country where fans will watch and bet on a live telecast of the race.

Of that $26 million, half is spread among the ten horses who are 7.5–1 or more, and the other $13 million rides on the three colts who are squarely the favorites for this race: Proud Truth, Spend a Buck, and Chief's Crown.

Proud Truth, who had been favored for the Derby most of the winter until he finished second in his last two starts, now was the third choice at about 5–1. A strapping, handsome chestnut-colored colt, Proud Truth was racing for his breeder, eighty-eight-year-old John W. Galbreath, who had been in the game for fifty years. Galbreath, who made his fortune buying up real estate during the Depression, is the only owner in the sport's history to have bred and owned winners of both the Kentucky Derby, with Chateaugay in 1963 and Proud Clarion in 1967, and the Epsom Derby, with Roberto in 1972. The latter colt was named for Roberto Clemente, the captain of the Pittsburgh Pirates, then a Galbreath family holding. The Galbreaths are hosting a large party today that includes former President Ford, and all of them are wearing little "I Like Proud Truth" buttons.

Proud Truth's sire, Graustark, had been heavily favored to win the 1966 Derby, but broke down ten days before the race while suffering his only career defeat. He had been retired and become a successful stallion at Galbreath's Darby Dan Farm, which has sprawling spreads in Kentucky and Ohio. Proud Truth's trainer, John Veitch, had been hired by the Galbreaths only a year earlier. Seven years ago, while training for Calumet Farm, Veitch had developed Alydar, who would surely have won the Triple Crown had he not been born the same year as

Affirmed. It was Alydar who beat Buckaroo by ten lengths in the 1978 Whitney Stakes.

The second favorite for the 111th Derby is the result of the mating between Buckaroo and Belle de Jour on that hot and dusty morning at Greentree Stud almost four years earlier, a colt born the following June 5 at 2:30 A.M.

Belle de Jour had gotten in foal on that second cover, but before long Harry Love had decided to sell her in foal instead of waiting another two years to sell her yearling. Love needed money, and put Belle de Jour into a January breeding-stock sale at Keeneland, Kentucky's main auction company. She caught the eye of Rowe Harper, a small-scale market breeder. Harper never intended to wait two or three years for Belle de Jour's unborn foal to make it to the races; his plan was to buy moderately priced stock that he could resell for a relatively quick profit, and he paid $33,000 for Belle de Jour.

Harper, thirty-seven years old at the time, had grown up on a small farm in the south-central Kentucky village of Edmonton. Graduated in 1967 from Georgetown College with a degree in political science, he spent four years as an administrative assistant in the State Highway Department, then five more in Dallas as national sales manager of a retail chain. In 1976, he moved back near home to Owensboro, Kentucky, in the western part of the state, where he established residency to run for state office. The role of a gentleman farmer seemed appropriate, and though Owensboro is on the opposite side of the state from the horse-breeding action, Harper bought two mares and decided to become a market breeder.

His plans failed all around. In 1979, he ran unsuccessfully for secretary of state on the Republican ticket. By 1982, when Belle de Jour delivered her foal, Harper was having serious cash-flow problems and selling off his horses. He moved his stock, including Belle de Jour and her newborn colt, to a leased farm in Paris, near Claiborne, where potential buyers were welcome to come and make him an offer.

In March of 1983, Dennis and Linda Diaz came to visit. Diaz, the son of a Tampa, Florida cattle farmer, had made a killing in Florida real-estate and insurance and retired to Tampa at the age of thirty-eight. A friend there, Elliott Hunter Fuentes, interested him in horses as a hobby, and before long he had purchased a 50-acre farm and begun looking for mares to stock it. A cousin by marriage living in Lexington told him about Rowe Harper's horses, and Diaz went to Lexington to see them. He liked the looks of Belle de Jour, and the mare was sold for the fourth time in six years. Diaz's interest had also been drawn by Belle de Jour's yearling colt.

"He seemed smart, even then," Diaz would recall. "He was using another colt in this field of yearlings as a kind of body-guard. He looked like a boss and I liked that."

Two days after buying Belle de Jour for $60,000, Diaz offered Harper an additional $12,500 for the colt, and the cash-strapped Harper accepted. The mare was sent to another Lexington-area farm, the Alchemy, to deliver the foal she was carrying. Diaz's new farm, which he had named Hunter after his friend Fuentes's middle name, was being rebuilt and renovated, so Diaz sent Belle de Jour's yearling Buckaroo colt to Fuentes's nearby spread.

An owner must submit a list of six suggested names for a horse to The Jockey Club before the horse's second birthday. Many names are rejected, most often because they already belong to one of the 300,000 active thoroughbreds The Jockey Club has registered at any given time. Others are rejected for violating the remaining rules, though The Jockey Club seems to enforce these lackadaisically.

A name may be no more than eighteen characters and spaces, which is why some names are run together, as in the filly Arewehavingfunyet. It may not be the name of a famous horse of the past, such as Man o' War or Seabiscuit, though the Club registrar recently allowed a duplication of the champion Wistful. It may not be the proper name of a person without that person's written consent, which has been given by the likes of Chris Evert and Don Rickles. It supposedly may not be a promotional name, though the Club has allowed Big Mac Attack and Go Quarter Pounder, and the owner of the Long Island Molding Company once got away with Limold. Finally, the name is not supposed to be vulgar or suggestive, though the Club recently allowed the registry of one colt as Drop Your Drawers, perhaps thinking it referred to clumsy furniture movers. The Club also approved one owner's naming a filly Cold as a Witch's, and then naming two of her foals Titular Feast and Bare Assets.

The best names are catchy or clever while taking into account the names of the parents. A crowning example is a son of Quadratic and Family Planning who was niftily named Four Kids Only. Mrs. Payne Whitney, a baseball fan, named Shut Out after his dam, Goose Egg. Alfred Vanderbilt's best horse was Native Dancer, a son of Polynesian and Geisha, but his best name may have been for a son of Shut Out and Pansy, whom he called Social Outcast. Later, when he bred Social Outcast to a mare named Court Jester, he named the result Village Idiot.

Diaz had all sorts of risque possibilities open with a son of Buckaroo and Belle de Jour, the latter being the French slang for a mistress. Instead, the retired young real-estate man seized on the greenbacks suggested by the buck in Buckaroo and submitted Money Talks, Pass the Buck, Pass the Hat, Raise a Buck and Turn a Buck. All those were taken, so he got Spend a Buck, his next choice.

Spend a Buck showed precocious talent even before being sent as a two-year-old to Miami and the Diaz's young trainer, Cam Gambolati, a thirty-five-year-old former statistician for football's Tampa Bay Buccaneers. Spend a Buck had won seven of his eleven career starts coming into the Derby and was coming off two very fast victories by wide margins in prep races at Garden State Park in New Jersey, which have made him the second choice in the Derby betting at 4–1. But he appears to be a speedball who might tire at the Derby distance. Also, he was beaten soundly the one time he raced against Chief's Crown, the overwhelming favorite to win today's race.

At odds of just 6–5, Chief's Crown is the heaviest Derby favorite since Spectacular Bid six years earlier and the first Derby starter since then to prompt as much anticipation of a possible Triple Crown. A determined colt who runs with his head down, Chief's Crown is the only proven champion in the field. He had been a near-unanimous choice as the best two-year-old in the country the year before when he had won the top races in New York, been flown to California and beaten the best youngsters there, then put the icing on his record by winning the first running of the Breeders' Cup Juvenile, a new year-end championship race, over Tank's Prospect and Spend a Buck.

In addition, Chief's Crown's pedigree is a particularly regal one. He is from the first crop of foals sired by Danzig, the colt De Kwiatkowski had purchased as a yearling who is also the sire of Stephan's Odyssey. Danzig, a son of Northern Dancer, currently the world's most expensive and fashionable stallion, won all three of his career starts as if he were going to be a champion but then was retired because of bone chips in his knee. Chief's Crown's dam is Six Crowns, so named because she is a daughter of two triple crown winners: Secretariat, the 1973 Triple Crown winner, and Chris Evert, who won the New York filly triple crown series a year later. Six Crowns herself was not much of a racehorse and Secretariat has yet to sire a Derby winner, but the richness of Chief's Crown's pedigree titillates the bettors.

Carl Rosen, the founder and president of Puritan Fashions, had raced both Chris Evert and Six Crowns, and bred the latter to Danzig to get Chief's Crown. Rosen died a year after the colt was born at Claiborne, where Danzig, Secretariat, and twenty-eight other blue-chip stallions stand and where select members of racing's elite board their stock. Rosen's widow, three sons, and a nephew now race the colt and named him for Rosen, who was known around his company as "The Chief."

After the colt's outstanding two-year-old season, the Rosen heirs had sold half of Chief's Crown to a syndicate headed by the Kentucky breeder Robert Clay for $10 million. Clay had syndicated most of his half of the colt, selling shares to breeders for $500,000 apiece. Each shareholder will be entitled to breed one mare a year to Chief's Crown when he is retired to Clay's Three Chimneys Farm near Lexington. A Derby victory, on top of everything he has accomplished, will make the price look like a bargain.

Chief's Crown still has his doubters on Derby Day, and even his biggest boosters are not ready to put him in the super-horse category along with the likes of Secretariat and Seattle Slew, but the colt has the solid and professional record of a likely Derby winner. He has won all three of his starts as a three-year-old, including two of the most prestigious Derby prep races, the Flamingo Stakes in Miami and the Blue Grass Stakes in Lexington.

As post time for the race approaches and the thirteen colts begin to enter the starting gate, Chief's Crown is holding steady at 6–5 and a trickle of late money knocks down Proud Truth's odds half a point, from 5–1 to 9–2. Tom Wagoner, the track's official starter, looks down from the small wooden stand over the gate to see that all the colts are loaded in and ready to break cleanly. He is just about ready to press the button in the palm of his hand that will break the electromagnetic field holding the doors on the gate closed, and the stalls will fly open for the 111th Kentucky Derby.

The owners of the thirteen colts, grouped together in boxes near the finish line, raise their binoculars, each focussing on his own horse at the start. At stake is a winner's purse of $427,000, though most of the owners would say this prize is inconsequential. It pales, they would surely say, next to the glory of winning the Kentucky Derby, of having their own names in the record books with the owners of the 110 previous winners, of seeing their colt's name painted in gold leaf on the walls of the Downs. No doubt they mean this sincerely. But what really makes the winner's prize extraneous is their knowledge that far more money than that rides on the outcome, a sum large enough to make the blood of even a John Galbreath or Brownell Combs run faster.

The owners know that whichever of the thirteen colts wins the Derby will instantly become worth at least $4 million, and possibly much more. The money will not come from a victory today or on any other day at any track, but from the eventual sale or syndication of the Derby winner as a stallion. In the previous ten years, every Derby winner who had gone to stud had been sold or syndicated for at least ten times the size of the purse he earned for winning the Derby. Seattle Slew, bought as a yearling for $17,500, had earned $214,700 for winning the Derby but was syndicated for $12 million in 1978. Two years later, Spectacular Bid, a $37,500 yearling, earned $228,650 on Derby Day and was syndicated for $22 million. Other horses who never raced in the Derby have been syndicated for more, but the Derby is the one race that immediately marks a horse as a multimillion-dollar stallion, whether or not he ever wins another race of consequence.

Seattle Slew and Spectacular Bid had been odds-on Derby favorites, so clearly dominant that more money was bet on them than on all of their opponents combined. Now Chief's Crown, though not backed quite as strongly, was the heaviest favorite since those two. He was in a different position, having already been syndicated at a value of $20 million, before even making a start as a three-year-old. His three victories before the Derby had made the investment look good, though, and clearly no one who had bought a share was going to get burned. Victories in the next two legs of the Triple Crown, the Preakness and the Belmont, could triple the value of those shares, making him worth more than any horse had ever been before going to stud and proving himself as a stallion.

The Rosen heirs had hedged their bets by selling half of their colt before the Derby, just as Brian Hurst had guaranteed himself a score, win or lose, by selling pieces of Eternal Prince to Steinbrenner and later to Spendthrift and John Post. Other owners had been approached about selling before the Derby. William Farish III, a Texas mining baron with old family ties to racing and a growing stud farm of his own, had been impressed with Spend a Buck's victories at Garden State and thought there was a chance the colt could stretch his speed to win the Derby. He had befriended the Diazes during Derby Week, helped them cut through some of the Churchill Downs red tape and done them small favors. He had one of his trainers, Neil Howard, bring the Diaz's baby to the track just before the race and return him to their hotel soon after.

He told them he was interested in buying a piece of their colt and eventually standing Spend at Buck at his Lane's End Farm near Lexington. The Diazes liked Farish and were flattered by his attention. Unfamiliar with the world of elite Lexington breeders, they had been pleasantly surprised to find Farish a soft-spoken, cordial, and considerate man and not a cigar-chomping wheeler-dealer. They promised him that he would get first crack at Spend a Buck as a stallion prospect, but decided not to sell any of their $12,500 colt just yet.

They figured they had a big shot at winning the race, and both the press and public agreed that Spend a Buck, along with Chief's Crown, Eternal Prince, Tank's Prospect, Proud Truth, and Stephan's Odyssey, were the Derby starters with realistic chances of ending up in the winner's circle. This was hardly a daring verdict, giving six of the thirteen starters a good chance at winning, but the Derby is one of racing's hardest events to decipher, in the absence of an obviously superior Secretariat or Seattle Slew. Most of the horses have been racing in different parts of the country, not against one another, and few have raced at Churchill. Picking the Derby winner is good for one's ego, but such a dicey proposition that few gamblers will stake their bankrolls or their reputations on it.

Tactically, this Derby figured to unfold with Spend a Buck and Eternal Prince sprinting away fastest and dueling for the lead, Chief's Crown stalking them, and the others coming from far back and making a late run. The question of the race was whether the two front-runners would burn each other out. When two horses run full tilt early, vying for the lead, they tend to expend more effort than they would if running unchallenged. The natural competitive urge and the pressure exerted by a rival makes them try harder. This extra effort will usually take its toll in the late stages of the race, weakening dueling leaders for the rush of a stretch-runner.

To see if this was happening, the sharpies and insiders today would be watching the fractional times posted on the infield scoreboard, seeing how quickly the leaders had run each quarter-mile of the 1¼-mile race. If the early pace was fast, they could figure that the leaders were burning themselves out. The race would then probably go to a stretch-runner, a colt who was allowed to relax early and make a late, fresh run from the back of the pack.

Of course, if Chief's Crown or one of the others were indeed much the best horse, a potential Triple Crown winner, such subtleties would make little difference. But if this was in fact a closely matched bunch, these small factors could end up deciding which colt would be worth $20 million after a little more than two minutes of work.

◆　◆　◆

Eternal Prince was in the sixth starting stall from the rail, and Spend a Buck was in post 10. Both had always shown outstanding speed from the gate, getting a quick jump on their opponents, and here they figured to blast out together. Eternal Prince had one advantage in being on the inside, in that he would be able to get to the rail and have a little less ground to cover around the first turn. On the other hand, the outside horse in a speed duel has an extra bit of control, putting pressure on his rival, who is trapped between the rail and a horse racing alongside.

When Tom Wagoner pushed the button to open the gates, Spend a Buck shot out to the lead as usual. But Eternal Prince hesitated in the stall for a split second. Films would later show that he might have been distracted by an assistant starter on the gate crew who was trying to keep the colt's head steady. Whatever the reason, by the time Eternal Prince got going, the horses on either side of him were a step in front and closing the hole. Eternal Prince's chance of winning the Derby, his owners' chance to make a windfall, and the colt's prestige and opportunities as a stallion had vanished in as much time as it had taken the race caller to say "They're off."

Just as quickly, Dennis Diaz and Spend a Buck's backers knew they had gotten the best possible break. Spend a Buck was winging it by himself now, and he had the services of Angel Cordero, Jr., the oldest and shrewdest rider in the race. Cordero, forty-two years old, is a master at putting a horse on the lead and nursing him through the slowest possible early splits in order to keep something in reserve for the finish.

Donald MacBeth, riding Chief's Crown, reacted quickly. Seeing Spend a Buck alone in front, he realized instantly that the prerace plan of waiting to inherit the lead from the tiring, dueling pace-setters was gone. His only hope now was to keep close enough to Spend a Buck to have a chance at running by him late if the leader tired a bit on his own, though now Spend a Buck would have less reason to tire at all. MacBeth quickly maneuvered his colt into second place, and the race was on. After just thirty seconds, it was clear that only two of the 38,523 foals of 1982 had any chance to win this Kentucky Derby. Either Spend a Buck was going to lead every step of the way, or Chief's Crown would stay close and then catch him down the stretch. Without a battle for the lead up front, closers such as Proud Truth were already too far back to win because Spend a Buck was not going to tire that badly.

Those who had been planning to watch the scoreboard for the early fractions of the race might now have thought they could safely ignore it, since there was no question of Spend a Buck and Eternal Prince pushing each other too quickly too soon. But those who looked may have found a surprise that quickly converted them into Chief's Crown fans. Spend a Buck had traveled his first half mile in 45 ⅘ seconds, the first three quarters of a mile in 1:09 ⅗ and, entering the stretch turn, a mile in 1:34 ⅘. No horse, even alone on the lead, had set fractions that fast and gone on to win the Derby.

As that one-mile time went up on the board and Spend a Buck rounded the far turn, Chief's Crown looked for a moment like he was advancing and would gain ground with every stride. But just as quickly, his bid was over. Spend a Buck was still going, not as fast as in the early stages but just as smoothly, and Chief's Crown was flattening out and falling back. Nearing the wire, the only battle was for second place, as Stephan's Odyssey made a late rush up the rail, catching Chief's Crown in the final stride. Fast Account, the 92–1 shot, was up for fourth, and Proud Truth, forced extremely wide on the stretch turn, was fifth. He was followed, in order, by Skywalker, Tank's Prospect, Floating Reserve, Rhoman Rule, Encolure, Irish Fighter, Eternal Prince, and I Am The Game.

It was one of the most boring Derbies ever, over the instant it had started, yet also one of the most impressive. Spend a Buck's winning margin of 5¼ lengths was the largest since 1946, and his time of 2:00 ⅕ was the third-fastest ever, behind only Secretariat's 1:59 ⅖ in 1973 and Northern Dancer's two minutes flat in 1964.

Dennis Diaz hugged his wife, Linda, kissed their nineteen-month-old son, Elliott, and embraced Gambolati. They rushed to the winner's circle, where Diaz ceremonially took the reins of the colt he had bought for $12,500.

"I'm scared to death I might wake up," Gambolati said a few minutes later. "This is the whole Cinderella story, the whole underdog story. This is the dream come true."

The dream right now meant the glorious inconvenience of posing for endless photographs and interviews in the winner's circle, a trophy presentation from the governor, a congratulatory telegram from the president. Diaz was hyperventilating, his adrenalin surging. Bored, burned out, and looking for a hobby only two years earlier, he had wandered into horse racing and won the grand prize in the sport's biggest lottery. He wanted to bask in it and he would, at least for a few hours.

Spend a Buck winning the 1985 Kentucky Derby.

But already a question was gnawing at him, one that he had foreseen for two weeks but had not really thought he would have to confront. It was a decision that no other owner of a Derby winner had faced.

♦   ♦   ♦

In almost the same breath that the world's sporting press announced Spend a Buck's Kentucky Derby victory, they posed a question that would have been academic in any other year: Where would the colt race next?

The answer would usually be the Preakness two weeks later, the second leg of the Triple Crown. If the Derby suggested greatness, the Triple Crown certified it, since only eleven of the previous one hundred ten Derby winners had gone on to victories in the Preakness and Belmont. Virtually every healthy Derby winner had gone on to the Preakness, as the only horse still eligible for the Crown, the game's most glorious prize. The consensus of opinion was still that the Preakness would be next for Spend a Buck, but this year there was a unique alternative: the Jersey Derby at Garden State Park, where Spend a Buck had won his two prep races before the Derby.

Garden State, which had been almost destroyed in 1977 by an electrical fire that razed the grandstand, had been rebuilt into a modern showplace and had reopened for the first time in eight years on April 1, 1985. The force behind the renovated high-tech track was Robert Brennan, a securities salesman who had gotten into racing in 1980, first as the owner of his own small stable and later as president of a huge publicly held company that owned and bred horses and bought Garden State. To attract the attention of the racing world, thoroughly consumed by Derby fever in April, Brennan had carded two rich Derby preps at Garden State, races which would compete for top horses and attention with New York's traditional Derby preps.

He also was looking ahead to the track's best-known race and potentially biggest money-maker, a race for three-year-olds called the Jersey Derby. It had usually been run on Memorial Day, almost exactly in the middle of the three weeks between the Preakness and the Belmont. Only one iron horse, Citation in 1948, had won the Triple Crown and run in the Jersey Derby too, but the race had served a useful role in the Triple Crown process, especially as a springboard to the Belmont for a horse who had skipped the Preakness.

So Brennan devised a complex scheme of bonuses that he hoped would attract better horses not only to the Jersey Derby but to the two Kentucky Derby prep races in April, the Cherry Hill Mile and the Garden State Stakes. Brennan announced a month before reopening the track that the 1985 Jersey Derby winner would be awarded a $1 million bonus if he had won any two of the following three races: the Cherry Hill, the Garden State, or the Kentucky Derby. The last was thrown in on the wild chance that, in its first year, Garden State might send a Kentucky Derby winner out of one of its prep races. In that spirit, Brennan added, almost as an afterthought, that if a horse won all three of those races and then the Jersey Derby, he would get a $2 million bonus.

Million-dollar bonus arrangements for winning three specific races had come into vogue over the previous three years. Track managements know that dollar signs command attention from the news media and thus generate free publicity for the track. Eight tracks had gotten involved in such arrangements, in some cases with the backing of commercial sponsors who saw a way to get their names into print repeatedly without paying for advertising space on the sports page. Such was the hope of the sponsors of the Jim Beam Challenge at Latonia in Florence, Kentucky, which was not won, and the Ballantine's Scotch Challenge at The Meadowlands in East Rutherford, New Jersey, which was. Interest in the Triple Crown was predicated on the question of whether one horse could sweep three races, so the new bonuses created that drama every time a horse won the first leg of one of the new series.

Brennan had hoped for one of two possible scenarios in which the bonus situation might come into play and thus keep the new Garden State track in the headlines during Triple Crown season: A horse might win the Cherry Hill and Garden State, then get beaten in the Kentucky Derby. With a chance to win a $1 million bonus at Garden State, that horse might skip the Preakness to run in the Jersey Derby instead. Better yet, a horse might win one of the prep races and then the Kentucky Derby, but lose the Preakness. Again, with no Triple Crown to shoot for, that horse might run in the Jersey Derby instead of the Belmont.

But now the unlikeliest scenario had come true. Spend a Buck, having won the Cherry Hill, Garden State, and Kentucky Derby, would get a $2 million bonus if he went on to win the Jersey Derby, a race that also offered a first-place prize of $600,000. The odds of any horse winning those Garden State races and then the Kentucky Derby, in the first year of the bonus arrangement, had been astronomical. Brennan had been blessed.

Diaz and Gambolati, along with a majority of sportswriters and racetrackers, initially had misunderstood the bonus system. The owner and trainer arrived in Kentucky thinking that a $1 million bonus was theirs if they won the Kentucky Derby. Then it was explained to them that everything hinged on winning the Jersey Derby. Once they understood that, they had decided that if their colt lost the Kentucky Derby, they would skip the Preakness and shoot for the Jersey Derby. If they won the Kentucky Derby? The only thing they were sure of was that they would not try to follow Citation's path. Spend a Buck would definitely not run in all four races, the Kentucky Derby, Preakness, Jersey Derby, and Belmont. It was too much racing for a colt who had already undergone knee surgery once and, while far from frail, was not the kind of iron horse Citation had been. They knew the colt would lose one of the four races if they pushed him that hard.

So the lines of choice were drawn sharply after Spend a Buck won the Kentucky Derby: go for the Triple Crown or go for a $2.6 million payday in the Jersey Derby. As NBC-TV's Bryant Gumbel put it in a nationally televised interview with Diaz, "It sounds to me like there are 2.6 million reasons to run in the Jersey Derby and none to run in the Preakness."

The reasons to run in the Preakness were slightly less quantifiable. For more than half a century, the dream of every owner had been to win the Kentucky Derby, and the dream of every owner of a Derby winner had been to win the Triple Crown. It had become ingrained in the heart of the sport. Beyond the glory of the challenge was the role of the Triple Crown as the arbiter of real quality. A Triple Crown winner was far more valuable than a mere Derby winner because while one race might be won on a fluke, only the truly top horses could win the three races.

Diaz had given every indication he would follow convention. Three nights before the Derby, he and Linda had been among the few owners of Derby horses to attend the annual awards banquet thrown by the National Turf Writers Association. The Diazes had wanted to go everywhere Derby Week, knowing that most small owners get only one real chance at a Derby, and their shyness and modesty had won over almost everyone they met. They seemed awed by the experience of having a horse in the Derby. When Diaz was asked about the Jersey Derby–Preakness dilemma if Spend a Buck were to win the Derby, he answered quickly, "My gut feeling is that we'd run in the Preakness because if we had a horse good enough to win the Derby, of course we'd want to win the Triple Crown."

Of course. But now, having won the Derby, he was wavering. The morning after the race, fielding the same question more than one hundred times by his own estimate, he said only that Spend a Buck would return to Garden State, where he had been training all spring, and a decision would follow later in the week.

The choice was not as simple as prestige versus money. It was unclear where the real money was, which race would win the most prestige, or even what that term meant anymore. Diaz had happened to arrive at the crossroads of the sport's own development, and the decision he would make would reflect as well as influence the changing nature of the game.

Only a few years before, every representative of the sport's power and wealth would have told him to go for the Preakness, to stoke the flame of tradition, and indeed he was getting plenty of advice along those lines in the days after the Derby. Now, though, there were also other voices telling him to strike out in a new direction, that the sport had changed irrevocably, and those voices came from powerful insiders as well. It was also getting harder to tell where the sport's real power was, for that power had been spreading and shifting in recent years.

Dennis Diaz, owner of Spend a Buck.

BILL MOONEY

Diaz would make his decision on the Monday after the Derby, four days earlier than he had planned. He would explain that he had arrived at his choice after thinking a lot about tradition and value, and the meaning of those words in a changing game: "I can only say what's right for me, but I'll say this. Ten years ago, there would not have been any issue, any choice. The fact that there was one should tell you that racing is a whole new game now."

2

Big Red and the Blue Bloods

Twelve years to the day before Dennis Diaz watched Spend a Buck win the Kentucky Derby, Seth Hancock, then just 23 years old, was sitting in that same row of seats at Churchill Downs, training his binoculars on a colt in the same tenth stall of the starting gate. Hancock did not own this colt, had not bred him, and had not bet on the race. But the horse was carrying much of Hancock's future and that of the sport's leading breeding dynasty and bloodline.

As the gates opened and the colt came away last in a field of thirteen, it seemed for a moment that Hancock's fears and all the rumors were true. Secretariat, acclaimed as a wonder horse the previous year as a two-year-old, had been beaten badly in his final Derby tuneup, the Wood Memorial. The colt had not run a dismally bad race, something that could have been shrugged off as a fluke. Instead, he had run a listless third so absolutely unremarkable in its mediocrity that his earlier victories seemed like illusions.

Now Secretariat was eleventh heading into the first turn, and the glare of the racing world's power brokers, gathered in the upper reaches of Churchill Downs, was on Seth Hancock. There was disappointment and accusation from some, vindic-

tive joy in his apparent failure from others. For the first time
in ninety-nine Kentucky Derbies, someone other than an
owner or a bettor had more to lose by the race's outcome than
anyone else at Churchill Downs. And for the first time, it was
a sum far greater than the Derby purse that was at stake.

♦   ♦   ♦

Seth Hancock and Secretariat were both descendants of
lineages that had begun to influence horse racing a century
earlier, and both were the products of the history those bloodlines had wrought. The two lines had been intertwined before,
often shaping the direction of the sport that was now reaching
a watershed with Seth and Secretariat.

The Hancock breeding dynasty began with Seth's great-
grandfather, Richard J. Hancock, who grew up on his father's
farm in Louisiana and served in the Confederate Army under
Stonewall Jackson. While recovering from a wound in 1863,
Hancock met Thomasia Harris, daughter of a Virginia plantation owner. They married in 1864 and went to live at her
father's plantation, Ellerslie, a 1,500-acre spread near Char-
lottesville. Like most landed Virginians, the Harrises kept
horses.

One of the things the early Virginians brought with them
from England was a love of racing, and Virginia soon became
a center of racing and breeding. The sport quickly evolved
from short dashes down paths cut through the woods to longer
contests around the perimeter of tobacco fields, and by the late
1700's the state had three formal race courses. Like the rest of
the South, Virginia was hit hard during the Civil War, and
much of the racing stock there was stolen, lost or killed in
battle. Thoroughbred racing and breeding in Virginia faced a
rebuilding process after the war, and when Richard Hancock
moved into Ellerslie he devoted himself to improving the stock
by trading with other locals. In the process, he turned the

Ellerslie horses from a genteel hobby into a business, supplying well-bred stock to the expanding American racing industry.

Recovering from the disruption caused by the Civil War, racing began to flourish again, with new tracks opening in the East, South, and Midwest. Saratoga in upstate New York held its first meeting in 1863, Pimlico opened in 1870, and Churchill Downs held its inaugural meeting in 1875.

Ellerslie quickly became a successful commercial nursery, thanks largely to the stallion Eolus, who was acquired by Hancock in a straight trade for Scathelock, the first stallion Hancock had purchased after taking over Ellerslie. Eolus sired several American champions in the 1880's and 1890's, including the 1884 Preakness winner, Knight of Ellerslie. Richard Hancock had decided early on that the trick to the horse-trading game was selling quality bloodlines in volume instead of using them to try to get lucky and breed a champion for one's self. The theory that power and wealth lay in controlling the bloodlines would sustain the success of the Hancock family.

Richard Hancock's son, Arthur, who stood six feet six inches tall and weighed less than 180 pounds, was graduated from the University of Chicago in 1895 and went home to Ellerslie to breed horses with his father. In 1907, Kentucky Senator Camden Johnson invited Arthur Hancock to Lexington to judge a horse show, figuring the young Virginian would be an impartial observer in the closely knit Kentucky horse community. While there, Arthur met Nancy Clay, whose father owned a 1,300-acre tobacco and livestock farm near Paris. They married in 1908, and when her parents died in 1910, Arthur took over the land. He now was the master of two farms, having assumed the operation of Ellerslie from his aging father earlier that year. In 1912 he consolidated them by moving much of the prime stock to his new Kentucky home. He had named the place Claiborne for his wife and converted it to a horse farm, acquiring more neighboring land in the process.

Arthur Hancock threw all his energies into improving the

breed of the racehorse, and he was immediately rewarded in an industry that had rarely seen much boldness or innovation. In 1913 he paid $20,000 for the stallion Celt, who quickly emerged as a successful sire of fast-developing two-year-olds. Celt died prematurely at the age of fourteen, but Hancock was ready with a substitute: Wrack, an English sire he had purchased for $8,000 four years earlier. Hancock felt that American breeding stock had become too inbred, since the British importation of horses had been slowing down ever since the Revolutionary War. He decided it was time for another large-scale infusion of European blood, and began buying other European sires at the bargain prices that followed the economic ravages of World War I.

He gradually got more ambitious. In 1926, Hancock formed a syndicate with three partners, including Chicago department store magnate Marshall Field, and bought the French stallion Sir Gallahad III for $125,000. This was more than anyone had been known to pay for a horse, but Sir Gallahad seemed to merit it. A son of the great French racehorse and sire Teddy, he had been one of the best colts of a vintage crop in France, winning the Poule d'Essai des Poulains, France's equivalent of England's Two Thousand Guineas, and placing third in the Prix du Jockey-Club, the French Derby. In addition, he was a naturally fast breaker, an indication that he would do well as a sire in America, where the races are shorter and there is a greater premium on early speed.

One of the first mares bred to Sir Gallahad was Marguerite, a daughter of Celt owned by New York financier William Woodward, Sr., a member of the syndicate which had purchased Sir Gallahad. Woodward, who raced a powerful stable under the name of Belair Stud, named the foal Gallant Fox, and the colt swept through the Kentucky Derby, Preakness, and Belmont Stakes of 1930 to become the sport's second Triple Crown winner. Sir Gallahad's influence proved even stronger as a "brood mare sire," meaning that his daughters produced superior runners. For ten straight years from 1933 to 1942, horses foaled by Sir Gallahad's daughters won more races and money than the progeny of mares sired by any other stallion.

Hancock's next big plunge came in 1936 when he and four partners paid $250,000 for Blenheim II, the 1930 Epsom Derby winner. Five years later, Blenheim's son Whirlaway won the Triple Crown and came to be regarded as the best horse of the era.

Horses such as Gallant Fox and Whirlaway were so superior to their contemporaries, and the breeding statistics reflecting the influence of Sir Gallahad and Blenheim were so persuasive, that the entire racing world knew that the breed had been changed by Hancock's imports. These strains had reinvigorated the American breed.

They had also made Claiborne an unusually powerful farm, and from the start Claiborne had used that power to form alliances with top-class stables, who bred their mares to the Claiborne stallions and boarded their breeding stock at the farm. Attracting top outside mares to the Claiborne stallions boosted their success and reputations as sires.

Arthur's son, named Arthur, Jr., but known throughout his life as Bull for his demeanor as well as his build, always aspired only to taking over Claiborne from his father. Bull subscribed to the *Racing Form* in prep school and returned to Claiborne after graduation from Princeton in 1933, following the family tradition of coming home to learn the business. His father put him in charge of Ellerslie, and after World War II Bull came home to Claiborne for good.

In 1945, Arthur Hancock suffered the first of a series of heart attacks and Bull began to take an upper hand in running the farm. He faced the same situation his father had thirty years earlier: stagnation had set in at Claiborne. Arthur, Sr., had become complacent in success, failing to sustain his pursuit of European blood, and allowing the Claiborne brood mare band to swell in size without culling the mares who were producing inferior runners.

It was time for some new blood. Bull was particularly concerned with replacing the aging Blenheim with a new European stallion who would carry on his bloodlines and restore Claiborne's cutting edge in the breeding world. He found a perfect candidate in Nasrullah, a fiery Irish colt who had been bred by the Aga Khan. Nasrullah was a son of Nearco and one of Blenheim's daughters, Mumtaz Begum. With his father's health now faltering badly, Bull took command and put together a syndicate that included some of the society stables who were Claiborne clients, such as those of Gladys and William Woodward. In 1949, the group purchased Nasrullah for a record $340,000. With so many partners involved and each wanting various percentages, Bull Hancock divided the horse into thirty-four shares at $10,000 a share. Each share would entitle the holder to breed one mare a year to Nasrullah.

The designation of thirty-four shares was not a strict reflection of the stallion's capacity to breed. Stallions today are bred to as many as sixty mares a year. Theoretically, by using artificial insemination, stallions could be bred to hundreds of mares a year.

Artificial insemination, however, is prohibited in thoroughbred racing, even though it would be safer and more efficient than nature's way, and stallions are still syndicated into no more than forty shares. Both of these moves are mechanisms by which the breeders retain their power and control and maintain the value and exclusivity of the top bloodlines. If there were more than thirty-five or forty of any expensive stallion's progeny each year, the stud fees immediately would be proportionately reduced and eventually would plummet, since the most desirable bloodlines would be flowing through so many more horses.

The syndication of Nasrullah by Bull Hancock in 1949 was among the first modern instances of stallion syndication, the process that would tie Bull's son, Seth, to Nasrullah's grandson, Secretariat, a generation later. The Nasrullah syndication followed two similar deals for imported stallions set up by Leslie Combs II, the master of nearby Spendthrift Farm. Combs, a sweet-talking dealmaker known as "Cousin Leslie," and the determined Hancock were feisty rivals throughout their careers. Combs would say of women he disliked that he "wouldn't kiss her with Bull Hancock's lips," and sometimes he extended the image a few feet lower.

Hancock and Combs would dominate the stallion industry for the next thirty years, landing most of the nation's top stud prospects and carving up much of racing society as their clients. They made their showplace farms the twin towers of the American breeding industry.

Gladys Phipps, wife of Henry Carnegie Phipps (the son of Henry Phipps, who with Andrew Carnegie built Carnegie Steel Company into the United States Steel Corporation), and her brother, Ogden Livingston Mills, ran a powerful racing stable under the *nom de course* of Wheatley. Gladys Phipps had often consulted Arthur Hancock for advice on pedigrees and conformation and eventually began breeding her mares to Claiborne stallions and boarding them there. Her son Ogden later became good friends with Bull, and in 1950 Gladys Phipps persuaded Bull to sell her a mare named Miss Disco, a daughter of Alfred Gwynne Vanderbilt's outstanding handicap horse Discovery. Using one of her shares in Nasrullah, Gladys Phipps bred Miss Disco to him in 1953, and named the foal born the following year Bold Ruler.

Bold Ruler was a top racehorse but had the misfortune to have been born in what is still considered the strongest foal crop of modern times, the class of '54—a group that included Gallant Man, Iron Liege, Gen. Duke, and Round Table. Bold Ruler finished fourth to Gallant Man in the 1957 Derby, won the Preakness, and was third in Gallant Man's Belmont. He was troubled by injuries and soreness throughout his career and frequently raced with painkillers, leaving the impression that some of his potential was never tapped. He went to stud at Claiborne in 1958 amid high hopes, but no one could have foreseen the success he was to enjoy. Bold Ruler was to dominate breeding in America for the next fifteen years.

When Bold Ruler was retired to stud, Gladys Phipps entered into foal-sharing arrangements with some of her friends who owned more and better mares than she did. Also, she was more interested in getting quality racehorses to carry the Wheatley colors than in collecting stud fees. In a typical arrangement, a partner would breed two mares to Bold Ruler, and then Mrs. Phipps and the partner would flip a coin to see who would get first choice of the foals.

One of the breeders she made such an arrangement with was Christopher Chenery. Born in 1886, Chenery had risen from a poor boyhood in Ashland, Virginia, to make a fortune as a financier in New York. In 1936 he purchased his family's ancestral homeland, 2,500 acres between Washington, D.C., and Richmond, named The Meadow. The place was run down and the land needed work, but Chenery was determined to build a great breeding farm. He started small, buying a mare named Hildene for $600, breeding her to Princequillo, another imported European-bred though American-raced stallion standing at Ellerslie (which the Hancocks were about to sell), and getting a colt named Hill Prince, who became a champion. Pleased with the results, he sent another mare named Imperatrice to Princequillo in 1951, and the result was a filly named Somethingroyal.

She turned out to be an ordinary race horse but something special as a brood mare at The Meadow. She produced Sir Gaylord, the favorite for the 1962 Derby until he broke down a week before the race. In 1968, Somethingroyal was designated as one of the mares who would be bred to Bold Ruler for two consecutive years. The choice was not made by Christopher Chenery, whose health was failing, but by his forty-six-year-old daughter, Penny, the youngest of his three children and the only one with an interest in the sport.

The coin tosses between Mrs. Phipps and her partners traditionally took place in August at Saratoga, where the racing world's elite gathers each year for a month of classy racing and nightly high-society functions. By 1969, Mrs. Phipps and Christopher Chenery were in the process of passing their fortunes on to their children, so Penny Chenery and Ogden Phipps met for the coin toss in the offices of James Cox Brady, the track president. This time, what was at stake was more complicated than usual, so much so that neither party wanted to win the toss.

They were flipping for two years' worth of offspring. Under normal circumstances, the winner would get first choice of the two Bold Ruler foals that had been born that spring of 1969, and the second choice of the two expected to be born in 1970. The loser would get second choice of the 1969 foals and the first choice of the 1970 foals. But while both mares had delivered healthy 1969 foals that spring, now only Somethingroyal had gotten pregnant again. There would be only one 1970 foal, and it would go to the loser of the coin flip. The winner, therefore, would get just one horse over the next two years while the loser would get two horses.

Brady tossed the coin and Phipps was the disappointed winner. From the 1969 pair, he chose the Bold Ruler–Somethingroyal filly over the Bold Ruler–Hasty Matelda colt, following his usual pattern of picking fillies. That meant that Penny Chenery automatically got the colt, as well as the lone foal that would be born the next spring. The following March 29, Somethingroyal delivered a colt at The Meadow, where he would stay as the Chenerys' property instead of being sent to Claiborne as the Phippses'.

The Phippses' Bold Ruler–Somethingroyal filly from 1969 was named The Bride. She raced four times as a two-year-old, finishing sixth twice, ninth once, and tenth once, failing to earn a nickel before being retired to Claiborne as a brood mare prospect. The Chenerys' Bold Ruler–Hasty Matelda colt came up with numerous physical problems, and they considered themselves lucky to sell him privately for $50,000 before he ever started.

The Chenerys' Bold Ruler–Somethingroyal colt from 1970, of the identical parentage as The Bride, was named Secretariat.

♦   ♦   ♦

The first time Penny Chenery watched Secretariat as a young foal playing in the Meadow Stud paddocks, she entered a one-word comment in her notebook: "Wow!" Racing history is filled with stories of ugly-duckling horses who look hopeless until they race, but Central Casting could not have improved on Secretariat's looks. The colt had a gleaming, coppery chest-nut-colored coat and bold, sassy patches of white: three white stockings, on all but his left front leg, a star in the center of his forehead, and a narrow stripe running down his nose. He was a big colt, and so precocious that he fired dreams a year before he made it to the races. When Secretariat was just a yearling and another Meadow Stud colt, a two-year-old named Riva Ridge, was winning major races and becoming the favorite for the following year's Derby, the help back at The Meadow were saying they had an even more promising colt on the farm.

Secretariat went north to New York to prepare for his racing debut in April of his two-year-old year, two weeks before Riva Ridge won the 1972 Kentucky Derby. The Chenerys' Canadian-born trainer, Lucien Laurin, loved the looks and manners of the big chestnut. Everyone was expecting an easy victory when Secretariat made his debut on July 4, 1972, at Aqueduct Race Track in Queens.

He broke well from the starting gate, but then everything went wrong, and he was solidly thwacked by three horses in a chain reaction that took less than ten seconds. He dropped far back, but then made a late charge, picking up seven lengths down the stretch in the short race to finish fourth, beaten by only 1¼ lengths. A first-time starter almost never makes such a recovery and late rally, so it was as impressive a debut as a romp to victory could have been.

Secretariat would not finish behind another horse for nine months, breezing through the rest of his two-year-old season like few colts before him, his record blemished only by a disqualification to second place when he brushed a rival en route to an easy victory in the Champagne Stakes. He was more than simply 1972's best two-year-old. His times were brilliant, and his flashy looks and dramatic come-from-behind style had made him the most popular two-year-old in years. He was everyone's early pick for the following year's Kentucky Derby. In addition to being voted the champion two-year-old, he was given the additional title of Horse of the Year, which in the past had almost always been won by an older horse.

The breeding world was already talking excitedly about his potential as a stallion. Secretariat had shown the blazing speed that breeders like most in a sire, and his come-from-behind style also suggested that he would be just as dominating when the races got longer the following year. Those doing the talking were thinking pretty far down the road, since they figured it would be at least two years before Secretariat would go to stud, after racing as a three-year-old and as a four-year-old.

In the three years following Secretariat's birth, power was being passed down one generation through deaths in all the dynasties surrounding the colt. His own sire, Bold Ruler, had died of cancer in 1971, leaving Claiborne without a leader of its dominant sire line. Gladys Phipps had died the previous fall at the age of eighty-seven, bequeathing control of her powerful racing and breeding operations to her son Ogden, who had managed much of Bold Ruler's stud career. Two years later, on September 14, 1972, Bull Hancock's death muddied the future of Claiborne Farm's operation. Finally, on January 3, 1973, two days after Secretariat officially became a three-year-old, Christopher Chenery died, throwing the colt's future into question.

Bull Hancock's will had left control of Claiborne to his two sons, twenty-nine-year-old Arthur III and twenty-three-year-old Seth, but he had set up an advisory committee to approve all Claiborne business. Bull had died without confidence that one of his sons could do the job right or that the other son could do it right away. Arthur had seemed more interested in performing his country-western compositions at Lexington nightspots than in carrying on the business of Claiborne. He had badly disappointed his father a year earlier. To give him a taste of running a business, Bull had set him up on a 100-acre spread named Stone Farm down the road from Claiborne, sent him some mares to board, and helped him buy some mares for himself. Then, in the middle of the crucial and busy foaling season, Arthur got an invitation to go fox hunting in Ireland and took off. Bull was infuriated and took back the mares. Arthur returned quickly but the trust had been broken.

The alternative, Seth, was too young. Born the same year his father had arranged the purchase of Nasrullah, he had been graduated from the University of Kentucky with an agriculture degree in 1971, and come back to Claiborne the following February. Bull structured a two-year apprenticeship program for Seth to learn all about Claiborne, but then died just seven months into it.

So Bull's will had stipulated that Arthur and Seth run the farm jointly, with all their decisions subject to the approval of three of their father's most trusted advisers: Ogden Phipps, Charles Kenney, and William Haggin Perry. The arrangement rankled Arthur, and it quickly proved unworkable. Four months later, the advisers recommended to the estate executors that Seth run the farm alone. Arthur told the executors he would prefer to do things his own way down the road, and he decamped to Stone Farm with $3.5 million, his share of the trusts established in Bull's will. Suddenly, Seth Hancock was in charge of Claiborne, a duty he had thought would rightfully become his, but not so soon.

Nor was he prepared for the task Penny Chenery was about to propose.

Christopher Chenery's estate consisted largely of The Meadow and its eighty horses. The inheritance taxes, in the 70 percent bracket, amounted to at least $6 million. To raise that, Penny and her two older siblings would have to sell much of the value of the farm and horses, and the majority of that value resided in Riva Ridge and Secretariat.

The family sought the advice of John Finney, president of the Fasig-Tipton auction company and an expert on the values and sales of horses. Finney's advice was to hold on to as much of the breeding stock as possible, and not to sell Riva Ridge, whose value had plummeted during a poor post-Triple Crown campaign. If the colt had any kind of a year as a four-year-old, Finney said, he could regain much of his value. The answer, he advised, was to syndicate Secretariat. The colt was already a sensation off his brilliant two-year-old campaign. His current value, which Finney estimated at $5 million to $7 million, could appreciate only 20 percent. But a bad year, a failure in the Derby, could easily cut his worth in half.

Penny Chenery liked the idea. She did not really believe that Secretariat was going to win the Derby. His sire, Bold Ruler, had dominated American breeding for more than a decade, yet had never sired the winner of a Derby or Belmont. The conventional breeding wisdom held that Bold Ruler's sons, though blessed with superior speed, could not quite go 1¼ miles in the Derby, much less 1½ miles in the Belmont. Also, Penny Chenery had always preferred Riva Ridge, a homely but spirited colt and a grandson of Christopher Chenery's $600 mare Hildene, to the flashy, royally bred Secretariat. Figuring that Riva Ridge's value could only rise and Secretariat's only fall, she agreed to syndicate the younger horse.

The question now was which breeder to turn to and where

the colt should stand. Finney, unbeknownst to Penny Chenery, was dealing with some Irish breeders who wanted to bring the colt to their country. It would be Europe's greatest import catch ever and a bit of an overdue payback for the American breeders' having taken Nasrullah a generation before.

That deal had little chance of succeeding, though, because from the start Penny Chenery had Claiborne Farm in mind. There had been a long connection between the farm and her family. Christopher Chenery had bred his mares to the last Ellerslie stallions before the Hancocks had finally shut down that Virginia branch, and had since sent his mares across the Appalachians to Claiborne stallions. More recently, when her father's health had begun to fail, she had turned to Bull Hancock for advice about every aspect of the business. Now it was time to give Bull's son a chance.

They were an unlikely couple to engineer the sport's richest stallion syndication. Penny Chenery, though devoted to her father and The Meadow since childhood, had spent the previous seventeen years as a Denver housewife, married to an attorney named Jack Tweedy. An attractive woman with neatly coiffed hair and an outdoorsy glow, she had the look of a veteran horsewoman but neither the experience nor contacts to be putting together this deal. Seth Hancock, unfailingly polite and earnest but more given to an aw-shucks manner than high-powered salesmanship, had just begun to settle into his job. Both of them had been suddenly thrust into playing at the highest level of the game by the recent deaths of their fathers. This created a natural bond between them, despite Seth's being exactly half her age.

Seth already wanted Secretariat to be a Claiborne stallion. The colt seemed to have the potential to become a sire who would move the breed along, as Blenheim and Sir Gallahad had done in his grandfather's day and as Nasrullah and Bold Ruler had in his father's day. Now that those stallions were gone, Secretariat was just what Claiborne needed. When, over dinner in Lexington, Penny Chenery asked Seth if Claiborne would syndicate and stand the colt, he accepted like a shot.

The Chenery family lawyers had already drawn up a syndication agreement that would raise about $5 million. The plan was to sell twenty-eight of thirty-two shares in the colt, with the Chenery estate retaining four shares. Claiborne would receive three free stud services the first year and four per year thereafter in exchange for standing Secretariat, and Lucien Laurin would be entitled to breed one mare per year to the stallion, a courtesy extended by custom to a top colt's trainer.

The lawyers had figured on between $175,000 and $200,000 a share. Seth set the price at $190,000, figuring $200,000 might scare off buyers. The next day, Seth went into Bull's office, now his, and sat down in front of the telephone. All that the twenty-three-year-old president of Claiborne Farm had to do now was sell a colt who had yet to race as a three-year-old for more money than anyone had ever paid for any horse.

◆　　◆　　◆

Bull Hancock, it has been said without much exaggeration, could syndicate a horse by strolling through the box-seat section at Belmont Park or Saratoga between races and chatting with his friends. The members of his syndicates were drawn from the pool of powerful owners and breeders who already dominated the sport. Leslie Combs sold his Spendthrift stallions the same way. For two generations, the power in the sport, the control of the bloodlines, had stayed in the same relatively small group.

It was February 12 when Seth set out to syndicate Secretariat. There was no box seat section open to stroll through, and Seth could not have pulled off face to face sales anyway. He was just Bull's younger son, and he had not yet proven himself. Bull's way was the only way he knew, however. He sat down with a list of telephone numbers of the most important and long-standing Claiborne clients. He picked up the telephone and started to go through the list, trying to sell shares in Secretariat for $190,000 each.

The first call he made was to Ogden Phipps. Seth began by asking Phipps, as the most active member of the advisory panel that still approved all Claiborne business, for permission to syndicate Secretariat. Phipps agreed. Then Seth offered Phipps the first share. Phipps said $190,000 sounded like a lot of money. Seth swallowed hard and told him it would not look like much of a vote of confidence in either Claiborne or Bold

Arthur B. "Bull" Hancock and Seth Hancock at Saratoga, 1968.

BERT AND RICHARD MORGAN

Ruler to turn him down. Phipps agreed and took a share, though he would later advise his son, Ogden Mills Phipps, not to buy one. Phipps, like Penny Chenery, had his doubts about Bold Ruler's ability to sire a Kentucky Derby winner, despite the fact that his mother had bred the horse and prized him above all her other thoroughbreds.

Seth sold the second share a few minutes later after peering out his office window. Dr. William Lockridge was sitting in his Cadillac outside the Claiborne main office. He had driven over from his nearby Walmac-Warnerton Farm because a mare he owned was going to be bred that morning to another Claiborne stallion. Seth knew Lockridge was a Secretariat fan and asked him if he wanted in. Lockridge said yes.

The remaining twenty-six shares did not all go so easily. Seth's confidence was shaken a couple of times when longtime Claiborne clients and supporters put him off and complained about the price. Some may have doubted Seth's abilities and Claiborne's future, though others tried to support the young man. John Galbreath, then seventy-five years old, said he really did not need any more stallion shares but offered to take one if it would help, Seth's efforts. Seth thanked Galbreath and declined.

That morning, as the word spread that Secretariat was for sale, Seth began getting some calls in addition to the ones he was making. Only a few hours after he had started selling the colt, he received a call from a bloodstock agent who had heard the news in the stable area at Hialeah Park in Miami, a thousand miles away. The agent wanted a share for a Japanese client, Zenya Yoshida, a prominent buyer at yearling auctions. Sold.

It took three days to complete the syndication, and some who wanted in were shut out. Some of the biggest names in the business turned down the offer, including Calumet Farm, whose runners had won a record eight Derbies and two Triple Crowns; Robert Kleberg, whose gigantic King Ranch in Texas had bred and raced 1946 Triple Crown winner Assault; and

Peter Fuller, whose Dancer's Image had won the 1968 Kentucky Derby but then became the only Derby winner ever disqualified, when a post-race urine test turned up a then-prohibited analgesic.

A larger and loftier list, though, said yes. With so much potential in the brilliant colt, few wanted to be left out. Especially for Claiborne's newer and younger clients, this was a chance to get in on the ground floor of controlling a bloodline, the way that previous generations had done with Blenheim, Nasrullah, and Bold Ruler.

The twenty-eight paying members of the syndicate included such major old-line stables as those of the Phippses; Allaire duPont, the Maryland chemicals heiress who had campaigned the popular gelding Kelso in the early 1960s; Paul Mellon, the multimillionaire philanthropist whose Rokeby Stable is based in Upperville, Virginia; and Alfred Gwynne Vanderbilt, who had raced Native Dancer and now was the president of the New York Racing Association. Vanderbilt would later sell half of his share to Greentree.

Also among the early invitees to the syndicate were less dynastic owner-breeders, who had raced top horses and who now had access to top mares, such as E. P. Taylor, the Canadian breeder whose Windfields Farm had raced Northern Dancer; William McKnight, former chairman of the board of 3-M, who had campaigned Dr. Fager; and Mrs. Paul Hexter, whose father, John Hertz, had founded Hertz Rent-A-Car and Yellow Cab and raced 1943 Triple Crown winner Count Fleet.

A third group was composed of less experienced investors, who were just getting into the game or had done business with Claiborne before: Will Farish, the polo-playing Texas mining tycoon whose Bee Bee Bee had won the Preakness, defeating Riva Ridge, the previous spring; Bert Firestone and Howard and Charles Gilman from the world of real estate; Zenya Yoshida and Tamao Tamashima, who had been speculating in blue-chip bloodstock with a few other Japanese investors; and a syndicate of Europeans acting through the British Bloodstock Agency.

Most of the buyers in the latter group had been among the last to join. Seth Hancock was eager to sell Secretariat, but only to buyers he thought had access to the kind of mares that would build the colt's reputation at stud. He had, of necessity, gone slightly beyond the old guard. The syndication agreement itself also went beyond the old rules.

The terms of the syndication mandated that the colt begin his career at stud the following year, meaning Secretariat would be retired at the end of his three-year-old season. Penny Chenery had insisted on maintaining control of the colt's racing career, but there was no argument that Secretariat would be retired by the end of the year. Those who had paid $190,000 a share wanted to start getting a return on their investment soon, and if the colt were to do well in the Triple Crown races, he would reach the peak of his value. If he failed to thrive, it was better to get him off to stud before his reputation could suffer any more, before the Horse of the Year title and his brilliance as a two-year-old were tarnished by more than one disappointing season.

It was the first time such a decision had been made about a major American horse so far in advance, and the first time such a decision was the result of a syndication agreement. The trend in the past had been the opposite, to give a horse every opportunity for additional victories and earnings. Citation, the 1948 Triple Crown winner, had been campaigned excessively, up to the age of six, in order to make him the sport's first million-dollar earner. This did not significantly increase his value at stud, but was a sporting gesture, an attempt to set a milestone. Bold Ruler had been kept going on sore legs as a four-year-old to allow as much of his innate talent as possible to shine through.

But now Secretariat, win or lose, was going home at the end of his three-year-old season. The equation between racing and breeding had changed overnight. A horse who had not even raced as a three-year-old was worth over $6 million, almost three times what any horse had ever earned by racing. Three years earlier, Bull had syndicated a three-year-old son of Northern Dancer named Nijinsky II for $5.4 million, but that colt had already won the Epsom Derby and would win England's Triple Crown for the first time in thirty-five years. Secretariat now had been sold for a higher value.

The sale of so young a horse for so much money marked one historic point in the development of the industry, but an equally significant one was marked by the mandated early retirement. The decision had nothing to do with sport and everything to with money, and it could only prove unpopular with racing fans. A line had been drawn between the racing game and the breeding industry, and the gap would widen over the next dozen years, up through the next and last time Seth Hancock would syndicate a horse who had yet to race as a three-year-old, a colt named Devil's Bag.

♦   ♦   ♦

The syndication process stalled Lucien Laurin's program to get Secretariat ready for the Triple Crown. The colt had been sent to Florida in late November and Laurin planned to give him a brief vacation, run him there twice in late February and March, then send him to New York for his final Derby prep, the Wood Memorial. But neither Seth Hancock nor Penny Chenery wanted Secretariat to run while the syndication negotiations were going on. What if the big colt should turn in a dull effort or injure himself before the papers were signed?

By the time the syndication was completed and announced at the end of February, Secretariat had run out of time for a Florida campaign. He would need a short prep race to contest the longer 1⅛-mile Flamingo Stakes, and those preps had all been run. Penny Chenery and Lucien Laurin decided to bring him to New York, where a three-race series that was not yet underway would set him up perfectly for the spring classics.

Secretariat made his debut as a three-year-old in the Bay Shore Stakes at Aqueduct Race Track, and the syndicate members breathed a sigh of relief as he crossed the wire an easy 4½-length winner under what the official *Daily Racing Form* chart of the race called only "a mild drive." His time of 1:23 ⅕ for seven furlongs was nothing spectacular, but perfectly creditable for a horse making his first start in four months. Three weeks later, in the Gotham Stakes at Aqueduct, uncharacteristically going for the lead from the start, he ripped off his first six furlongs in a frighteningly fast 1:08 ⅗ and finished up the mile in 1:33 ⅖, the fastest ever recorded by a three-year-old at the track and equaling the track record.

Two weeks later in the Wood Memorial, he figured to enjoy another romp, though he was meeting a highly regarded colt from California named Sham, who had gone up for sale the previous November in a dispersal auction of Bull Hancock's racing stock. One of the stipulations of Bull's will had been that Claiborne sell its yearling colts and race only the fillies, the best of whom would join the farm's brood mare band. He did not want his sons to get too involved in the risky business of racing; he figured the breeding operation alone would be difficult enough for them to run. Sigmund Sommer, a New York real estate developer, had paid $200,000 for Sham, and sent him to California for the winter. Now the Claiborne-bred colt had emerged as the biggest threat to the horse that Claiborne had syndicated for $6.08 million.

For the Wood, Laurin entered both Secretariat and another horse he trained for a different owner, an undistinguished colt with some early speed named Angle Light. Laurin was hoping to ensure an honest pace, and enhance Angle Light's value if he ran second or third to Secretariat. Angle Light's owner, Elmer Whittaker, knew his colt was no Secretariat, and Lucien

Laurin assured Penny Chenery that she had nothing to fear from Angle Light.

On the day of the Wood, Angle Light took the lead easily, but everyone in the place was waiting for Secretariat and Sham to come get him. Sham went after him first but couldn't get by him, and Secretariat never came close. When jockey Ron Turcotte asked the colt for his customary burst of speed nearing the stretch, Secretariat continued along like an ordinary horse, failing to fire his jets. At the finish, it was Angle Light a head in front of Sham with Secretariat four lengths back in third place. Rarely has a man looked so miserable in a winner's circle as Lucien Laurin did that day.

Neither Laurin nor Penny Chenery had known that Secretariat ran with an abcess the size of quarter on his upper lip, and even when that condition was discovered several days after the race, no one could be sure it had caused his defeat. The Wood had been Secretariat's longest race and his first around two turns, so perhaps the problem had been what some breeders had predicted all along: The colt was a typical son of Bold Ruler, brilliant at a mile and suspect going farther. Whatever the case, the fourteen days until the Derby were tense ones for everyone around the colt, especially those who had agreed to pay $190,-000 a share for his breeding rights, and for Seth Hancock, who had orchestrated that deal as his entry by fire into running Claiborne Farm. Seth had always believed that "when a horse doesn't run his race, there's a reason," which made him optimistic that the colt would run a truer race in the Derby.

♦　♦　♦

"I knew the second I got on him in the paddock there was nothing wrong with him," Ron Turcotte, who is now confined to a wheelchair as a result of a 1978 riding accident, remembers. "I'd been getting on him all week and I knew he was going to win. He had been wrong in the Wood and I didn't find out about the abcess until a week later. I was thrilled when I heard that because it finally gave a reason, and then he was his old self again. Nobody knew the horse like I did, not Lucien, not Mrs. Chenery. They didn't know that as good a two-year-old as he was, he'd gotten better over the winter. Horses that fast at two, sometimes that's as good as they get. But Secretariat went on, got bigger and stronger and better."

Last at the start of the Derby, Secretariat took the overland route going wide around the first turn and began picking off horses as if they were tied to a post. He was sixth after half a mile, second after a mile, and closing fast on Sham, who had overtaken the pacesetter, Shecky Greene.

"I thought I was going to win it, win it big," remembers Laffit Pincay, Jr., Sham's jockey. Sham would run a faster final time that day than any of the ninety-eight previous Derby winners. "Then I see this thing coming up on the outside of me and it just went, whoosh. I couldn't believe it."

It was Secretariat by half a length in midstretch, and Secretariat by $2\frac{1}{2}$ lengths at the wire. The time was 1:59 $\frac{2}{5}$ for $1\frac{1}{4}$ miles, three-fifths faster than the Derby record Northern Dancer had set nine years earlier over a slightly faster track. Sham also had run faster than Northern Dancer and fast enough to win any Derby before or since, but not against Secretariat.

As impressive as the final time were the succession of quarter-mile splits the big red colt had turned in: :25 $\frac{1}{5}$, :24, :23 $\frac{4}{5}$, :23$\frac{2}{5}$, :23. The last one was the fastest closing quarter in the race's history, and no colt had ever run each quarter progressively faster than the last. Horses almost always slow down at the end, but Secretariat was speeding it up at every pole.

That was enough to scare off all but five challengers for the Preakness two weeks later, where only the winner's style was different. Once again, Secretariat broke last, but this time he charged to the lead early in the race, taking command and beating Sham by the same margin, $2\frac{1}{2}$ lengths. It should have been recognized as another track-record performance, but the electronic timer at Pimlico had been malfunctioning all week and gave him an official time that was one full second slower than the record time he really ran, according to independent clockers, television films, and the *Daily Racing Form.*

Secretariat was now on the verge of winning the Triple Crown. It had been twenty-five years, the longest gap since the series had been recognized, since Citation had done it in 1948. The sport had three weeks to wait for what looked like the cinch of the century, and that allowed plenty of time for coronations. Secretariat became the nation's favorite story in the midst of the dispiriting Watergate scandal, and made the covers of *Time, Newsweek, Sports Illustrated,* and the *National Observer* during Belmont Week. Penny Chenery, fulfilling every outsider's notion of what a horse owner should look like, fit the part perfectly as her colt's spokesman, and racing was enjoying more attention than ever before in this country.

Even so, no one was prepared for Secretariat's Belmont Stakes, a race that still gives veteran racegoers the chills. He and Sham both went for the lead, and they dueled for half the race as if certain to kill each other off. They went a half mile in :46 ⅕ and three quarters of a mile in 1:09 ⅘. No horse had ever run that fast that early and won the race, even running unchallenged. For Sham it was too much. Secretariat, though, was just beginning, accelerating anew when he should have been fading. Turcotte looked over his shoulder and could not see the competition. The roar for the first Triple Crown winner in a quarter of a century began at the top of the stretch, and Secretariat crossed the wire an astounding 31 lengths in front of Twice a Prince, with Sham struggling home last. Secretariat's time of 2:24 flat had a similarly otherworldly quality, being 2 ⅗ seconds or about 13 lengths, using the rule-of-thumb that a length translates to one-fifth of a second, faster than any horse had run the race before.

Secretariat was now bigger than both life and his $6.08

million pricetag. Some syndicate members thought he should be retired at once, since he could not possibly exceed his accomplishments, but Penny Chenery and Seth Hancock wanted to keep going. There was no reason to think he would ever lose again.

On a somewhat subtler note, Secretariat was helping the entire racing and breeding industry every time his name appeared in print. His Triple Crown sweep had put his name on the lips of people who had never known or cared about the sport. Penny Chenery had to hire a William Morris agent to field the commercial offers pouring in. Secretariat's continued activity could only draw new fans through the turnstiles and, perhaps, new owners to the yearling sales several years down the road when Secretariat's sons and daughters would begin selling in the auction ring.

The colt raced six more times. At Arlington Park near Chicago, he drew 42,000 fans to watch him win by nine lengths. His next stop was Saratoga, where a track-record crowd of 38,000 piled in to watch him run in the Whitney. The colt came up with a virus the morning of the race, but Penny Chenery decided to run him anyway, reluctant to disappoint the crowd and hopeful he could still win. But Secretariat weakened in the stretch to finish second to an improbable longshot named Onion, trained by H. Allen Jerkens.

His next start came in the inaugural Marlboro Cup at Belmont Park. The New York tracks had been trying to attract commercial sponsors for years, and Secretariat provided the needed bait. The event originally was conceived as a match race between Secretariat and his four-year-old stablemate, Riva Ridge, but since both were coming off defeats it was turned into an invitational that drew five other horses. Secretariat collared Riva Ridge in the middle of the stretch and drew off to an explosive 3½-length victory, setting a world record of 1:45 ⅖ for 1⅛ miles.

Two weeks later, he ran in the Woodward at a mile and a

half, the same distance at which he had posted his historic 31-length Belmont score. Running on a sloppy track, he was near the lead through a slow pace and then tired badly late, finishing second by 4½ lengths to another Jerkens trainee named Prove Out.

That was no way to end a career, and Chenery and Hancock decided that a no-lose proposition was to try him on the grass. Grass racing was just beginning to gain real popularity in America, having been introduced as something of a novelty twenty years earlier, a taste of European racing. If Secretariat

(left) **Secretariat, after winning the 1973 Preakness, with jockey Ron Turcotte, trainer Lucien Laurin, and owner Penny Chenery.**

Secretariat winning the 1973 Belmont Stakes by 31 lengths.

N.Y.R.A.

went well on the grass, it would increase his appeal to foreign breeders, who might want to race his offspring in Europe. If he didn't, he had the ready-made excuse of not liking the surface, and it would not damage his value.

He liked it just fine, ending his career with two smashing victories that gave him another dimension. In the Man o' War Stakes at Belmont, he led all the way to beat the two best older grass horses in the country, Tentam and Big Spruce, by five lengths, breaking the course record by three-fifths of a second. On October 28, he closed out his career at Woodbine Race Course in Toronto, winning the Canadian International Championship by 6½ lengths from Big Spruce.

Nine days later, he was paraded at Aqueduct for a farewell he found confusing.

"He hasn't run, he hasn't worked, and he hasn't won, so he doesn't know why he's in the winner's circle," said Mrs. Chenery.

In a career that spanned just sixteen months, he had shown more brilliance than any horse before him. While some fans and journalists bemoaned his early retirement, there was little left for him to do. He had won sixteen of twenty-one races, swept the Triple Crown and broken the track record each time, beaten older horses in the fall, and been just as sensational on the grass. Penny Chenery had generously showcased him around the country and helped the sport's popularity and image more than anything else in decades.

It was time to go home, to begin a new career at Claiborne Farm, a career that was to prove a bit more complicated than running fast.

♦ ♦ ♦

When Secretariat arrived at Claiborne on November 15, 1973, and bedded down in the stall that for thirteen years had housed his father, Bold Ruler, his new owners had only paid a 25 percent down payment on their $190,000 per share. Penny Chenery had borrowed the money needed to pay Meadow Stud's estate taxes by providing banks with the syndication agreement and the insurance policies that covered anything going wrong. If Secretariat proved a fertile and able stallion, the syndicate members would pay the balance by February, and the insurance companies would pay off in the case of injury or infertility.

Secretariat and Riva Ridge, who had been syndicated for $5.1 million, arrived at Claiborne and within a week underwent fertility tests, based on analysis of their sperm. It was expected to be a routine certification, but both tests came back negative: the semen of both horses contained immature and unstable spermatozoa. This occasionally happens with young horses coming off the race track, but it was still upsetting to the breeders who planned to send their mares to Secretariat in the coming months.

The syndicate members agreed to give Secretariat a couple of months to acclimate to farm life, and then test him again. In the meantime, to get him used to the breeding act before introducing him to expensive thoroughbred mares, he was test bred to three nonthoroughbred mares in early December. Two of the three got in foal, but results of a second lab test still showed the immature sperm. The news media had a picnic with the story, betraying for the first time a kind of populist resentment of the breeders. It wasn't that anyone wanted to see the beloved Secretariat fail, but that everyone enjoyed the possibility of the monied breeders taking a beating. This could not have been the case, since everyone was insured against infertility, but the public liked the idea.

Seth Hancock had a gut feeling, based on the results of the test breedings, that Secretariat would do better in the flesh than under the microscope, and gambled by revising the syndication contract. If everyone would agree to dispense with lab tests and just go ahead and breed the horse as if nothing were amiss,

Hancock would guarantee that at least 60 percent of the mares would get in foal. If that did not happen, anyone with a barren mare who wanted to drop out could get a full refund with interest; those whose mares were in foal but still wanted out would have to forfeit the $47,500 they had already paid, but could back out thereafter. All but one member of the syndicate agreed to the revision.

Secretariat got thirty-three of thirty-six, or almost 92 percent, of his mares in foal, far better than the national average of 66 percent. Now all the shareholders could do was to sit back and wait. The foals would be born in 1975, sold as yearlings in 1976, and begin to race as two-year-olds in 1977. Only then would anyone know if Secretariat could advance the breed the way his own immediate ancestors had done, reproducing some of the brilliance he had added to the game's standards or perhaps even exceeding it.

♦   ♦   ♦

"Breed the best to the best and hope for the best." The motto is needlepointed on pillows that sit in the parlors of more than a few Kentucky breeding farms, and is repeated throughout the industry as a credo. It applied particularly in Secretariat's case. Usually, the trick in breeding is to match a sire and dam who will compensate for each other's deficiencies and combine their strengths. Breeders often want to match a stallion with brilliant sprinting speed to a mare with stamina, a stallion with a docile temperament to a mare with a fiery nature.

With Secretariat, though, there were no such deficiencies or personality quirks to compensate for, so breeders simply sent their best-bred, best-producing mares, hoping to add layers onto layers of talent. The mares breeders sent to Secretariat his first year at stud were probably the strongest group ever sent to a stallion. Most of them were accomplished both as racemares and as producers of top horses. They included mares, some of them veterans old enough to be his grandmother, who had foaled such luminaries as Northern Dancer, Dahlia, Majestic Light, Arts and Letters, and Reviewer.

Secretariat's first foal was born January 1, 1975. There is not much on which to judge a newborn foal, and most horses do not show their talent until they reach the race track. But in Secretariat's case, the foals were immediately scrutinized, as if they should be bigger, taller, and faster at birth than any in history. The breeders were also anxious to know how much they resembled their sire. If the foals were born looking like little Secretariats, perhaps they would run like the old man.

The first foal fit the bill, emerging into the world with three white stockings and a narrow stripe down her face, but most of the others looked as if they could have been sired by any of the other stallions at Claiborne. Word began to get around that Secretariat was not "stamping his get"—not reproducing himself—and Seth Hancock decided it was best to admit it right off and begin lowering everyone's expectations. In the eyes of some syndicate members, he went too far, saying as early as March that he hoped the second crop would look better than the first.

Secretariat "has not reproduced himself with anything like the consistency we hoped for," he said.

By that summer, some of the shareholders whose mares were now in foal with Secretariat's second crop decided to sell the mares in foal rather than waiting another two years to sell those foals as yearlings. The prices fetched were far below expectations, though the buyers, most of whom had been unable to get a share in Secretariat, were delighted to get a piece of the action. Tom Gentry, a flamboyant Kentucky breeder who woos prospective buyers with lavish parties featuring paid appearances by celebrities, bought the in-foal mare Levee Night for $225,000; Artists Proof was purchased by Stavros Niarchos, the Greek shipping magnate, for $385,000; and Raymond Guest, a cousin of Ogden Phipps and the millionaire owner of Powhaten Plantation in Virginia, bought Color Me Blue for $220,000.

That fall, two of Secretariat's first foals were put up for auction as weanlings. The majority of horses are sold the following summer as yearlings, but weanling sales appeal to a small speculative market. They sell for less than yearlings, since they are less developed and show fewer signs of possible talent, and many buyers purchase weanlings in the hope that they can be resold at a profit as yearlings. With a new stallion's first crop, it is often decided to sell one or two as weanlings and bid up high prices, setting a tone for the prices that might be expected the following summer at the yearling sales.

That was the thinking of E. V. Benjamin, who consigned his Secretariat colt out of Chou Croute, hoping to break the world weanling record of $202,000. He got the record but the top bid of $250,000 was far short of his expectations. The other weanling, a filly out of Zest II, went for $200,000 and was accidentally bought back by Nelson Bunker Hunt, who had owned the filly in partnership and consigned her through an agent. The agent was trying to raise the bidding on Hunt's behalf when he got stuck with the filly.

A cool market analyst might have urged caution about Secretariat as a sire, but coolness does not apply to the most select summer yearling sales, held first in July in Lexington and then in August at Saratoga. The sales are as much a social as a business function, with the elite of the breeding world assembled under one roof to bid on the best-bred and best-looking yearlings in the entire foal crop.

Amid such an atmosphere, the ten Secretariat yearlings consigned to the auctions broke every possible record. The seven sold at Keeneland brought in $2.61 million and three more went at Saratoga for a flat million. The total record average was $371,000, almost double what each share in the colt had cost. Those who had waited to sell had been amply rewarded.

The biggest winner was Hunt, who more than made up for

his buyback weanling by selling the most expensive yearling ever: a colt out of Charming Alibi went for $1.5 million to John Sikura, a Canadian horseman bidding on behalf of a partnership of Canadians who wanted to get into racing at the top.

Suddenly, the $190,000 Secretariat shares and the horse's total pricetag of $6.08 million looked cheap at twice the price. If the breeders could get $371,000 per Secretariat yearling, they had almost doubled their investment in one year, and now the Secretariat foal they would get each succeeding year to race or sell was gravy. It was nothing new in principle. The old-line breeders and society owners who had bought into Blenheim and Nasrullah generations earlier had realized similar scales of profit early on, but it was a money-making secret they had kept to themselves, and the numbers were relatively small. The public neither knew nor cared about these obscure investments, but now, a $1.5 million yearling was national news, and not just on the sports pages.

The sale of a yearling for $1.5 million when the previous record had been $715,000 was as much a quantum leap as Secretariat's time of 2:24 in the Belmont Stakes. An unraced horse now could be sold for almost as much money as a horse had ever earned by racing, and that simple fact suddenly skewed the appeal of the sport to investors. Dreamers and sportsmen would still want to buy a horse for $10,000 and fantasize about his winning ten or one hundred times that much while carrying their colors. But now horse trading appealed to the kind of investors who had always shunned the sport because of its high risk. Financiers looked at racing economics, and they saw an industry on the launch pad. Secretariat, they figured, would carry the entire industry upward.

♦   ♦   ♦

The gold rush was on, though no son or daughter of Secretariat had yet to set foot on a racetrack. Their performances became almost incidental to the revolution he had prompted, since expectation rather than results had changed the scope and scale of the industry.

The first to race was Sexetary, a chestnut filly out of Spa II. She had been purchased at the Keeneland sales by Andrew Adams, a Kentucky coal man, for $75,000, a cheap price that reflected a crooked knee. Many of the syndicate members did not intend to race their two-year-olds from Secretariat's first crop until after the summer yearling sales, lest failure on the track detract from the auction prices of the second-crop yearlings. Some people who had purchased first-crop Secretariats, including Adams, were approached by syndicate members and asked not to race them until after the sales. But Adams liked his filly, had no vested interest in protecting her sire's reputation, and went ahead and ran her at Keeneland on April 16, 1977, in a short "baby race" for two-year-olds. Sent off a heavy favorite at 1–2, less on good information than on the bettors' hunch that the first Secretariat foal to run just had to be a winner, Sexetary broke sharply, led for about a quarter-mile, and faded to fourth.

Secretariat's first stakes winner was Dactylographer, who was sent to England and took the William Hill Futurity on the grass in October. His first American winner was Sacrebleu, whose dam had been purchased in foal by Raymond Guest. He won a maiden race at Laurel Race Course in Maryland in late December, 1977.

From Secretariat's first crop, twelve horses eventually won races, two of them winning stakes races. For any other stallion, it would have been a promising start, but for Secretariat it was a severe disappointment.

One colt in particular seemed to embody the gap between expectation and results. Paul Mellon had used his Secretariat share in the first season to breed him to All Beautiful, who had already produced Arts and Letters, the Horse of the Year in 1969. Mellon named the resulting foal Debrett, and the colt was one of the few to resemble his sire in appearance and conformation. He had an awful disposition, though, and Mellon had to choose between gelding him, which would make him more tractable but eliminate the possibility of a career at stud, or retiring him immediately and cashing in on a good-looking son of Secretariat. Mellon, a sportsman with an immense personal fortune, decided the colt had too much ability never to run and went ahead and had him gelded.

"It was more important to see what a horse who looked so much like Secretariat, and seemed to have talent, could do," he said.

But Debrett's lone distinction would be that in 1984 he was the only product of Secretariat's first crop who was still racing. He was out of Mellon's hands, and had passed through many other owners, winning nine races and $150,000. But he had sunk to the bottom of the racing hierarchy, running in claiming events in which any owner could purchase him for $4,000. As an nine-year-old in 1984, he won one of twenty-one starts.

After the first crop, Secretariat's record began to improve steadily. By 1985, he had sired thirty-two stakes winners, good enough to place him in the top 5 percent of the world's sires, but still a disappointment for a horse who had been expected to be as dominant a sire as he was a racehorse. Sham, who went to stud the same year as the colt who beat him in all the Triple Crown races, had sired thirty-four stakes winners in the same time, and by 1985 neither was among the hot, fashionable sires whose offspring were setting new sales records. Secretariat's yearlings in 1985 sold for an average of $137,775.

Secretariat's best offspring have included Medaille d'Or, a champion two-year-old in Canada; General Assembly, who was second to Spectacular Bid in the 1979 Kentucky Derby and set a track record winning the Travers; and such standout fillies as Lady's Secret, who won eight stakes in a row in 1985, Terlingua, Secrettame, and Viva Sec.

His best fillies have opened a ray of hope that he may

ultimately have a major influence on the breed. They have begun producing extraordinary foals, raising the possibility that Secretariat's greatest influence, like Sir Gallahad's, may be as a brood mare sire. In 1984 Secreto, a son of Secretariat's daughter Betty's Secret, won the Epsom Derby, and in 1985 his daughter Six Crowns's son, Chief's Crown, was favored in all the Triple Crown races and won the Travers and the Marlboro Cup. Some of Secretariat's most loyal fans have advanced a theory that perhaps his own foals were overbred, that their own pedigrees were too rich. Breeders sent their best and classiest mares to him regardless of whether they were particularly good matched. A generation later, the theory goes, Secretariat's blue-blooded daughters are now being bred more selectively.

Wayne Lukas, a quarter horse trainer who was just beginning to train thoroughbreds when Secretariat's first crop was three, has had more success with the stallion's progeny than any other trainer, conditioning twelve stakes winners by Secretariat. He has a related theory about the horse's career at stud.

"The mistake everyone was making was breeding those classic distance mares to a classic distance horse like that," Lukas said. He believes that mares with an early burst of speed made better mates for a stallion whose stamina was apparently limitless.

Neither Hancock nor anyone else can explain Secretariat's failure to reproduce himself except to say that it was an unreasonable expectation in the first place. Although he certainly fit the role of "the best" in the breeders' equation of "breeding the best to the best," the science is neither that simple nor that exact. After all, The Bride, with parentage identical to Secretariat's, could not win a single race.

Yet Secretariat's success by any standards but his own proves the fundamental soundness of the equation. It was his potential, rather than his performance, that revolutionized the breeding industry, as far-reaching an effect as he had as a racehorse.

Among Claiborne's current roster of thirty stallions, Secretariat ranks only seventh among the twenty-four who have had foals to race. But in public popularity and affection, he is still number one at the farm. Seth Hancock says that 90 percent of the farm's visitors, even among clients who come to do business involving other horses, ask about Secretariat and want to have a look at the horse they can still remember seeing win the Belmont Stakes by 31 lengths. He is 100 pounds heavier now, but his coat is sleeker than ever and his massive stride when he gallops through a field still makes other horses look smaller, slower. He spends most of his days prowling his showcase paddock disdainfully, preening and then dismissing and intimidating visitors. He still gets fan mail, and in four or five years he will be retired from stud service and given his pension to roam and graze without a duty. He will not breed but he will run, still feeling and looking like the best of the best.

"You look back," Seth Hancock says today, "and regardless of how he turned out, Secretariat was a steal. Considering my position at the time, I wouldn't have tried to syndicate him for $10 million. But in retrospect even $15 million would have been a good investment."

3

Sangster and the Sheiks

At the 1983 Keeneland sales, seven years after a yearling from Secretariat's first crop had drawn a record $1.5 million, the 308th colt catalogued for sale drew an opening bid of $1 million. The next bid was $2 million, and the action was just beginning.

The $1.5 million record at first had grown slowly, nudged by inflation and a prosperous market. There were no million-dollar babies in 1977, one who fetched $1.3 million in 1978, five who went for between $1 million and $1.6 million in 1979, and five for between $1.05 million and $1.7 million in 1980. Then suddenly, the market went wild.

In 1981 there were thirteen million-dollar yearlings, including three for more than $2.9 million and one for a record $3.5 million. In 1982, twenty-one yearlings went into seven digits, one of them setting a new standard of $4.25 million. Now, at the 1983 sales, twenty-eight had already sold for at least $1 million when the 308th colt in the catalogue walked into the ring.

It took eight bids on the colt to set a new world's record of $4.3 million. Two minutes later, the price was up to $7 million, the number of bidders down to two. Twenty-four bids later, the duel of checkbooks ended, and the final price was a staggering $10.2 million, a number so unexpectedly large that it could not even fit in the spaces on the electronic tote board in the sales pavilion.

More than the prices had changed since Secretariat's first yearlings had gone into the ring seven years earlier and prompted the first great rise in the sales market. Only one of the seventy-four million-dollar yearlings sold since then had been sired by Secretariat; and almost all of the top purchases had been made by two teams of newcomers to the game, the two bidders who had just offered small fortunes to buy an unraced, year-old horse.

One of the bidders was a team headed by Robert Sangster, a British soccer-pools operator who had raced a few horses in England in the 1960s and begun buying American yearlings in 1972. He began with one partner, John Magnier, the son-in-law of Britain's top trainer, Vincent O'Brien. Now he was the heaviest investor in a syndicate that included a Greek shipping magnate, several European horsemen, and a Los Angeles attorney.

The Sangster group had failed to answer the $10.2 million bid made by their rivals, three brothers from the tiny but oil-rich Arab sheikdom of Dubai in the Persian Gulf. The youngest and most active of the brothers, Sheik Mohammed ibn Rashid al-Maktoum, had caught the horse bug while attending Cambridge University in the 1970s and drawn his two older brothers into the game.

The bidding war that ended in the $10.2 million record was less than a realistic reflection of the market but more than just a duel of egos. It was the culmination of a revolution in American breeding, in which the dominant players and pedigrees had changed. It also marked an international shift in the horse trading game that was restoring bloodlines and money to regions of the world where the thoroughbred had originated centuries earlier.

Secretariat's earliest ancestor was Eohippus, the "dawn horse," which appeared during the Eocene era, about 50 million years ago. Eohippus was about the size of a modern Shetland sheepdog and had four toes on the front feet and three toes on the rear feet. Centuries of evolution produced the ancestor of the modern horse, *equus caballus,* a larger hooved animal which existed during prehistoric times. This horse is thought to have developed in Asia and spread from there to Europe and North Africa.

Bones and drawings found in Paleolithic caves suggest that these horses were for eating and not riding. But the ancient Egyptians used horses in war, according to carvings on the walls of the tombs of Pharoahs that show horses pulling chariots and carrying weapons. Chinese paintings dating back 5,000 years suggest the same purpose. In 312 B.C., the Romans built the first military road, the Appian Way, largely to make traveling easier and more efficient for their horse-drawn chariots and cavalry.

The events which led to the development of the thoroughbred strain began more recently, with the Battle of Hastings in 1066. The English were fighting the Norman invaders to a draw when suddenly the Normans unleashed their superior cavalry, scoring a decisive victory and elevating the importance of a well-bred horse to the realm of national security. During the Hundred Years' War between England and France in the fourteenth and fifteenth centuries, the military role of the horse was so vital that both countries set up royal studs to improve the breed.

Similar programs developed all over the continent in the next few centuries, with English, French, and Spanish breeds being crossed in search of the right combination of speed and sturdiness for battle. With the passing of heavy armor, the emphasis shifted from a stout, sturdy type of horse to a lighter, faster one, and the development of firearms and artillery accelerated that trend.

The royal stud farms inevitably produced some horses who were exceptionally faster than their contemporaries, and royalty just as inevitably raced them for pleasure. Racing found its greatest monarchical enthusiasts in England's Stuart Kings, James I, Charles I and Charles II. James I established Newmarket as the headquarters for his hunting trips in the late 1500s and also began to race there, building a palace and stables. His son, Charles I, also loved racing and patronized Newmarket, which survives today as the site of Britain's National Stud.

Racing suffered a setback in the Great Rebellion. Beginning in 1649, the Council of State banned racing throughout Britain, but it went on anyway. Although Oliver Cromwell broke up the royal stud and those of wealthy private breeders, Cromwell continued to import horses and breed them for battle. In addition, some private breeders began returning to their estates to breed horses.

In 1660, the Stuarts were restored to the throne of England, and a crucial era in the development of the modern thoroughbred followed. Charles II was a racing enthusiast and a small-scale breeder. He also was a notorious womanizer and his exploits earned him the same nickname as his stallion, "Old Rowley."

In the years that followed the Restoration, British breeders started importing more horses from the Middle East and North Africa to improve their stock. Horses known as Arabs, Barbs, and Turks already had come to England in various ways in previous years, being purchased, captured in battle, or presented as royal gifts and parts of dowries. The Arab was an ideal choice to be mated with Britain's sturdy mares because of its burst of speed and relative lightness.

Since it was hard to get pure Arabs, English breeders also took related breeds such as Turks and Barbs. Keeping their precise lineages straight proved difficult since horses at that time were named after their owners. The same horse might be called by a different name each time he changed hands. However, equine geneticists agree that all modern thoroughbreds trace their ancestry back in direct male line to one of three imported stallions: the Byerley Turk (foaled about 1680), the Darley Arabian (1700), and the Godolphin Arabian, or Barb (1724).

The Byerley Turk was captured in battle at Buda in 1688 by Captain Richard Byerley. Like many other horses called Turks, he was believed to have been an Arab who was bought or stolen by a Turkish officer. His male line survived through a dominant eighteenth-century stallion named Herod.

The story of the Godolphin Arabian is the most romantic and difficult to substantiate. Foaled in the Yemen in 1724, he was exported to Tunis, via Syria, and was sent to the king of France as a royal gift. According to some stories, he was rejected as a gift and was later found pulling a water cart in Paris. He eventually ended up in the hands of the second earl of Godolphin, who stood him at his Gog Magog stud near Newmarket. He was used sparingly and sired only about ninety foals, but his male line survived through a successful grandson, Matchem.

The Darley Arabian was purchased by Thomas Darley, a Syrian merchant, in 1704, and sent to Darley's brother, Richard, who operated a stud farm at Aldby in Yorkshire. The Darley Arabian is the male ancestor of about 80 percent of modern thoroughbreds. His line had six main branches, the most important of which flowed through thirteen generations before reaching Phalaris, founder of the dominant strain of the best twentieth-century thoroughbreds.

Phalaris sired Pharos, whose son Nearco sired both Nasrullah and Nearctic. Nasrullah was the horse Bull Hancock imported in 1949, and he sired Bold Ruler, Secretariat's sire. Nearctic, Nearco's other key son, sired a colt named Northern Dancer.

Robert Sangster's initial purchases included horses whose pedigrees were rich with the blood of Nasrullah. But within a few years, his interest, and that of the other international buyers who would join or compete with Sangster, was focussed on the other branch from Nearco, through Nearctic and finally to Northern Dancer.

♦ ♦ ♦

E. P. Taylor, the Canadian industrialist who would build a fortune based on oil, precious metals, and Northern Dancer, in 1936 was a horseplayer and brewery owner who wanted a profitable way to combine his business and pleasure. Beer advertising in Canada was severely restricted by government regulations, and Taylor hit on the idea of getting the name of his beer into print by racing a stable under its name. Thus began Cosgrave Stable, which started with a bankroll of just $4,000.

There was racing in Ontario for only six months of the year, and it was Taylor's plan to pick up some cheap American horses and bring them to Toronto for the beginning of the season, where they would have a bit of an edge on the locals. It worked like a charm. One of his first bargains was Nandi, a filly he got for $1,500. After winning a dozen races for Taylor, she was retired and produced Windfields, his first homebred stakes winner and namesake of his farm. Nandi would also be the great-great-granddam of Right Chilly, who in 1977 would become the 193rd stakes winner Taylor had bred, making him the most prolific breeder of stakes winners in the sport's history.

The early Cosgrave Stable did better than Taylor had expected, easily winning races in Canada, expanding into the States, and getting plenty of free exposure for his beer. He curtailed his racing during World War II, when he represented his country in Washington for $1 a year and was eventually named president of the British Supply Council in North America by Winston Churchill and Lord Beaverbrook.

Taylor began breeding more horses after the war and started buying top bloodstock at the Keeneland sales, making his breeding operation at Windfields Farm near Toronto an even bigger fish in the small pond of Canadian racing. His power in the sport grew with his stature. He was behind the consolidation of the major tracks into one circuit, which increased the number and value of stakes races. A lot of them were being won by Taylor's horses, especially the Queen's Plate, Canada's version of the Kentucky Derby. From 1949 through 1985, twenty Taylor-breds won the Plate.

Determined to prove that Canada could produce world-class runners, Taylor asked his chief racing contact in England, George Blackwell, to pick him out the best mare in the 1952 Newmarket December Sale. In Blackwell's opinion, it was Lady Angela, a daughter of Hyperion, an English sire from outside the Phalaris line. Lady Angela was in foal to Nearco, Nasrullah's sire, and Taylor bought her and arranged to breed her back to that stallion the following year. Her first foal by Nearco was nothing special, but the next year she produced a good-looking brown colt Taylor named Nearctic, combining the sire's name and the local geography. Taylor put the colt up for sale at a private auction, but nobody bid the price Taylor had put on him, and he took the colt back to race.

Nearctic was born the same year as Bold Ruler and they met twice in New York as two-year-olds, with Bold Ruler winning both times. For the most part, though, Nearctic stayed in Canada. He won twenty-one of forty-seven races and was Canada's Horse of the Year in 1958, a superstar by that nation's standards, a solid and professional racehorse measured against the best in America. Taylor brought him home to stud and in 1960, his first year as a sire, he was scheduled to be bred to twenty mares. An additional mating was tacked on in June, when Taylor's star three-year-old filly, Natalma, was injured while training for the Kentucky Oaks and was vanned home. The mating of Nearctic and Natalma was a late one, and her foal was not born until the following May 27, meaning he would be spotting several months to some of his competitors in the same foal crop.

The colt, Northern Dancer, was small but strong, a bay with a crooked white blaze and three white feet. He was offered for sale at Taylor's annual yearling sale, which was less an auction than a gallery showing. Since Taylor kept some of his yearlings and raced others, he did not want buyers to think he was culling the best for himself and selling the rejects, or using phony bidders to inflate the final prices. So he put a pricetag on each yearling, and invited buyers to take them or leave them.

Nobody took the Nearctic–Natalma colt, priced at $25,000, just as no one had taken Nearctic himself seven years earlier. So he joined the Taylor racing stable, carrying the colors of his breeder's Windfields Farm. The colt had a feisty personality, and Taylor even considered gelding him for a while, but decided not to when early training reports said that Northern Dancer was coming along quite nicely.

The colt became Canada's top two-year-old in 1963, winning three stakes there and then vanning into New York to take the Remsen Stakes at the end of the year. He went south for the winter with the trainer Horatio Luro, an Argentine whose own successful career had started in 1942 when he claimed Princequillo for $2,500. Princequillo had gone on to multiple stakes victories and an outstanding career at stud, first at Ellerslie and then at Claiborne, where among others he sired Somethingroyal, the dam of Secretariat.

As a three-year-old, Northern Dancer bloomed. A cracked hoof cost him a few weeks of training, but he then won the Florida Derby, the Flamingo, and the Blue Grass in succession, and came into the 1964 Kentucky Derby as the second favorite behind Hill Rise. Bill Shoemaker had his choice of riding the two favorites and went with Hill Rise. Shoemaker's mount had an awful trip in the Derby, getting bumped twice early and going wide on both turns, while Northern Dancer, under Bill Hartack, saved ground on the rail and proved best by a diminishing neck. His winning time of 2:00 flat was a Derby record, two fifths faster than the undistinguished Decidedly had run two years earlier over an unusually fast track to better the record Whirlaway had set in 1941. It would stand until Secretariat's 1:59 ⅖ nine years later, and by 1985 it still was the second-best winning time posted.

Many racetrackers did not believe the Derby outcome had been genuine, and two weeks later in the Preakness, Hill Rise was an even heavier favorite than he had been in the Derby, going off at 4–5 to Northern Dancer's 2–1. Northern Dancer went to the lead after six furlongs, and once he got there Hartack took a strong hold on him and gave him a breather. When Hill Rise came to him at the top of the stretch, Hartack just let out a notch and Northern Dancer spurted clear, winning by 2¼ lengths over The Scoundrel with Hill Rise a head back in third.

Racing was on the verge of its first Triple Crown winner since Citation in 1948, but Luro did not even want to run the colt in the Belmont. Northern Dancer was not a speedball, but he was a small colt and Luro thought the 1½-mile distance would undo him.

"I was even surprised that he got a mile and a quarter," Hartack would say twenty years later. "He had talent but he was a small colt and built like a sprinter. It's hard to understand how he turned out the way he did as a sire because he just was not made to get a mile and a half." While there is generally little correlation between a thoroughbred's height and his success at the races, small horses are thought to be at a disadvantage in particularly long races such as the Belmont. The average thoroughbred stands 15–16 hands high, that is, 60–64 inches measured from the ground to the top of the withers. Northern Dancer is so unusually short that as a stallion, he climbs up on a nine-inch-high box when he is bred to mares. The box, coated with a rubbery padding, is known at Windfields as "the pitcher's mound."

Luro and Hartack were right in worrying about the colt's ability to get a mile and a half in the Belmont. Kept within striking distance most of the way, Northern Dancer made a

Northern Dancer at Windfields Farm, 1985

bold move at the top of the stretch but quickly flattened out and ended up a tired third, sixth lengths behind the winner, Quadrangle.

Northern Dancer raced just once more, going home to Canada for the Queen's Plate, where he romped as the heavy hometown favorite. He ruptured a tendon shortly thereafter, was retired, and at year's end was named America's champion three-year-old and Canada's Horse of the Year. He went to stud at Windfields in Canada, though five years later he was moved to Maryland after Taylor bought a spread there.

His initial stud fee was $10,000, and he seemed at first to be a good midlevel investment. Seven yearlings from his first crop went through the ring for an average of $38,357.

It took a few years to see what a bargain that was. Of those seven sales yearlings, all were winners and five became stakes winners. From his second crop, which averaged only a bit more in price, came five more stakes winners, including a colt named Nijinsky whose success would foretell his sire's future.

The only knock on Northern Dancer when he first went to stud was that he, like ten other near–Triple Crown winners before him, had failed the so-called "test of the champion," as promoters and stuffy traditionalists like to call the 1½-mile Belmont. The vast majority of American races are half that long. Even most important stakes races are between one mile and 1¼ miles, and a horse who wins the Belmont will often never race that far again. The inclusion of a 1½-mile race in the Triple Crown is a holdover from European racing. The distance of the St. Leger, the final leg of the English Triple Crown, is over 1¾ miles, and races at that distance, even for cheaper horses, are common. The horses are not necessarily sturdier. All racing there is on the grass, a less tiring and taxing surface than the hard dirt tracks on which the American classics are run, and the pace of European races is creeping by comparison, with most of the horses loping along for the first mile before launching strong late runs.

Still, the English Triple Crown—consisting of the one-mile Two Thousand Guineas, the 1½ -mile Epsom Derby and the 1¾ -mile-plus-127-yard St. Leger—is even more difficult than its American counterpart. Only three horses have won it in this century. The greater range of distances is a tough challenge demanding more versatility. Also, the races span nine weeks instead of the five in this country, demanding that a horse hold top form longer and guaranteeing fresh new opponents for each leg of the series.

In 1970, it had been thirty-five years since Bahram had swept the English Triple Crown, but after Nijinsky won the Epsom Derby, he was a heavy favorite to keep going. He was a Taylor-bred colt from Northern Dancer's second crop, out of Queen's Plate winner Flaming Page, and had been purchased at a Canadian yearling auction by Charles Engelhard, a precious metals dealer who raced extensively in America, Europe, and South Africa. Vincent O'Brien, who had trained several classic winners for Engelhard, spotted the strapping bay colt at Windfields while there to inspect another yearling and was bowled over by his physical presence. On the trainer's recommendation, Engelhard bought the colt for $84,000, at that time the highest price ever paid for a Canadian yearling, and sent him to O'Brien in Europe.

Although Northern Dancer had been tried just twice on grass, without success, his tall, long-striding son took to the turf beautifully, winning all five of his starts at two. The next year he won the Two Thousand Guineas, the Epsom Derby and, at odds of 1–2, the St. Leger as well, succeeding at a distance more than a quarter of a mile longer than that of the Belmont, in which his sire had failed.

Earlier in the year, E. P. Taylor had syndicated Northern Dancer, selling forty shares at $60,000 apiece for a total of $2.4 million. He probably could have gotten twice as much a few months later, and Northern Dancer's stud fee jumped from $15,000 to $25,000 after Nijinsky's triumph. European breeders tried to keep Nijinsky there for stud duty, but Bull Hancock pulled off his last major transatlantic raid and syndicated the handsome son of Northern Dancer for a then-record $5.44 million in 1970.

The old-line American breeders who bought shares in either Northern Dancer or Nijinsky that year had made the investments of their lives. They had no way of knowing that the Northern Dancer line was just beginning its ascendance in Europe, and that British owners such as Robert Sangster were beginning to envision a new order based on that sire line.

◆   ◆   ◆

Vincent O'Brien's daughter Susan had married a third-generation Irish horseman named John Magnier, who had taken over running the family stud farm at the age of sixteen when his father died. Six years later a mutual friend introduced him to Sangster, and the two hit it off immediately. They had been partners in buying and selling horses for years by the time Nijinsky emerged as the best horse in Europe, and were even more impressed when O'Brien, the trainer of six Epsom Derby winners, insisted that Nijinsky was something really extraordinary, a watershed horse. There seemed to be some special alchemy in Northern Dancer's blood. The horse was passing on his own speed, but his offspring also were able to cover the longer distances at which Northern Dancer himself had failed, perhaps because they were running on the grass.

Sangster and Magnier had begun buying yearlings speculatively in 1972, including their purchases at Keeneland, and they began increasingly to look for Northern Dancer yearlings. They also had begun acquiring available seasons each year and buying mares to send to him, but they did not yet have mares of their own as good as the ones who produced sales yearlings.

Sangster's involvement increased when he inherited control of $30 million of Vernon Pools, the bookmaking company that

R. H. WRIGHT

Robert Sangster

had been in his family for three generations. He became the main backer for a syndicate of experts that began launching a virtual siege on the American summer sales each year. Known widely as "Sangster's Gangsters," his team of investors, conformation experts, and trainers included O'Brien, who would train all the purchases, and Magnier, manager of the Irish stud farm where their horses would eventually go to be bred.

Sangster's investments began to pay off quickly, most notably with two 1975 yearling purchases. One, a flashy chestnut son of Northern Dancer named The Minstrel, won the Epsom Derby and Irish Derby in 1977. The other, Alleged, won back-to-back runnings of the Prix de l'Arc de Triomphe, Europe's most prestigious year-end race. The Minstrel was syndicated in 1977 for $9 million, then a world record, and went to stand at Windfields, the heir apparent to his sire. Alleged was syndicated the following year for $13 million.

The Minstrel's $9-million price tag certified the fashionability of the Northern Dancer line. Secretariat's first foals were not doing well, and the talk was that perhaps it was the Nearctic branch of the Nearco line, not the Nasrullah one, that would now dominate the sport. Strangely, this perception was being based almost purely on the results of European racing. To this day, Northern Dancer has not sired an American champion. The notion that he could sire only grass horses would diminish later with the success of Danzig, but the initial fever over Northern Dancer was European in origin.

Whatever the reason, it was beginning to transform the scope of the summer sales. It was inevitable that other horse traders with Sangster's kind of money would begin bidding against him for Northern Dancer yearlings, in the hopes of getting a Nijinsky or The Minstrel of their own. At first, the competition came from a few other leading Europeans such as Stavros Niarchos, the Greek shipping tycoon.

The first million-dollar yearling had been the Secretariat–Charming Alibi colt from Secretariat's first crop that Nelson

Bunker Hunt had sold for $1.5 million in 1976. The second came two years later, with a Northern Dancer colt that had been bred by Claiborne. Niarchos bought the colt, produced by the Claiborne mare Special, for $1.3 million at the 1978 Keeneland sales. Sangster was the underbidder.

The following year, three more Keeneland yearlings went for over $1 million, and two of them went home with Sangster: a $1.4-million colt by Nijinsky out of Syrian Sea, the latter a full sister to Secretariat; and a colt by Northern Dancer whom Sangster took for $1 million. Niarchos was the underbidder on both.

Sangster and Niarchos were both doing their bidding through the same agent, the British Bloodstock Agency, and decided after the 1979 sales to join forces rather than fight. They formed a series of partnerships with several other investors, including Danny Schwartz, a Los Angeles attorney who had helped structure their agreements. Different horses would race in individual partners' names, but they would share ownership of all of them.

At the 1980 sales, three of the five yearlings who went for over $1 million were signed for by the BBA, one each in the name of Sangster, Niarchos, and Schwartz. The two Europeans were no longer competing, but there were new players in the ring who were keeping the prices high.

The new group was three brothers from Dubai, one of the seven city-states on the Persian Gulf that joined in 1971 to create the United Arab Emirates, a nation the size of Maine. Dubai's ruling family, the Maktoums, is headed by aging patriarch Sheik Saeed ibn Rashid al-Maktoum, and his three eldest sons: Maktoum, the deputy prime minister; Hamdan, the minister of finance and industry and representative to OPEC; and Mohammed, the minister of defense, and the primary buyer of horses.

"Racing is in our blood," Sheik Mohammed likes to say. "When we came to England we saw a lot of care being taken, both with the horses and the racing. We do a lot of our business here, and America is too far for us to see our horses. So we chose Europe as our base."

The first year the Maktoums, quickly dubbed the "Dubai brothers," came to the summer yearling sales, they merely dabbled, purchasing eighteen yearlings for $4.6 million. They did some sharp buying, largely on the advice of some royally paid British agents who did their picking and bidding. Their first round of buying yielded Touching Wood, who would win the 1982 St. Leger, and Awaasif, a top filly who would run third in the Arc. They liked the action and they came back with more money in 1981, buying twenty-seven yearlings for $10.7 million.

Their bidding that year caused an overhaul of all the sales records. No yearling had ever been bought for more than $1.7 million, but in 1981, three went for between $2.9 million and $3.5 million. All of them were colts by Northern Dancer, and all of the final bidding was between Sangster and the Sheiks. Sangster's group won out on two of the three, but the Sheiks ultimately came away the winners. Sangster's two colts, Ballydoyle and Fulmar, were flops on the race course and eventually sold as stallion prospects for less than their purchase prices. Ballydoyle, the record $3.5 million yearling, now stands at Green Pastures Ranch in Oklahoma for a $5,000 stud fee.

The $3.3 million yearling was purchased by Sheik Mohammed and given to Sheik Maktoum. Named Shareef Dancer, the colt raced only five times but did enough to be named England's three-year-old champion of 1983. The Sheiks retired him to their new Dalham Hall Stud in Newmarket, and had little trouble getting an unprecedented $40 million for him, in forty shares at $1 million per share. American breeders now wanted in on the ground floor of a Northern Dancer-line syndication, especially those who had missed out on the earlier ones.

The popularity of the bloodline grew with the success of

Northern Dancer colts in Europe each year, reinforcing its desirability. In June of 1982, Golden Fleece and Assert, Sangster-owned grandsons of Northern Dancer, combined to sweep the English, Irish, and French Derbies in the space of three weeks. It was not surprising that the record price for Ballydoyle was topped the next month at Keeneland.

In 1982, Sangster and the Sheiks went at it again, one or the other buying the five top-priced yearlings in the sales. Sangster again got the topper, going to $4.25 million for a Nijinsky colt. Sheik Mohammed's Aston Upthorpe Stud came out as the

Sheik Mohammed ibn Rashid al Maktoum (left), **with advisers John Leat and Col. Richard Warden.**

leading buyer at Keeneland, though, and spent a total of $29.6 million for sixty-one yearlings at the three blue-chip summer sales.

The bidding by the two groups changed the sales virtually past recognition. There had been four $1 million-plus yearlings in 1979, the year before the Sheiks joined the action, twenty in 1982, and by 1984 there were thirty-eight. In 1983, foreign money, most of it Sangster's or the Sheiks', was accounting for over 60 percent of the gross receipts.

The sheer amount of money, which suddenly made horse trading a hot story in newsmagazines, seemed to matter little to either of the two big camps. They would go to any price to get what they wanted, and an extra million here and there seemed like a few extra chips at a big gaming table.

One year at Keeneland, Sheik Mohammed was talking with some associates near a television monitor displaying sales results, and he noticed a colt being purchased for $675,000.

"Who bought that?" he casually asked one of his advisers.

"Why, you did, your highness," he was told.

"Ah, very good," the Sheik said with a smile.

In 1983, he smiled again after outduelling Sangster in the bidding for the $10.2 million yearling, a Northern Dancer-My Bupers colt. That year, the two big bidders accounted for the six sales toppers and twenty-one of the twenty-nine who sold for $1 million or more.

In 1984, the two bought the nine most expensive yearlings of the year, failing to break the $10.2 million mark but accounting for the second through sixth highest prices ever paid for a yearling. Six of the seven top prices were for colts by Northern Dancer.

Their similar strategies were working, and they did not mind each other's presence in the ring. The market conditions they were creating were the same ones they were exploiting. It had been the Maktoums' purchases of Northern Dancer blood for seven-digit sums in the early 1980s that made it possible for them to syndicate Shareef Dancer for $40 million a few years later. American breeders were willing to pay $1 million a share for that stallion because they figured that any of his sons might fetch $1 million or more as yearlings and get them out quickly.

The American breeders reacted to the new market with a typical mixture of greedy satisfaction and paranoid unease. It was swell having these free-spending foreigners come over and pump such ridiculous sums into the American game, but the Americans were beginning to feel frozen out of their own market, unable to compete for the top horses they liked, reduced in effect to being left to bid only on those yearlings that Sangster or the Sheiks didn't want.

The unease took a predictably racist turn. Cartoons in racing and breeding publications began depicting the Arabs with crude stereotypical strokes, flying on magic carpets with harems in tow and oil-spattered greenbacks oozing from beneath their turbans. Another incident was more revealing: The Sheiks had always flown in for the sales on a private 747 that sat at the Lexington airport for a week, its Arabic lettering visible from the road leading into Keeneland. In 1984, some anonymous patriot rented a hot-air balloon to block the public's view of the plane, a gesture that seemed to capture the American breeders' reluctance to admit that perhaps they had been reduced to manufacturing luxury goods for foreigners.

The irony of it all, one that did not escape the proud Arabs, was that the game had finally come full circle. The foundation stallions had been Arabian, and had sired the thoroughbred when crossed with English mares. The best of the bloodlines had come to America in the first half of the century, but now the distillation was heading back to where it had all started.

The question then became whether it was going home to stay. Amid Lexington's enthusiasm for the foreigners' bottomless bankrolls, there emerged an undercurrent of worry: What would happen if, suddenly, Sangster and the Sheiks were to stay home one year?

It seems inevitable that it will eventually happen, though

the industry has been slow to see this. Sangster and the Sheiks now own nine breeding farms in England and Ireland, and over a thousand horses that will begin producing homebred runners. Having virtually cornered the market on Northern Dancer's blood, they are running out of reasons to come over and buy more each year. Northern Dancer turned twenty-four in 1985, and is not expected to survive the decade. Nijinsky turned eighteen the same year. Most of Northern Dancer's top sons and daughters are now owned by Sangster or the Sheiks.

This was not the first time that the breeders were fearing a collapse of the market in the absence of big spenders. A decade earlier, the death of Charles Engelhard, Nijinsky's owner and the dominant buyer at select sales in the late 1960s, prompted the same concerns. But along came a series of new players, first a flurry of Japanese investors, then Sangster, Nelson Bunker Hunt, Niarchos, and the Sheiks. The top market breeders remain confident that there will always be new money attracted to the glamour of the sales.

"It's a quick way for a rich man to get his name in all the papers," says John Nerud, the legendary trainer of Dr. Fager and president of Tartan Farm. "It's like buying a baseball team. There's always going to be someone with too much money who we can get interested in horse racing."

The breeding community's anxieties were amplified by another upsetting thought: What would happen to yearling prices if Sangster and the Sheiks got together, as Sangster and Niarchos had done in the late seventies, and decided not to bid against each other? This fear was fanned early in 1985 when Sangster, Magnier, and O'Brien boarded one of Sheik Mohammed's private 727's and took off for a weekend at his palace in Dubai, where the Sheik introduced his visitors to two of his other passions, camel races and falconry. Even before this summit, Sangster had announced that Sheik Mohammed had agreed to buy a half interest in the two most expensive Northern Dancer yearlings purchased by the Sangster syndicate at the 1984 Keeneland sale. The colts would continue to be trained by O'Brien but would race in Sheik Mohammed's colors.

The growing friendliness between the two camps did not rock the 1985 Keeneland sale, where records fell once more, Sangster and the Sheiks were again the leading buyers, and the Northern Dancer line continued to command the top range. But there were some new elements as well, ones that signaled renewed strength for American pedigrees and bidders.

◆   ◆   ◆

On the afternoon of Tuesday, July 23, a bay colt was led into the ring at Keeneland. Most yearlings fuss and whinny when being exhibited, and the green-jacketed grooms often have their hands full keeping them from rearing or drowning out the auctioneer. This colt, though, was mild and calm, his only interest being in playing a game of grab-the-shank with his handler.

The tote board to the left of the ring lit up with 215, the number pasted on the colt's flanks and corresponding to his page in the sales catalogue. Most of the buyers in the packed pavilion settled back to watch, knowing this colt was going to be beyond their means. While it is usually impossible to predict exactly which yearling will be the sales topper, number 215 was one of the half dozen considered most likely to bring a huge price. A buzz filled the crowded amphitheatre.

The tension could even be seen at the front of the pavilion as the tuxedoed auctioneers prepared to sell a million-dollar baby. Tom Hammond, the announcer, leaned toward the microphone to begin his introductory pitch, and Tom Caldwell, who would be calling the actual auction, quietly cleared his throat. Charlie Richardson, one of the six bid-spotters who would be watching the key players in the pavilion for discreet signs, tapped his sales catalogue against his leg. Richardson had been with Keeneland since 1950, when he started out changing the paper numbers on the manually operated bid board.

"Hip number 215, property of Warner Jones, is a bay colt by Nijinsky out of My Charmer, by Poker," began Hammond in a formal voice with just a touch of the circus barker in it. "By the great Nijinsky, European Horse of the Year and among the leading sires, sire of more than eighty stakes winners. He has sired more Grade I and Group I winners than any other sire except his sire, Northern Dancer, and his stakes winners this year include Shadeed."

As Hammond continued reciting the colt's lineage, detailing the accomplishments on the female side of the pedigree, the audience stirred in anticipation. When Hammond was done, Tom Caldwell took the microphone. He already was watching the hand signals being given him by the bid-spotters, and listening through a tiny earpiece to Rex Jordan and Dale Rouk, two more bid-spotters who worked the circular holding area behind the pavilion where yearlings are walked around before being led into the sales ring itself. Some buyers prefer to bid from "out back," shunning the fishbowl scrutiny of the glass-enclosed pavilion, and everyone knew that Sangster's Gangsters would be bidding and caucusing there. The floor had just opened and two spotters had already signaled a seven-figure opening bid.

"Rex beat you, Charlie, I think, if that's what you were about to do," Caldwell said. "Rex says one million to start him."

The auction had begun. The rest of Caldwell's patter until the colt was sold would be more song than speech. While auctions of this level in other commodities, such as artwork, tend toward understatement, even the highest grade of thoroughbred auctions retain a countrified flavor with a lot of hustle to it. Even though the bidders are multimillionaires who know precisely what they are bidding on, there is an underlying informality and humor about the proceedings, a lot of drawling talk about a "fine-lookin' animal there" amid million-dollar sums. Almost no one but the auctioneers wears a necktie, and the look is more country club than Wall Street.

At one Saratoga sale, an auctioneer became mildly annoyed when a woman in the audience began working her charms on a wealthy bidder, distracting him in the midst of a six-figure duel for a yearling.

"Young lady, we're trying to conduct business with that gentleman," one auctioneer said over the loudspeaker.

"I think she's trying to conduct some business, too," another auctioneer said.

When the bidder finally dropped out, the second auctioneer had a final comment: "Young lady, I hope you're more successful with that man than we were."

The heart of the auction, though, is the singsong of the ever-rising price, an unbroken cadence of numbers and encouragement for bigger numbers. For Tom Caldwell, it was just beginning now at $1 million on hip number 215.

"Would you bid two?" he asks the crowd. "One million, two. Would you bid two? Two . . . Oh, I thought you meant two million, five hundred thousand, that's what I was waiting to clarify." Caldwell's voice, for just a moment, dripped mock disappointment at how slowly things were going. "All right, one million two-fifty, one million five. Got a million two-fifty, a million FIVE. A million two fifty, I need a five, a million FIVE, I got it. Two million, sir. Two, two million five, a two million five, now three. Would you bid three million, two million five, would you bid three?"

It has taken less than half a minute for the bidding to reach $2.5 million on this colt, and everyone in the pavilion knows the action is just beginning. Only when the bids slow down is the final price in sight, but so far they are coming rapidly.

"Three, three million five," Caldwell continues. "Three million five, three million five, FOUR. At three million five, make it four. Would you bid four, would you bid four, would you bid four, FOUR, ho, four-five. At four-million five, he beat you, Rex! At four million five, six, now seven! Seven million, at six, would you bid seven? Would you bid seven, would you bid seven, thank you, six million five hundred, now seven. I've got it ahead of you, Rex, catch up!"

In less than sixty seconds, the bidding has climbed to $7 million, and the battle is down to two bidders. One is working from behind the podium, out of the public view, and it is no surprise that Sangster's Gangsters are still in it.

The other group is not, however, the Maktoums. Their agents had sat watching, having received instructions to pass on this colt. Instead, the competition is coming from the upraised hand of Wayne Lukas, the California-based trainer who is bidding on behalf of two wealthy clients: Eugene V. Klein, former owner of the San Diego Chargers, and L. R. French, a Texas oilman. Few Americans have bid this high for a yearling, but now as Lukas looks over to Klein and French for approval, they are nodding at him to go on.

"That's seven, thank you, seven million five," Tom Caldwell is singing. "At seven million, would you bid five, seven million five hundred thousand, that's five, EIGHT. At seven million five, eight, eight million five, NINE, thank you! Now, you're all right, I'll take care of you. At eight million five, nine. Eight million five, nine."

The giddiness of the prices is about to take over the auction. Caldwell's bid-spotters are signaling that both bidders are wanting to go on, but Caldwell mistakenly reads these signals as actual bids.

"Ten, thank you, eleven million," Caldwell says quickly, skipping over bids that have not been made. "At ten million, would you bid eleven million—I had nine, Charlie, when you said 'yep.' Now do you wanta be ten? Okay, I've got nine million in back on Dale. Nine million, would you bid ten. Nine million five, would you bid ten? At nine five, would you bid ten? Nine million seven, would you bid ten million, would you do it? At nine million seven, would you bid ten million, sir?

Nine million seven, would you bid ten? At nine million seven. The Lord loves a cheerful giver. Nine million eight, ten million. Nine, now ten. At nine million nine, would you bid ten million. At nine nine, would you bid ten?"

The last bid, $9.9 million, has come from Lukas, who has been leaning over to huddle with Klein and French.

"TEN, in back!" Caldwell shouts, recognizing the Sangster group's bid. "Ten million five hundred. At ten million, ten million one, ten million two. At ten million one, would you bid two? Now two, at ten million one, do you want him, two. At ten million one, do you want him at two. At ten million one, two, THREE!"

Lukas has just topped the $10.2 million record set by Sheik Mohammed two years earlier, and there is a ripple of recognition in the audience. That $10.2 million bid had been a shock at the time, and there weren't enough digits on the electronic bid board to accommodate the eight-figure price. The next year Keeneland had cut an extra digit on the lighted board. It had not been used in 1984, but it was needed now as the price on the Nijinsky colt continued to climb.

"At ten million three, FIVE, thank you. At ten million three, ten million five, would you do it at—Oh, you ain't seen nothin' yet—ten million three, ten million five. At ten million three, would you give five, ten million three, ten million five, at ten million three, what do you say? At ten million three, ten million five, do you want five, thank you, eleven million? Ten million five, eleven million, at ten million five, ten million SEVEN, now eleven million. At ten million seven, would you bid eleven million for him? At ten seven, would you bid eleven? At ten seven, eleven million, would you do it. At ten seven, ten eight, thank you, now eleven million. At ten eight, eleven million. At ten eight, eleven, would you do it? At ten eight, eleven, eleven, thank you, eleven million five. At eleven million, would you bid five. Eleven million, five hundred thousand, eleven million, do you want him at five. What do you say,

Dale? At eleven million five—be bold!—at eleven million five, do you want him at five. What'd you say? Eleven million one. Eleven million two. At eleven million one, eleven million two, would you do it? Eleven million one, do you want him at two. At eleven one, eleven two, TWO, thank you."

Despite all his exhortations, Caldwell has reached that part of every sale where the increments start slowing. With most other horses, he will interrupt the flagging bidding to recite some of the yearling's good breeding again and remind the audience what a good-looking physical specimen they are bidding on. In some cases, where he thinks the price is low, he will chide the bidders, sometimes even telling them that they are "stealing money at the price" or "dead wrong on this one." But with number 215, it would be redundant and insulting to remind the two bidders what they are bidding on. In fact, it might just break the flow of their game and remind them that this is, after all, just a horse, and an unraced one-year-old at that. Caldwell does not know how much farther this one can go, so he gently continues urging the two bidders up. Back and forth it goes, from $11.2 million to $11.5 million to $11.7 million to $12 million to $12.3 million. The increments are getting erratic and the pace is slowing.

The Sangster camp, sensing indecision to continue on their unseen rival's part, decides to keep going but to drop the increments from $100,000 to $50,000, to show their determination but perhaps save $50,000 on the final price.

"Dale, I'd love to accommodate you," Caldwell says to the spotter taking the bids from the back. "All right, now you're talkin' my language! Twelve million three fifty."

The bidding has hit a crawl now. Caldwell works hard to get the price up to $12.4 from Lukas, then $12.5 from Sangster's group. He tries for $12.6 from Lukas, who is looking over at Klein intently. Caldwell, somewhat whimsically, changes gears. "How about thirteen million dollars and let's just stop this? Thirteen?"

Lukas looks over at Klein a final time, and the owner nods. This is their last big shot. They will jump the bid $500,000, hoping that Sangster's Gangsters will look at one another and decide they are beaten. Lukas speaks for the first time in the bidding.

"Yeah!" he says.

"Thank you!" says Caldwell in a booming voice, then picks up the singsong again. "Thirteen five. Thirteen million five hundred thousand. At thirteen five, thirteen million, five hundred thousand. At thirteen million, are you all through? Do you want him at five any more? At thirteen million five, Dale? Did that plum choke you down? Okay, I'll wait for you, thirteen five. Thirteen five, what do you say. At thirteen million five hundred thousand, let's go, at thirteen million five—"

There is a final bid from out back.

"Thirteen million ONE, thirteen million two. I have thirteen one, two, thirteen one, would you bid two. Thirteen two, at thirteen one, do you want him at two. At thirteen one, two, would you bid two, would you bid two, would you do it. Should we try that one more time, thirteen five. That might stop 'em this time."

He is talking directly to Lukas now, suggesting a jump like the one from $12.5 million to $13 million a minute earlier. Lukas leans toward Klein, and his intensity is almost palpable. Straightening up again he stares straight ahead, looking dejected now. Finally he shakes his head and utters a simple "No." That had been their final offer, and Sangster was still ready to go higher. Someone close to the podium says something unintelligible about the Lukas group. It sounds like "They've got the money."

"They sure have," Caldwell responds with a laugh. "Football team, oil wells, you name it. Thirteen five? Thirteen one. Thirteen five, would you do it. Thank you sir, thirteen one and—"

He picks up the gavel, sensing the bidding is over. He holds it aloft for a moment amid dead silence, then brings it down with a crack.

"Sold him back there, Dale, to your man. Thirteen million one hundred thousand. Can you tell me offhand who it might be, Dale?" Caldwell knows full well and is really asking Dale to see if the Sangster group minds having it announced, even though their names will be released to the press momentarily. There is no problem.

"BBA, Joss Collins," Caldwell says, giving the shorthand for the British Bloodstock Agency and its representative who is signing the sales slip on behalf of the Sangster group. "Our contending bidders—Mr. Lukas, Mr. Klein, Mr. French, and associates. Thank you all. Let's give them a nice hand, ladies and gentlemen—new world record."

A few minutes later, the two bidders are surrounded by microphones.

"Most of the best horses that have been bought here go to Europe," Sangster is saying, "and I would not like to see him in an opposition camp. We didn't know who was bidding. Wayne Lukas was a very brave bidder. We didn't want to see him in Europe taking on our best colts."

Sangster had assumed he was bidding against the Sheiks and realizes now that had Lukas won the bidding duel, the colt would have stayed in this country. Still, he says, his group was committed to getting the colt at any price.

"We wanted him here," Lukas says. "We wanted one like that kept in the United States. Fortunately they breed a lot of them every year, and Keeneland is held every year and we'll be back."

The involvement of American bidders at so high a level was a signal of new vigor after four years in which Sangster and the Sheiks had carved up the market unchallenged. But more important was the breeding of this particular colt and the fact that his being a son of Nijinsky may not have been the most appealing part of his pedigree, to either Sangster or to Lukas.

Had the Nearctic–Northern Dancer branch of the Phalaris line emerged alone in the 1980s, and its best representatives all been owned by Sangster or the Sheiks, the balance of international breeding power might finally have swung back to those parts of the world where the thoroughbred has its roots, Britain and the Arab world. But after the relative disappointment of Secretariat, two other American stallions from different branches of the Phalaris line had come along to influence the breed and change the game once more. One of them had been foaled by My Charmer, the dam of hip number 215, and he had cost less than one-seven-hundredth of what his yearling half-brother fetched exactly a decade later.

4

A Slew of Gold

In January 1973, a few weeks before Penny Chenery asked Seth Hancock to syndicate Secretariat, Hancock got a call from Ben Castleman, a small-scale local breeder. Castleman, the owner of the White Horse Tavern in Florence, Kentucky, just south of Cincinnati, had bought a 69-acre farm in Lexington in 1967 and named it White Horse Acres. His spread was tiny compared to the sprawling nurseries surrounding it, but he loved the racing game and wanted to breed a few horses of his own. He began with a brood mare band of one, a mare named Fair Charmer, whose first foal was a Poker filly named My Charmer. In Castleman's racing colors, My Charmer had won six of thirty-two starts in 1971 and 1972, including the respectable Fair Grounds Oaks in Louisiana, and now she was about to begin life as a brood mare.

Twelve years later, My Charmer's yearling colt by Nijinsky would sell for $13.1 million. Now, Castleman was looking to breed her to a stallion whose fee would not put him out more than $5,000.

Castleman was calling "out of the blue," as Seth remembers it, to ask for advice on a stallion to breed to My Charmer. His original choice was Jacinto, a young son of the recently de-

ceased Bold Ruler, but Seth told him Jacinto's mating calendar
was all filled. Castleman asked for another affordable suggestion, and Seth quickly named Bold Reasoning, a grandson of
Bold Ruler who was standing his first season at Claiborne for
$5,000.

Castleman agreed, figuring he was still getting the Bold
Ruler blood and for a reasonable fee, and Seth Hancock was
pleased to book another mare to Bold Reasoning, as there was
not yet much demand for the colt's services. Bold Reasoning
had been brilliant when right, setting a track record of 1:08
⅘ at Belmont Park as a four-year-old and winning eight of
twelve career starts including the 1971 Jersey Derby. But Bold
Reasoning did not race at all as a two-year-old, was held out of
the Triple Crown races and was retired in the middle of his
four-year-old season. Chronic throat problems often left him
tired during races, and repeated attempts to clear up the ailment
failed.

Ben Castleman sent My Charmer to Claiborne in March,
and she delivered a colt eleven months later on February 15,
1974. "He was the ugliest foal we'd ever seen," Castleman
recalled later. "He had a head that looked about two feet long."

The ugly foal got a little better-looking as he grew to be a
yearling, and was popular with the White Horse staff for his
eagerness. They joked that the coarse and awkward colt always
made it to the feed tub first at mealtime.

Castleman's plan as a breeder had been to sell his colts at
auction to pay the bills and keep and race his fillies, eventually
bringing them home as brood mares. So the Bold Reasoning–
My Charmer colt was going to auction. The question was
where.

Of the 28,127 foals born in 1974, 4,905 eventually were
auctioned, for prices ranging from $200 to $450,000. The latter
price and almost all of the other big ones came from the two
major select sales, the July sale in Lexington run by the Keeneland Association, which operates the track there; and the Au-

gust sale in Saratoga run by the Fasig-Tipton auctioneering company, which also conducts a dozen other yearling sales in Kentucky, New York, Maryland, and Louisiana.

Fasig-Tipton, which started out selling trotting horses in the late 1890s, branched out into thoroughbreds in 1901, and by 1943 its annual auction at Saratoga had become the largest yearling sale in the country. Many of the horses sold there were bred in Kentucky, so when wartime travel restrictions interfered with its Saratoga sale, Fasig-Tipton shifted the site to the grounds near the track at Keeneland, and put up a big circus tent in the paddock for the sale. Local breeders liked having an auction in Lexington so much that they built a permanent sales pavilion at Keeneland the next year and formed an auction company of their own, which was eventually taken over by the Keeneland Association. Fasig-Tipton continued its Saratoga sale, which served mainly Virginia and Maryland breeders, and by the late 1970s Keeneland's July sale had emerged as the premier yearling auction in the country. With the size of the nation's foal crop growing every year, the selection committees at Keeneland and Saratoga got tougher on their evaluation of both pedigree and conformation, and many breeders suddenly found some of their better yearlings being excluded from the two blue-chip sales. Fasig-Tipton saw the need for a new auction, one that would have some of the appeal and ambiance of the select sales while offering much less expensive runners. So in 1974, Fasig-Tipton moved into Kentucky, starting a sale of horses one cut below those who would be auctioned two days later at Keeneland. Their first sale, like Keeneland's 31 years earlier, was held in a tent, but by 1975 Fasig-Tipton had built its new sales pavilion on Newton Pike, less than a mile down the road from White Horse Acres.

For a Kentucky breeder like Castleman, just getting a horse accepted by the Keeneland cataloguing committee would have been a certification of success, because Keeneland picks only the best-bred and best-looking applicants. Castleman's Bold Reasoning–My Charmer colt was one of about 1,200 nominated to the sale. Like 850 others, he was rejected. His pedigree was not compelling enough to make up for his coarse looks, and the Keeneland judges also noted that his right front foot "toed out," or turned out slightly from the ankle down.

Most thoroughbreds have physical flaws of some kind. Detecting any but the most glaring ones is a subtle art that takes a practiced eye and almost a sixth sense. Assessing the importance of these flaws is often a guessing game.

Many potential buyers descend on the summer sales with a retinue of advisers, veterinarians, and conformation experts. They spend hours and sometimes days sizing up those youngsters whose pedigrees have already attracted the buyers' fancy on the pages of the sales catalogues, which are sent out a month earlier. The yearlings, brushed, combed, and polished to perfection, are led out of their stalls for inspection. Prospective bidders scrutinize them with narrowed eyes, sometimes stepping forward to run their hands over a horse's legs with the delicacy of a diamond cutter appraising a stone.

Experienced judges of horseflesh have a checklist of ideal characteristics: a bright, bold eye, indicating intelligence and spirit; a strong, wide jaw for plenty of breathing room; a long, well-proportioned neck set at the proper angle, essential for good balance; a wide, deep chest to allow the lungs to expand; strong shoulders and hindquarters to provide power; most important of all are straight, strong feet and legs to withstand the pounding of the racetrack.

Finding all these qualities is no guarantee that the horse will be able to get out of his own way when he gets to the track. Secretariat and Buckpasser came close to physical perfection and ran to their glorious looks, but some of the handsomest horses ever to go through a sales ring have been flops in competition. Other horses have succeeded in spite of their flaws. Seabiscuit, a grandson of Man o' War, was born with a big head, short legs, and large, knobby knees, but the colt went on to become the world's leading money winner. Assault's right foot never grew properly and the hoof wall was so thin that the blacksmith had trouble finding a spot to hammer in a horseshoe nail. That did not stop the colt from winning the Triple Crown in 1946.

Sales yearlings are fattened up with special feed mixes that make them look older and more like racehorses. This practice may sway unsophisticated buyers, but experienced judges know that the fat will have to be burned off before the horse can get to the races.

In general, though, the sales are relatively free from outright trickery and deception. Consignors do not try to unload bad horseflesh, even though responsibility rests with the buyer, because their reputations would be ruined.

Buyers and sellers, in fact, sometimes go to great lengths to demonstrate to the public how much they are on the up-and-up. At the 1984 Keeneland select sales, E. P. Taylor's Windfields Farm consigned a Northern Dancer–Ballade colt who fetched a sales-high bid of $8.25 million from Robert Sangster's group. A week later, Sangster's veterinarians discovered a problem with one of the colt's feet that had obviously been there for at least a month. Windfields issued a statement offering to buy back the colt any time within a year if Sangster was at all dissatisfied. Sangster never took them up on it.

The Fasig-Tipton judges accepted Ben Castleman's Bold Reasoning-My Charmer colt for their 1975 sale after giving him six out of a possible ten points on conformation and a seven on pedigree, and noting that the toeing out which had bothered the Keeneland judges "should not preclude a racing career." The physical inspection sheet, rating him in thirty-six conformation categories, closed with the comment, "Strong colt. Shoulder developed well. Good angle. Strong back, good through middle." On a scale of 100 on which 91 was "outstanding" and lower than 30 "unsuitable for sale," the Bold Reasoning–My Charmer colt earned a 75.

Castleman had decided his colt was worth at least $15,000 and that he would buy him back if the bids failed to go that high. Consignors almost always make such a decision or, in more expensive cases, put an actual reserve price on a yearling through the auction company. Many horses hammered down later are revealed to be buybacks or "RNA's," the shorthand for "reserve not attained." At the 1985 Keeneland summer sale, a Northern Dancer colt who had apparently been sold for $7.4 million turned out to be the top-priced RNA ever. Ralph Wilson, Jr., the former Buffalo Bills owner who bred the colt, thought he could get more, and decided to take his chances racing him instead. Sending the colt through the ring cost Wilson a 5 percent commission to Keeneland on the buyback bid, amounting to $370,000.

Ben Castleman's colt went into the Fasig-Tipton ring on a rainy Saturday night that kept many potential buyers at home. The bidding began at $3,000, increased at increments of $500 and $1,000, and stalled at $17,500. Fasig-Tipton president John Finney, sharing the podium with the auctioneer, Ralph Retler, tried one final time to get the action going again, at least up to $20,000.

"First foal of a stakes-winning dam and by a *runnin'* horse," he implored the buyers, but there were no more bids.

The sales slip was signed by a Karen Taylor of White Swan, Washington, on behalf of herself and her husband, Mickey, a Yakima logger; it would turn out that they had two other partners, Jim Hill, a New York racetrack veterinarian originally from Florida, and Hill's wife, Sally.

Karen Taylor named the colt to reflect the transcontinental nature of the dual ownership. For the Hills, she thought of the swampy, alligator-infested sloughs or "slews" of Florida's Everglades. For herself and Mickey she initially wanted their hometown, but White Swan Slew didn't sound right. Alliteration won out, and the colt was named Seattle Slew.

◆   ◆   ◆

Mickey and Karen Taylor were still living in a house trailer in White Swan, a town of 600 near the Yakima Indian reservation, when they purchased Seattle Slew. A third-generation logger, Mickey had started out driving a truck and then gone on to cut and haul timber. In 1970 he married his high-school sweetheart, Karen Pearson, who was in the midst of a five-year stint as an airlines stewardess for Northwest Orient.

As part-owner of a logging company that had been started by his grandfather in the early 1900s, Taylor obtained the rights to 95 percent of the pulpwood on the Yakima Reservation. In 1973 the Canadian pulp industry, which controls the price of pulp in the Northwest, was hit by a strike, and the resulting pulp shortage made Taylor's rights a sudden bonanza as prices tripled.

Taylor, who had grown up around quarter horses, had raced a few of them at nearby Yakima Meadows with his brother, Quirt, while still in high school. Now he had the money to invest in thoroughbreds.

He bought two fillies at the 1973 Keeneland sales but also wanted to have something running while waiting for those yearlings to grow up. Bob Penney, a Washington veterinarian who was a friend of the Pearson family's, heard that the trainer Allen Jerkens had a horse for sale in New York. His name was Triangular, and Jerkens, who sent out Onion and Prove Out that year to beat Secretariat in separate races, thought the horse would fare better out west.

Bob Penney recommended that the Taylors ask Jim Hill to check out Triangular in New York before buying him. Hill, the son of a Ft. Myers, Florida, rancher, had attended veterinary school at Auburn. He decided to specialize in racehorses after working at Claiborne as a veterinary assistant in the summer of 1959, and served his residency at the prestigious New Bolton Center at the University of Pennsylvania. Practicing near the New York tracks, he had gained a reputation as a superior judge of horses and was frequently consulted about potential purchases.

He gave the Taylors the green light on Triangular, and the horse won two races for them in California. The first time the two got a chance to know each other was the next fall, when Hill saw Taylor kicking a newspaper machine at 6 A.M. in a Lexington hotel lobby. The two men hit it off immediately and soon were spending hours talking horses.

"We both drank Jack Daniel's—that helped," Mickey Taylor says with a laugh. "I don't know, I guess the chemistry was just right. We've never had an argument, and it's been a partnership made in heaven."

Taylor asked Hill to look at a few yearlings he was interested in buying at the 1974 fall sales. The seeds of their partnership were planted when Hill refused to take a fee for recommending a colt Taylor bought for $16,000.

The colt, named Lexington Laugh for the fun the Taylors and Hills had together in Kentucky, looked like he might be a good one. He finished second in the Del Mar Futurity the next summer, a major race for West Coast two-year-olds, and Taylor turned down an offer of $175,000 for the colt. Two months later, Lexington Laugh fractured a leg during a stakes race and eventually had to be destroyed.

Taylor was impressed with Hill's eye for a horse and by the veterinarian's assertion that many owners were robbed blind by trainers and veterinarians who buffaloed them with excuses and ailments. Hill liked Taylor's enthusiasm and willingness to spend money. They meshed well. Taylor is the more gregarious of the two, the salesman and the spokesman, given to large Western belt buckles and cowboy boots. Hill, a shy and somewhat nervous man, is more comfortable with horses than crowds.

The two couples decided to put together a more formal partnership. Karen Taylor's father, an accountant, drew up a plan for what they called Wooden Horse Investments, the deal calling for an eventual fifty-fifty split, with Taylor putting up most of the money and Hill contributing his time and knowledge to pick the horses and keep an eye on them.

The horses all ran in Karen Taylor's name, because in some states veterinarians are prohibited from owning horses in the same jurisdictions where they practice. The thinking is that their integrity, or the appearance thereof, might be compromised by caring for their horse's rivals. So Hill was publicly known only as the Taylors' veterinarian and adviser, and the nature of his involvement as effectively an owner of Seattle Slew was not disclosed until midway through the colt's three-year-old year.

For the 1975 sales, the plan was that Taylor would select the pedigrees he liked from the catalogue and Hill would inspect the horses. They were especially interested in the first crop of yearlings by Bold Reasoning, whom Hill had examined and treated several times during the horse's racing career.

"We thought he had tremendous ability, and really liked him," says Taylor. "And Jim thought My Charmer's colt looked a lot like Bold Reasoning."

Hill liked the dark bay colt's strong bone structure, athletic appearance, and overall balance, ignoring the fact that he wasn't the prettiest horse on the grounds. He put him at the top of his "most wanted list" of eight horses in the sale.

Taylor agreed to go as high as $22,000 for him, and was happy to get him for $17,500. Wooden Horse, under the name of Karen Taylor, bought thirteen yearlings at the 1975 sales, and the plan was to send them all to a training center in California. Taylor's racing strategy was to bring them along quickly and cash in fast by running them in early two-year-old sweepstakes races with inflated purses such as the Riley Allison Futurity at Sunland Park in New Mexico. Such events are particularly popular in the Southwest, where thousands of small-time horsemen put up a series of nominating fees from the time a foal is born in the hope that he will be precocious and talented enough to compete for these jackpots. The Hills and Taylors figured these races might be easy pickings for better horses.

But the California training center had only nine stalls available, so the owners decided to pick the four yearlings of the thirteen who looked least likely to develop quickly and send them east. One of them was Seattle Slew, still a big and gangly youngster who had not grown into himself. Hill recommended that Seattle Slew be sent to Billy Turner, a relatively unknown young trainer whose wife, Paula, worked with yearlings at a farm in Monkton, Maryland.

Billy Turner, who was then thirty-five years old, had grown up in Unionville, Pennsylvania, the heart of that state's horse country and a center for show jumping and steeplechasing. Turner worked with horses as a youngster and became a steeplechase rider, leading the circuit in 1960 as a regular rider for the top trainer W. Burling Cocks. He stopped riding when he got too big in 1962, and worked as Cocks's assistant for four years before forming a small public stable in Maryland.

Turner's best horse had been Dust Commander, a top two-year-old of 1969, whom Turner regarded as a possible Derby colt. After a successful two-year-old campaign, Turner thought it was time to give the colt a few months off, but the owners wanted to keep running him and fired Turner as their trainer. Dust Commander went on to win the Derby the following spring as a 15–1 longshot, but lost eighteen of nineteen subsequent starts.

Hill approved of Turner's style, his patience and his attention to possible physical problems, and Taylor liked the sound of him. They sent Seattle Slew and the three other immature yearlings to the trainer's leased farm in Monkton directly from the Fasig-Tipton sales. It did not take long for the colt to get a new name. Paula Turner took one look at him and started calling him Baby Huey, after the clumsy and pudgy duckling of cartoondom who did everything wrong.

Seattle Slew's company at the farm consisted mainly of an assortment of jumpers and steeplechase horses. Paula Turner's specialty was "breaking" yearlings, training them to get used to having a saddle and then a person on their backs, and to respond to basic commands like walking, stopping, and turning to the left or right. She figured that this particular colt was an overgrown baby who might take longer than some to learn his lessons, but Seattle Slew's behavior on his own soon convinced her that Huey had some redeeming qualities.

"There was this field that had what I called 'monsters,' " she would recall. "Tree trunks, broken walls, all sorts of things that would throw a young horse. He marched through it confidently without spooking or shying."

In February, he was sent to Turner in New York, and the workers in Turner's barn quickly saw why he had been called Baby Huey. Still more interested in playing and eating than racing, he did nothing but gallop for his first two months. In his first mild workout in April, though, he outran an older filly in the stable. Turner decided not to rush to run him, but instead to give him all the time possible to mature and develop. In August, the colt started working out more seriously, being pointed for a race, and he began to channel his juvenile energy into speed and eagerness on the track. He went five furlongs one morning in :58 $\frac{2}{5}$, a smashing move that would have made him the talk of the stables had the track clockers not miscredited the time to a nonexistent Seattle Sue. They subsequently missed reporting an even faster workout, six furlongs in 1:10 $\frac{1}{5}$ two weeks later.

This was a typical case of racetrack larceny as practiced all over the country. Morning workouts by unraced horses are recorded by clockers working for the track and the Daily Racing Form. Clockers are sometimes persuaded by gambling trainers to bury fast workouts, or they go ahead and do it on their own in the hopes of getting a good betting price on the horse when it gets to the races. Exercise riders often cooperate, planning to make a bet themselves. What usually happens, though, is what happened with Seattle Slew. Word leaks out as friends tell friends and the horse goes off as the favorite.

Seattle Slew had acquired his jockey by default. Turner had asked Eddie Maple, a leading jockey who rode most of his horses, to work the colt one morning, but Maple already had a commitment that day to work For the Moment, who at the time was considered the fastest two-year-old in New York. So Turner turned to Jean Cruguet, a Frenchman who had served in the French Army in Algeria and taken a shot at being a professional boxer before he turned to riding horses. Cruguet had arrived in the United States in 1975 and was considered best at riding in grass races, but Turner admired Cruguet's horsemanship and considered him a good choice for the colt.

Seattle Slew's debut was set back a month by a minor leg injury, and he finally made his first start September 20 at Belmont. He opened at odds of 7–5, crushing the dreams of everyone who had tried to keep his fast workouts a secret. At post time, he was the 5–2 favorite. He broke slowly but rushed to the lead in an instant and romped by five lengths in 1:10 ⅕, an outstanding time for any two-year-old. Fifteen days later, he won an allowance race by three and a half lengths in 1:22 flat for seven furlongs, one of the fastest times recorded at that distance by a two-year-old.

On October 16, he made his first stakes race appearance, in the Champagne, New York's major race for two-year-olds. For the Moment had won other stakes races and had been considered the leader of the pack, but Seattle Slew's times were faster and the bettors made him the favorite. They never had an anxious moment. Seattle Slew rocketed out of the gate and led at every pole, running up a 9¾-length advantage at the finish. His time of 1:34⅖ was the fastest ever for the race, three-fifths faster than Secretariat had run four years earlier.

He appeared now to have the nation's two-year-olds at his mercy and the two-year-old championship within his grasp, but Billy Turner thought he had raced enough. Turner's experience with steeplechasers, who compete far less frequently than

racehorses, had led to his strong feelings about running well-rested horses off training instead of excessive racing. The Taylors and Hills wondered whether Seattle Slew could be voted the divisional championship off only three races, but agreed with Turner and decided to stop on him for the year. No other two-year-old emerged in the remaining six weeks of the season, and Seattle Slew was voted the championship over Run Dusty Run and Royal Ski.

Seattle Slew went to Florida with Turner's stable just before the first of the year, and he was the focal point of the racing world for the next six months. As the champion two-year-old he was the early Derby favorite, and no colt had dominated his contemporaries so thoroughly since Secretariat. The comparisons began immediately, and few of them were favorable to Seattle Slew.

Secretariat had taken on such mythic proportions that most of the racing world and the press bridled at the very notion of there being another Secretariat so soon. There was also the feeling that Seattle Slew had promised a lot but accomplished very little. He had run only three times, never gone more than a mile, and never been challenged. Unlike Secretariat at that point in his career, he had yet to show any versatility, character, or courage, just more raw ability than a weak group of rivals. Secretariat had overcome trouble, won both on the lead and from off the pace. Seattle Slew, though, looked like he might be a one-dimensional speedball who had already peaked.

Also, Secretariat had been perfectly cast as a Triple Crown winner. His glimmering pedigree, smashing looks, and storybook owner contrasted sharply with Seattle Slew's moderate breeding, coarse appearance, and handlers who had little in common with the sport's establishment.

Seattle Slew (left) **with exercise rider Mike Kennedy and trainer Billy Turner** (on pony).

Mickey Taylor believed in his horse, though. He did not want to syndicate the colt at this point, figuring he could only become more valuable, but he had tried to sell an interest in him over the winter.

"We were negotiating with about four people to buy from one quarter to one half of Slew before he made his three-year-old debut, but we couldn't come to a satisfactory agreement," Taylor said. "It was just economics. The insurance was eating us up."

Seattle Slew's debut as a three-year-old proved he was no flash in the pan. Making his first start in five months on March 9 at Hialeah, the colt tore off seven furlongs in 1:20 ⅗, two fifths faster than the track record.

"After he won that race and broke the track record, everyone called back," Taylor recalls, "but he wasn't on the market anymore."

Taylor dug deeper into his pocket and upped the colt's insured value from $2 million to $3.5 million.

Seattle Slew came back two weeks later in the Flamingo, his first race around two turns or at more than a mile. He won easily, with Cruguet exerting little pressure, and turned in the third fastest time in the history of the race while winning by four lengths.

Seattle Slew returned to New York for the Wood Memorial, the race in which Secretariat had finished third, and while he won, his performance brought out all the doubters once again. The colt set relatively slow fractions and got away unchallenged, opened a six-length lead and coasted home, but his final time of 1:49 ⅗ was dull, and he came back visibly tired and blowing hard. His 3¼-length margin of victory was the smallest in his career. Turner, Taylor, and Hill shrugged and said the colt had been deliberately undertrained so that he would not peak before the Derby, but race track sharpies predicted that Seattle Slew would be vulnerable when he ran against better horses.

The doubters got more ammunition when everything went wrong in his final pre-Derby training. The Sunday before the race he went a mile in an extremely slow 1:41 ⅕, which left Turner saying that was all he had wanted and critics saying the Wood had knocked out the colt. A scheduled Thursday workout was cancelled after a heavy downpour and shortened to three furlongs since it had to be rescheduled for Friday, the day before the race, and Turner did not want the colt to work any farther.

On Derby Day, Seattle Slew slept until an hour before the race and left the stables calmly, but when he got to the paddock he was an angry version of Baby Huey. The small, hot Churchill Downs saddling area, surrounded on three sides by crowds shouting and pressing in for a look at the Derby horses, worked on his nerves, and the colt was dripping with sweat and snorting amid the cramped quarters and the noise. Cruguet could feel that Seattle Slew was taut but not trembling, which would have meant that he was falling apart completely, and told the colt's worried owners and trainer that he would try to settle him down on the way to the post.

When the gate opened, he broke slowly, worse than ever in his career, and for a moment he looked like he had already forfeited any chance as the horses in front of him began to shut him off.

The worry lasted only for the few seconds it took Seattle Slew to bull his way through the field and reach a contending position going into the first turn. He simply muscled his way past at least four other horses to reach second place, a length behind For the Moment. Once clear, Cruguet took a tight hold of Slew, content to be second for the first six furlongs. Rounding the far turn, Cruguet went to the whip and Seattle Slew sailed to the lead, opening a three-length margin and then coasting to the wire under intermittent urging, a 1¾-length winner over the late-rallying Run Dusty Run and Sanhedrin. His time of 2:02 ⅕ was mediocre at best, though, twelve lengths slower than what Secretariat had run, making his critics look good in defeat. The opposing argument was that Seattle Slew ran, and Jean Cruguet rode, just like Billy Turner trained —doing enough to win and nothing more. The best proof, said the colt's backers, was that Seattle Slew was now seven-for-seven and a camera had never been needed to declare him a winner.

The Preakness figured to be the easiest leg in Seattle Slew's Triple Crown bid, since the shorter distance appeared to play into his strong suit of early speed, but he had to contend with a talented speedball named Cormorant, who drew the inside post. Cormorant broke on the lead as expected, but Seattle Slew was at his throat from the start and gradually wore him down. Just as in the Derby, he drew clear by three lengths at the top of the stretch, then finished up without much push from his rider, scoring by 1 ½ lengths over Iron Constitution and Run Dusty Run. Seattle Slew was now eight-for-eight and one race away from becoming the first undefeated Triple Crown winner ever.

On June 11, Seattle Slew stepped onto a muddy track at Belmont, trying to accomplish what only Secretariat had done in the previous twenty-nine years. Mickey Taylor predicted it would be the easiest of the three races because Seattle Slew could set a slow pace against his speedless rivals, with Cormorant out of the race. Taylor was dead right. Seattle Slew loped out to his first uncontested and easy lead of the Triple Crown series, setting slow fractions in the absence of a challenge. After a half-mile in :48 ⅖ and a mile in a slow 1:38 ⅕, he had plenty left to increase his margin to four lengths at the finish, with Run Dusty Run second and Sanhedrin third, the same order of finish as the Derby.

The reception was as boisterous as it had been for Secretariat, though the time was almost 30 lengths slower. But Seattle Slew had become a grittier hero, the dime-store yearling owned by the logger and the stewardess. He was the only Triple

Crown winner sold at auction and the only one to be undefeated in his career by the end of the series. His unbeaten
record added a glow that somewhat made up for the lack of
Secretariat's aura. Here was a colt who might go through his
entire career without ever losing, something which no important horse in this century had done. The record of invincibility
and the colt's relatively humble beginnings and connections
had struck a different chord from the one Secretariat had four
years earlier, but it was equally compelling. Railbirds at Belmont were wearing "Slew Crew" T-shirts, and the picket fence
at Esposito's, a popular bar across the street from Belmont that
Billy Turner called his "office," was painted in Slew's silks of
yellow and black.

The Triple Crown had been won again, though in slow
time by a colt who looked ready for a rest. Billy Turner told
everyone that Seattle Slew would get some time off now and
then try to extend his streak in late summer or fall. Four days
after the Belmont, a farrier pulled off the colt's shoes, the official
beginning of a summer vacation.

♦   ♦   ♦

The image of the Taylors as simple folks from timber country had begun to crack several weeks before the Belmont, when
they casually told reporters that Jim Hill was more than just the
colt's veterinarian. He was, for all intents though not technically, a half-owner. Under a complex and canny scheme Karen
Taylor's father had drawn up, Hill held an option as the benefi-
ciary of his own paper corporation's pension plan to assume 50
percent of the stock in Wooden Horse Investments. The option was to be exercised June 1, 1977, ten days before the
Belmont. Since Hill would not technically be an owner until
then, he had retained his veterinary license and practice and not
taken an owner's license until May 25.

The disclosure did not bother racing officials in Kentucky

or Maryland, though it would later become a major problem in New York. But it began to suggest the kind of forethought and attention to detail that was going on behind the scenes of what the public had perceived as a Cinderella story with hillbilly players. In fact, the owners had been making plans on several fronts that were unprecedented in racing, drafting proposals and contracts to license and merchandise their colt. Penny Chenery had hired a William Morris agent to sort through all the offers she was getting from people who wanted to make a buck off Secretariat's name, but she had not gone out and pursued such schemes.

The irony of what the Hills and Taylors were doing was that they were, in a sense, beating the tycoons who controlled the sport at their own game. The kinds of business plans they were making drew snorts of disapproval from the sport's old-liners, though they were exactly the kinds of arrangements that racing's lords made in their own business enterprises all the time. They had not done so in their racing enterprises, and while they would say this was because of decorum, it actually was because they had not had the opportunity. Until Secretariat, the commercial possibilities had not existed. Some of the resentment the Taylors and Hills would engender was actually of the same sort one hears from star ballplayers of a generation ago about the salaries and endorsement revenues for today's athletes.

The Taylors copyrighted the name Seattle Slew and sewed up all the merchandising rights to the horse, including photographs, authorized biographies, and dolls. They made endorsement deals for pet clippers, horse feed, and commemorative coins from an ersatz mint. Karen Taylor's father, Delmar Pearson, Sr., had been installed as president of Seattle Slew Inc., which reportedly handled $1 million in gross volume in the two months following the Derby, most of it from the sale of T-shirts and from lithographs produced by Collier Graphic Services. X rays of Seattle Slew's legs would be featured in a series of ads

for Xerox and Mickey Taylor was going to be a spokesman for
Arrow shirts. These decisions set the tone for the next step in
Seattle Slew's career.

♦   ♦   ♦

As soon as Seattle Slew had won the Triple Crown, representatives of tracks from all over the country had begun calling
the owners, offering to put on any kind of a race or show that
would draw the colt to their tracks. Secretariat had drawn
record crowds to Arlington and Saratoga after his Triple
Crown sweep, and this time everyone wanted a chance to
profit.

The richest offer came from Marjorie Everett, the chief
operating officer of Hollywood Park in Los Angeles. That
track's Swaps Stakes for three-year-olds on July 3 already carried a purse of $200,000. She said she would raise it to $300,000
if Seattle Slew would run there. The Taylors and Hills decided
to put the colt's shoes back on him and send him to California.

Before the race, the worst that anyone could call the owners' decision was a slight case of pressing their luck. Seattle
Slew, after all, was lightly raced and in perfect health. Secretariat had gone to Arlington three weeks after the Belmont and
won easily, so why not a similar trip for a colt who had an easier
and slower Belmont victory and fewer races under his belt?

The decision later would be called an exercise in greed, but
the virtually unanimous verdict that the Taylors and Hills were
lusting after the $180,000 first prize in the Swaps never made
sense. Neither did the allegations, still widely believed, that
Everett had also privately given them an additional flat appearance fee of at least $100,000. (This rumor was so widely pub-
lished that the Internal Revenue Service investigated it and
found no evidence.)

The colt had already earned more than $800,000, and was
worth a minimum of $10 million as a stallion prospect; Secre-

tariat, after all, had fetched $6 million four years earlier before even beginning his three-year-old season. So it is difficult to see the owners' being seduced by an additional $180,000 or even $280,000.

The colt had two workouts the last week in June, looked good in both, and was flown to Los Angeles on Wednesday, June 29. Before he left, however, he was tranquilized twice for photo sessions for the Xerox ads, and once again for the flight west. Within two hours of his arrival, he was paraded for the fans with Jim Hill in the saddle. The move drew criticism from California horsemen, who thought the colt should have been rested after the long flight. During the next two days, he was subjected to several photo sessions, and on Saturday he had a short three-furlong blowout.

On Sunday, July 3, 68,115 people turned out at Hollywood, the third highest crowd in California racing history. The track had given away 125,000 bumper stickers, box seats were being scalped at $100 a chair, and at least 5,000 fans paid $6 apiece for Slew Crew T-shirts. Jean Cruguet sensed nothing wrong as Seattle Slew broke well from post two and sat two lengths off a fast early pace. But when Cruguet asked the colt to move after six furlongs, there was no response. J. O. Tobin, England's champion two-year-old the previous year but a dull fifth behind Seattle Slew in the Preakness, his first start on dirt, was setting a torrid pace but extending his lead rather than tiring. Seattle Slew fell back farther and farther, and at the top of the stretch he was through. Affiliate and Text had also gone by him, and he crossed the finish line a weary fourth, beaten an astounding 16 lengths.

"We stretched the Impossible Dream one act too far," Billy Turner said gamely, sharing in the blame for a defeat he was privately fuming over.

It was hardly the first time an eastern horse had run poorly in California. This is more the rule than the exception. The different climate and track surface throw many horses off, and for some reason going west has always been riskier than coming east. Some horsemen seriously believe that subtle ground tremors in California upset newcomers to the land of the San Andreas fault.

Seattle Slew had run so badly that he obviously had not been himself. But the unbeaten record was now blemished, so badly that a torrent of criticism began. The owners were lambasted for their greed, Seattle Slew was called a sham, and the Swaps was considered as much an unmasking as an aberration. The colt had folded when faced with real speed and pressure for the first time in his career.

No Triple Crown winner had fallen so far so quickly, and while all nine previous Triple Crown winners had been voted Horse of the Year at season's end, now there was strong sentiment that J. O. Tobin might be better even among the three-year-olds. The Taylors had already announced that Seattle Slew would race as a four-year-old instead of being syndicated and sent off to stud, and that decision saved them from having to do an about-face after the Swaps. Breeders were suddenly hesitant, and the talk in Lexington was that there was now no way that the colt would be syndicated for more than $10 million.

Seattle Slew headed back to New York, and the plan was finally to give him the two months off he should have had, then bring him back for the major fall races and reestablish his prestige and value. But it would be another ten months before Seattle Slew would race again.

♦   ♦   ♦

The defeat in the Swaps had made the entire Slew Crew edgy and defensive. Having a veterinarian as an owner was a situation few other trainers had to deal with, and Turner found himself being second-guessed by Hill at many turns. The colt had not handled his 6,000-mile round trip all that well, and came up with recurring coughs throughout the summer. Hill and Turner disagreed on treatments, and the battle of egos wore Turner down. He began drinking heavily, by his own admission, and his marriage fell apart. It did not help when the owners began saying that they hated to see Seattle Slew's earnings going into the cash register at Esposito's.

Slew might have raced in September, but was barred from running when the complex Wooden Horse scheme finally caught up with the owners. On August 25, the New York State Racing and Wagering Board ruled that Hill had violated state rules by not having been licensed as an owner. The board did not buy the loophole that Hill was not technically an owner until June 1, by which time he was licensed. Board members made it clear that they were not calling the owners unethical but citing them for a violation. The licensing of all actual owners has long been a bedrock of state racing commissions, a way to fight the constant fear that crime figures will buy horses and manipulate them for betting coups. Convicted felons and other "undesirables" are usually turned down for licenses. Some commissions take this very seriously. In 1985, George M. Steinbrenner III, principal owner of the New York Yankees and a licensed owner in numerous other states where he raced regularly, was denied an owner's license by the new Minnesota Racing Commission for his 1974 conviction on improper campaign contributions.

Hill disagreed with the ruling but chose not to fight it, partially because Seattle Slew was still not in peak health and it was beginning to look like he would not race again until he was four. By the time the suspension was over, the Jockey Club Gold Cup, the last major race of the year, was only two weeks off. There was no way to get the colt ready for that race and no purpose in pointing him for lesser events.

He headed south for the winter in early December, but on December 20, the owners announced Turner would be replaced by Doug Peterson, an unknown westerner Taylor hailed as the sport's next great horseman. What went unsaid was that Peterson, who had won the only stakes race in his career seven years earlier in New Mexico, would offer little resistance to the owners.

Turner would maintain that he advised against the California trip, and that the owners had been so embarrassed by the results that they drove him out of the job.

"The horse had been grinded to death and there was no reason to grind him anymore," Turner said, adding that he thought the owners had turned the colt into "a circus animal."

Every contemporary account reported that the owners had decided to take the colt to California, but Taylor maintains it was Turner's doing.

"This may come as a surprise after everything that's been written, but it was Billy's decision to go to California," Taylor says. "They worked the colt in New York after the Belmont, and Cruguet came back and said, 'He's not the same horse,' but Billy said he was just relaxing coming off the mile and a half, and not to worry, he'd be fine in California. It was Billy's decision, but we went along with it."

With Turner's firing came the loss of the traditional complimentary breeding right the trainer expected and says he was promised. He would eventually sue for it, only to settle privately without getting the breeding right.

"We did some things for Billy," is all that Taylor will say, and Turner will not discuss the matter further.

One of the few bright pieces of news came at year's end, when the balloting for the 1977 Eclipse Awards was announced. Through a combination of default and the tradition of honoring the Triple Crown winner, Seattle Slew had been voted the Horse of the Year title over Forego, the top older horse who had sustained an injury in the midst of a fall campaign, and Affirmed, a two-year-old who was being ballyhooed as a possible Triple Crown candidate for the following spring. J. O. Tobin had never duplicated his form of the Swaps, and the vote for the three-year-old championship had not been close.

Even in the midst of this one triumph, the bad feelings lingered on. On the day of the Eclipse Awards dinner, Mickey Taylor picked up a local newspaper and read that the trophy he would collect that night "represents a triumph of bad judgment, greed, and arrogance" and that "the Seattle Slew saga is a classic illustration of the way good people can be changed and corrupted by success."

♦   ♦   ♦

Seattle Slew was scheduled to return at Hialeah at the end of January, but on January 12 he was suddenly hit with a virus that would nearly kill him. He came down with a blood disorder, a fever, and colitis, and could not even walk for two weeks. Even after he passed the life-threatening stage, his owners had no confidence he would race again, and began talking to Kentuckians about syndicating him.

Time was crucial. The thoroughbred breeding season begins in mid-February, and it would take at least six weeks for the colt to wind down and acclimate to farm life and undergo fertility tests and test-breedings. Most top mares were already booked, and while their owners would have been happy to reschedule to get to Seattle Slew, they could not wait much longer.

The owners pondered several offers, but in the days they did so, Seattle Slew began to improve noticeably, as if the major illness had wiped out all the lingering ones from the year before. The owners needed more time to complete the kind of deal they wanted, and now it looked like the colt could run again. On February 2 they announced that Seattle Slew would not be retired, saying that they owed it to themselves and the public to run the colt as a four-year-old.

They had been scared badly enough, though, that they no

longer wanted to shoulder all the risk. On February 17, the Taylors and Hills announced that they had sold a half interest in Seattle Slew's breeding rights. They were selling twenty of forty shares in the colt, at $300,000 a share, to three breeders: ten to Joe Layman, Jr., a Washington lumber mill operator who campaigned a racing stable in California and boarded his mares at Spendthrift Farm in Lexington; five to Franklin Groves, whose family's Minneapolis construction company had built more of the nation's interstate highways than any other firm, and who had recently gotten into the game, spending millions on brood mares and boarding them at Spendthrift; and five to Brownell Combs, son of Leslie Combs, the founder and principal owner of Spendthrift. Part of the agreement was that Seattle Slew would be retired to Spendthrift to take up stud duty at year's end.

Spendthrift, Claiborne, and Gainesway Farm, the Big Three of the Lexington breeding nurseries, had all pursued the colt. Spendthrift won out largely because of Layman's ties to both the Taylors and the farm. "I grew up with Joe Layman, and that had a lot to do with it," says Taylor. "Joe brought Brownell and his wife and John Williams, the farm manager at Spendthrift, down to Florida, and they pretty much camped out down there for about a week. That's when Spendthrift got Slew."

Seth Hancock had been interested in the colt the year before, wanting the prestige of standing both living Triple Crown winners at Claiborne. He also needed a replacement for Bold Reasoning, who had died of a heart attack in the breeding shed in 1975.

"I tried real hard to get Seattle Slew after he won the Belmont, but they wanted to wait, and then he lost the Swaps, and they wanted to wait until he was four," Hancock recalls. "Then he didn't run again all year, and he went to Florida and got sick, they changed trainers, and everything was in a state of turmoil. He was sick, there was no telling how he was going to come out of that, and the man who was training him had never trained a major stakes winner. Maybe I didn't pursue him as enthusiastically as I would have if I'd known I really wanted him. Spendthrift really did want him, and they got him."

The Taylors' and Hills' decision to retain half of the shares in Seattle Slew seemed unusual, since they had no brood mare band of their own. Speculation was that they had been unable to sell them, but in fact it was a calculated risk. "Basically the

Seattle Slew after 1978 syndication with (left to right) **Mickey and Karen Taylor, Brownell Combs, Jim and Sally Hill.**

reasoning behind it was that I could always go back to chopping timber and Doc could always go back to vetting racehorses," Taylor says. "We took a hell of a gamble, but that's what life's all about. We fell in love with the horse, and if we were going to be involved in the breeding industry the way we wanted to, this was a once in a lifetime chance."

By the time Seattle Slew had recovered, the Florida season was ending, and it was decided to send him to New York and prepare for the Metropolitan Handicap, the Memorial Day fixture that unofficially begins the summer campaign for older horses. On May 14, Seattle Slew made his first start in forty-one weeks, easily winning in a seven-furlong race at Aqueduct as a prep for the Metropolitan. But Seattle Slew was to miss that race, coming back from his prep victory with a swelling in his right hind leg that would sideline him for another two months.

It was a minor injury, and the colt was back to full health by August. Now, a dream race was in the offing. That spring, Affirmed had become racing's eleventh and most dramatic Triple Crown winner, scoring narrow victories over Alydar in all three races. Affirmed's times had been faster than Seattle Slew's, and he had been tested by a superb rival, whereas Seattle Slew had cruised to victory against horses who had never been heard from again.

The target race for a first-ever showdown between Triple Crown winners became the Marlboro Cup, the race that had been invented to match Secretariat against his older stablemate Riva Ridge and had continued as an annual invitational event for the country's best horses. The Marlboro was now also part of what had begun to take shape as a fall triple crown series at Belmont Park, also including the Woodward Stakes and the Jockey Club Gold Cup.

Seattle Slew needed racing to get fit for the Marlboro, and made two starts to get ready. He breezed through another seven-furlong allowance race at Saratoga, turning in a sharp 1:21 ⅗. The owners found a spot for a final Marlboro prep in the Paterson Handicap at The Meadowlands, a futuristic glass-and-neon plant across the river from Manhattan in East Rutherford, New Jersey. Seattle Slew would have to carry 128 pounds, fourteen more than his main rival, Dr. Patches, but it looked like an easy spot.

Seattle Slew got to the lead easily enough and led comfortably turning for home, but when Cruguet asked him to draw off, he got no response from the colt. Dr. Patches was flying at him down the stretch, and in the final strides got up to beat him by a neck.

It was only the second defeat of his career, but unlike the Swaps it was not a race that could be thrown out as too bad to be true. It left everyone wondering whether the colt was as good as he had been the year before. Even Cruguet asked that question, and also volunteered the opinion that the colt was not fit for the race. The Hills and Taylors wondered whether Cruguet was the right jockey for the colt, and decided to replace him with Angel Cordero, Jr., who had ridden Dr. Patches.

It was an ideal and overdue match. Cordero, who dominates the riding colony in New York, is particularly skillful on front runners, using his excellent sense of pace to take control of races, his daring to intimidate rivals, and his physical strength to hold tiring speed horses together. In one of his most famous rides, he had managed to nurse a badly tired Bold Forbes to victory in the 1976 Belmont Stakes. His style seemed perfect for Seattle Slew.

Affirmed was coming into the Marlboro in top shape. He had two victories at Saratoga, in the Jim Dandy Stakes and in the Travers, though he had been disqualified in the latter for impeding his old rival Alydar.

The Marlboro was the first time in Seattle Slew's career that he was not the favorite. Affirmed was the 1–2 choice of the bettors and Seattle Slew was 2–1. Although older horses traditionally have an edge on three-year-olds, Affirmed was considered the more impressive Triple Crown winner, and his versatility figured to give him the option of staying close to Seattle Slew early or coming from off the pace if someone else could keep Slew from stealing away to an easy lead.

The Hills and Taylors were immediately vindicated in their choice of jockeys. Cordero figured that the way to beat Affirmed was to get the jump on him and have enough horse left to hold him off, and he executed the plan perfectly. He got Seattle Slew out of the gate on top but slowed the first quarter-mile down to 24 seconds flat, and the race was as good as over. Seattle Slew was relaxed and stronger than ever with enough in reserve for a three-length victory over Affirmed and a clocking of 1:45 ⅘, only two-fifths off Secretariat's world record.

In beating a more highly-regarded Triple Crown winner, Seattle Slew had silenced his critics and reestablished his value. In the following weeks, some of the twenty shares that had been sold for $300,000 apiece were being traded for $800,000.

Affirmed was held out of the Woodward two weeks later, and Seattle Slew had a new challenger in Exceller, California's top older horse. The race was a virtual rerun of the Marlboro, with Cordero getting Seattle Slew out to a comfortable two-length lead, letting out a notch on the reins whenever Exceller began to advance, and stretching his early lead into a four-length triumph. His time of 2:00 flat for 1 ¼ miles tied Kelso's 1961 track record.

The Jockey Club Gold Cup three weeks later posed a challenge because of the 1 ½-mile distance and because Affirmed was back with a stablemate to do his dirty work. Life's Hope, a fast Californian, was entered to push Seattle Slew early in the hope of preventing him from getting the kind of easy lead he enjoyed in the Marlboro.

This time, Slew was the 3–5 favorite, and the entry of Affirmed and Life's Hope the second choice at 11–10. Seattle Slew came into the paddock exuding an almost satanic energy, snorting and preening with anticipation. A few minutes later, he broke through the starting gate and had to be reloaded.

Nothing went as planned for either Triple Crown winner. Cordero's foot slipped out of a stirrup coming out of the gate and he nearly sprawled on the horse's back. It took him a few seconds to recover and get Seattle Slew to the lead on the rail. He quickly was challenged by a colt wearing the Harbor View Farm silks, but it was Affirmed and not Life's Hope. Affirmed's saddle was slipping out from under the jockey Steve Cauthen and the colt could not be controlled. He pushed Seattle Slew through a half-mile in :45 ⅕ and six furlongs in 1:09 ⅖. No horse had won a Gold Cup after dueling through such torrid fractions, and even after Affirmed began to drop back, it seemed unlikely Slew could keep going much farther.

Exceller, 22 lengths back after half a mile, was the fresh and strong horse who came running at Seattle Slew at the far turn. Seattle Slew was slowing down badly, and with a quarter of a mile to go, Exceller drew abreast and then forged ahead. He looked certain to whisk by him and win easily.

But this was to be Seattle Slew's finest display of courage. The moment Exceller got in front of him, he began to claw his way back. As they ran neck and neck to the finish, Seattle Slew was, almost unbelievably, gaining on Exceller. At the wire, he was still a nose behind, but two strides later he had scored his own unofficial victory. The final time of 2:27 ⅕ was mediocre at best, but the way the race had been run transcended the simplicity of the clock. Seattle Slew had shown more tenacity and character in defeat than he ever had in victory.

He made one final start, in order to go home a winner, and to gain one more ribbon, this time for carrying weight. Attempting to turn the relatively minor Stuyvesant Handicap at Aqueduct two weeks later into less of a mismatch, the handicapper loaded him down with 134 pounds, more than any other Triple Crown winner had ever carried in his career. He wore it like a feather, scoring a disdainful 3 ¼-length victory under a mild ride, and went into the winner's circle a final time with all the good feelings of one and a half years earlier restored. Hundreds of fans had taken out their Slew Crew T-shirts and ringed the winner's circle to watch the end of the long and stormy career that had ended so happily. Two weeks later the colt was vanned to Spendthrift.

The only slightly off note at the end came two months later when Affirmed was narrowly voted the Horse of the Year title over Seattle Slew despite having lost to him twice. The prevailing sentiment, however, was to reward a Triple Crown winner. Suddenly, the tip of Exceller's nose seemed particularly long, since an unprecedented sweep of Belmont's three fall races might have swung the balloting in Seattle Slew's direction.

♦   ♦   ♦

The Hills and Taylors now had twenty shares in Seattle Slew which they probably could have sold for $800,000 apiece, nearly three times what they had gotten for selling half of him eight months earlier. They decided instead to gamble on their faith in the colt as a sire. With Secretariat's first two crops already on the track and disappointing, it may have seemed like a particularly bold risk for them to hitch their fortunes to a Triple Crown winner heading for the breeding shed, but Secretariat's meek showing only encouraged them. If Secretariat, a son of Bold Ruler, was not going to fill the void left by the death of his sire, perhaps Bold Ruler's great-grandson Seattle Slew could do it.

Their problem was that they had only one mare worthy of their new stallion, and the way to make him a successful sire was to get him the best mares possible. With world-class brood mares selling for $500,000 and up, they could not go out and buy nineteen. So they turned to two plans for getting mares. The first was to form a syndicate to buy some top mares and race the offspring. The second was to enter into a series of foal-sharing agreements, such as the ones that Gladys Phipps had used a generation earlier to get top mares to Bold Ruler.

In 1978, the Hills and Taylors formed the Seminole Syndicate, whose members included Karen Taylor's father and brother; Glen Rasmussen, an accountant who handled their lumber and thoroughbred portfolios; Don Forbes, their insurance agent; William Gould, a Los Angeles attorney; and Murray McDonnell, a New Jersey investor. The syndicate spent about $3 million to buy seven mares who would be sent to Seattle Slew in his first season at stud. The Seminole Syndicate was the basis for a spinoff racing stable, with six more investors involved, called the Equusequity Stable.

The foal-sharing plans matched Slew with mares money could not buy, the old guard's blue-chip matrons who had records of producing one top runner after another. In many cases, the plan was for the mare's owner to get the foal one year and Equusequity to get it the next, or for a breeder to send two mares to Seattle Slew with a coin flip to determine who got which. These arrangements appealed to many top breeders, who were anxious to breed to Seattle Slew but not anxious to pay his initial stud fee of $150,000. The Taylors and Hills's foal-sharing partners included Ogden Phipps, Ogden Mills Phipps, Paul Mellon, Spendthrift Farm, Thomas Mellon Evans's Buckland Farm, John Hay Whitney's Greentree Stud, John Schiff, Louis Wolfson, owner of Affirmed, and Jacques Wimpfheimer.

The most successful foal-sharing deal would be one with Claiborne Farm that would yield Seattle Slew's two best sons to date. Equusequity got a colt from Seattle Slew's first crop from the Claiborne mare Alluvial, who would be named Slew o' Gold. The next year, Claiborne kept a colt from its mare Tuerta and named him Swale.

Since these arrangements were mostly with breeders who raced rather than sold their horses, only seven yearlings from Seattle Slew's first crop went through the Keeneland auction ring in 1981. They ranged in price from $75,000 to $700,000 and averaged $380,000. Since the yearling market had inflated almost 100 percent since Secretariat's first crop went through the ring, these prices were not very auspicious. His sales average was not even the highest for a new sire at Keeneland that year. J. O. Tobin, his conqueror in the Swaps, sired five yearlings who went through the ring at an average of $438,000.

For the 1982 sales, there were fourteen yearlings from Seattle Slew's second crop catalogued at Keeneland and Saratoga, and a month before the auctions their value began to soar. Seattle Slew's first runner was Slewpy, bred by the Seminole Syndicate and raced by Equusequity, and he won smartly in his debut at Belmont. More important was the performance of a filly named Landaluce, who the California trainer D. Wayne Lukas had bought for $650,000 a year earlier for two Texas oilmen, Lloyd French and Barry Beal.

Landaluce made her first start at Hollywood Park on July 3, 1982, and won by seven lengths in the sensational time of 1:08 ⅕. Before anyone could fully research whether that was the fastest time ever turned in by a two-year-old filly, she came back a week later and won the Hollywood Lassie Stakes by 21 lengths in 1:08 flat. No two-year-old filly had ever begun a career so spectacularly, and the timing was perfect for her sire.

The fourteen Seattle Slew yearlings who went through the sales ring in the next three weeks brought an average of $554,-643, almost 50 percent higher than the previous year and the highest average ever for so young a sire. Two of them were sold for more than $1 million, including a full sister to Landaluce who went for $1.5 million to Dolly Green, the Beverly Hills Standard Oil heiress.

Three months later, after winning three more races in similarly astounding style, Landaluce contracted a bacterial infection and died. Slewpy and Slew o' Gold finished out of the money as the favorites in the Remsen Stakes for two-year-olds that fall at Aqueduct, but the following spring Slew o' Gold began to improve dramatically, winning the Wood Memorial, finishing fourth in the Kentucky Derby, and second in the Belmont Stakes. Seattle Slew's third crop to go through the ring showed another gain, with fifteen yearlings averaging $624,333 at the 1983 sales and three of them going for more than $1 million. The same year, thirteen Secretariat yearlings averaged just $296,692.

In the next twelve months, the two colts that had been bred through foal-sharing arrangements with Claiborne would secure Seattle Slew's position as Bold Ruler's rightful heir. That fall, Slew o' Gold continued to mature, and started looking like his sire in the flesh and on the track. Still a three-year-old, he began to show some of the frenetic energy his sire had flashed before races and started to flesh out in the same muscular way. He bid for Belmont's fall championship series and virtually duplicated his father's performance, winning two legs, the Woodward and the Gold Cup, and losing one, the Marlboro in this case, by a neck. Just as had happened five years earlier, that narrow defeat in one leg of the fall series probably swung the Horse of the Year balloting, as Slew o' Gold was named champion three-year-old but lost the major title by a whisker to a French grass filly named All Along.

That fall, Swale emerged as the second-best two-year-old in the country, overshadowed only by a stablemate named Devil's Bag. The following spring, Devil's Bag failed to continue developing as had been expected but Swale showed steady and significant improvement and won the Kentucky Derby and the Belmont. Eight days after the latter victory, he suddenly collapsed and died of an apparent heart seizure that was never fully explained.

The early deaths of Swale and Landaluce prompted some crackpot speculation about a possible genetic flaw in the Seattle Slew line. But the success of Landaluce, Slew o' Gold, and Swale had stamped Seattle Slew as the most important new sire in a generation. As impressive as his progeny's overall successes was their variety of quality. Landaluce was brilliant and precocious, while Swale and Slew o' Gold started slowly and they improved as they went along.

The breeding world caught the same Slew fever that had touched New York seven years earlier when the colt won the Triple Crown. At the 1984 sales, seventeen Seattle Slew yearlings sold for $22.382 million, an average of $1.316 million apiece, including a $6.5 million colt and a $3.75 million filly, both bought by the Maktoums. In comparison to those prices for unproven Seattle Slew offspring, the reported sale of two lifetime breeding shares in Seattle Slew—for $3.5 million and $3.1 million—almost seemed cheap. Only Northern Dancer, who was twenty-three years old at the time and already a sire of fifteen successful crops, had been considered worth as much. Now, though, the Europeans and Arabs who had been trying to corner the Northern Dancer bloodline had a bold new bloodline to chase.

The Taylors and Hills, no longer hustling endorsement contracts for pet clippers and lithographs, moved on to bigger deals, having negotiated to buy the Citizens Union Bank in Lexington, Kentucky, in 1984, and established breeding farms of their own in Kentucky and Florida. They also have carried their faith in Seattle Slew as a sire one step further by keeping half the shares in Slew o' Gold, who went to stud in 1984 after doing what he and his father had so narrowly missed, sweeping the 1984 Woodward, Marlboro Cup, and Jockey Club Gold Cup as a four-year-old. The sweep earned him a $1 million bonus and made him the richest horse to go to stud up to that time.

Their management of Seattle Slew as a stallion has served as a model for other owners. In 1985, the owners of Spend a Buck and Chief's Crown sold half-interests in their colts and decided to keep the remaining shares and set up breeding syndicates and foal-sharing plans.

The ferocity of spirit that made Seattle Slew battle back in the Jockey Club Gold Cup, and which he is apparently passing on to his sons and daughters, necessitated an unprecedented routine when he was retired to stud. Seattle Slew still had the enthusiasm for eating he showed in his Baby Huey days, and his weight ballooned. He also was showing a bit too much spirit for anyone's comfort, kicking, lunging, and running off at every opportunity. The solution was to let him do what he likes best: three times a week, Seattle Slew is galloped under full tack. He puts his head down and plays the racehorse again, and he seems as determined as ever to come back and beat Exceller before the wire.

Had the Hills and Taylors sold Seattle Slew, they could have walked away from the game with $10 million or $20 million. Instead, by believing in their horse at every turn and gambling that his fire on the track would burn as brightly in the breeding shed, they became permanent players at the highest level of the game.

One horse had given them the clout and independence of the dynasties that had been built on generations of horses. A definitive show of their power came in September 1985. A year earlier, the Combses had gone public with Spendthrift Farm, selling its shares openly on the American Stock Exchange. The experience had been an unhappy one. Frustrated by disclosure requirements and other burdens of answering to stockholders, Leslie Combs decided he wanted out. He announced that Spendthrift was up for sale.

The Hills and Taylors were unhappy with the prospect of Seattle Slew being in the midst of an unsettled situation. Most owners whose stallions are taken by a major farm feel obliged and grateful for life. But the Hills and Taylors simply went ahead and yanked their horse, moving him to Three Chimneys Farm, where Slew o' Gold was standing and Chief's Crown would be arriving soon.

"He's more relaxed there," Taylor said a few weeks after the move. "Three Chimneys doesn't have all the public tours and visitors that Spendthrift did."

They could have moved him anywhere. No one was breeding to him because he was a Spendthrift stallion, but because he was Seattle Slew.

"Brownell Combs was the syndicate manager, but Jim Hill and I basically controlled Slew," Taylor says. "We had the say over how the horse was handled. When Brownell told us he was selling the farm, we called a meeting of the syndicate, not about moving him, but to name a new syndicate manager. But in the end we had to move him, just because of circumstances. There were bad feelings about the sale."

Ironically, the Spendthrift sale never came off. Manuel Mayerson, one of Rhoman Rule's namesakes, made the most serious offer, but could not come to final terms with the Combses. Spendthrift valued its holdings at nearly $100 million, including land, stallion shares, broodmares and facilities, but none of the offers were for even half that much. Seattle Slew alone, figured on the basis of $3 million a share, was worth $120 million, half of that still belonging to the Hills and Taylors.

Taylor and Hill even briefly considered buying Spendthrift themselves. Their one horse had made them rich enough to afford it.

"We looked at it but that's all we did," Taylor said, laughing. "We've got enough alligators, and that farm is a little alligator, just sitting out there gobbling up money."

The Hills and Taylors had been consistently unorthodox owners, but every move they made, including moving Seattle Slew and passing on Spendthrift, had embraced the old wisdom of the breeding game: Power is in controlling the blood, not the money.

5

The One-Two Finish

The 1982 Keeneland and Saratoga sales catalogues listed twenty-four yearlings by two new sires named Affirmed and Alydar. If breeding correlated precisely to the outcome of horse races, the sales results should have been easy to predict. Of the twenty-four, a dozen should have been sired by each stallion, and for every $1,000 the Affirmed yearlings fetched, Alydar's should have brought $999.

The two colts had been so closely matched in two seasons of track rivalry that their names seem woven together as one. Affirmed-and-Alydar, in the order they usually finished. In ten career matchups, spanning two seasons of racing and the 1978 Triple Crown, Affirmed had won seven times, but his net margin after more than ten miles of racing was under five yards. Four times it had taken a photo finish to separate them, and it had always been daylight back to the rest of their contemporaries. Even their breeding was similar. Alydar is a son, and Affirmed a grandson, of Raise a Native. As stallions, at first glance, they should have been virtually interchangeable and inseparable once more.

As close as they had been as racehorses, they would end up being worlds apart as sires. The relationship between performance on the track and in the stud had been a key theme of their pasts, in both the bloodlines that preceded them and the people who surrounded them. The two colts, inches apart as runners, would once again demonstrate the chasm between expectation and performance.

♦   ♦   ♦

On the race track, Affirmed wore the flamingo pink and black silks of Louis Wolfson's Harbor View Farm, a real farm in Ocala, Florida, from 1958 to 1977 and only a stable name thereafter. Alydar wore the devil's-red and blue silks of Lucille Parker Wright Markey's Calumet Farm, founded in Lexington in 1932. Any similarity between the owners ended with their using shades of red in their silks.

Wolfson, a controversial activist in racing, law, and politics, spent much of his career fighting the establishment, on Wall Street and in The Jockey Club. He maintains that his 1970 conviction for selling unregistered securities, which landed him a one-year prison sentence, was the result of an establishment conspiracy to frame and discredit him. Calumet, by contrast, was a white-fenced old Kentucky home, owned in 1978 by a dowager in declining health who was wheeled to trackside to see her beloved Alydar.

Much of Calumet's sentimental popularity at Alydar's time stemmed from its unaccustomed role as an underdog. Once the New York Yankees or Boston Celtics of racing, it had fallen far by the early seventies.

Calumet had started modestly and with a breed apart. William Monroe Wright, who made his fortune in the first two decades of the century with Calumet Baking Powder, raised standardbreds, the trotters and pacers who pull sulkies in the sport of harness racing, as a hobby in Libertyville, Illinois. He moved his horses to Lexington after buying five-hundred acres there in 1924, and envisioned Calumet as a Claiborne of harness racing. In 1931, his Calumet Butler won the Hambletonian, harness racing's Kentucky Derby, but Wright died six months later.

His son, Warren, preferred racing without buggies. He disposed of his father's stock, replaced it with thoroughbreds, and bought brood mares and yearlings, building up bloodstock rather than ready-to-race runners. In 1932, Calumet won only one race all year, but by 1934 the stable ranked seventh in the country in earnings, due largely to the success of Nellie Flag, a Wright homebred who became the country's top two-year-old filly.

Two purchases in 1936 would lay the foundation for Calumet's future success. That was the year in which Arthur Hancock bought Blenheim, and Warren Wright bought in for one quarter of him. Wright's other key purchase was a yearling named Bull Lea, a son of Bull Dog, who was a full brother to Sir Gallahad, Hancock's major import of a decade earlier who had sired Gallant Fox. Wright now was tapped in to the European bloodlines that would revolutionize the sport.

The final key to Calumet was Wright's hiring in 1939 of Ben Jones, a fifty-six-year-old Missourian who had won the previous year's Kentucky Derby with a colt named Lawrin. Wright had run through five trainers in six years and wanted a proven winner. Jones took the job over breakfast at the Drake Hotel in Chicago.

The shares in Blenheim, the purchase of Bull Lea, and the hiring of Jones set the stage for two decades of dominance. Calumet would lead the nation's owners in earnings twelve times; become the first stable to crack the $1 million mark in a year; campaign the sport's first equine millionaire, Citation; win the Triple Crown twice and the Kentucky Derby an astounding five more times; win the Horse of the Year title with four different horses in one seven-year span, and win a total of twenty-eight divisional championships.

Its two Triple Crown winners were Whirlaway, a son of

Blenheim, and Citation, a son of Bull Lea. Whirlaway, a stretch-runner with a flowing tail, swept the 1941 classics with more flair than any of his predecessors. He set a Derby track record of 2:01 ⅖, which stood for twenty-one years. He raced through his four-year-old year, winning thirty-two of sixty career starts, and retired with record earnings of $561,161.

Bull Lea, brilliantly fast but unable to win over classic distances as a three-year-old, had gotten off to a smashing start at stud. His first crop included Armed and Twilight Tear, both of whom would go on to be named Horse of the Year. Bull Lea would sire a total of fifty-eight stakes winners, none better than Citation, considered the horse of the century until Secretariat

Warren Wright, founder of Calumet Farm (left), **with trainer Ben Jones at Hialeah, 1941.**

BERT AND RICHARD MORGAN

came along. Citation's main competition for the Triple Crown was a Calumet stablemate, another son of Bull Lea named Coaltown. After beating Coaltown handily in the Derby, though, he breezed through the rest of the classics. Those races came in the midst of a three-year-old season that has never been approached for longevity and success. After nineteen victories that year, Citation had won 27 of 29 races and $865,150.

His career should have ended there but Wright wanted to make him racing's first millionaire. Citation never raced as a four-year-old, sidelined with injuries that should have retired him. At five he won only two of nine starts in California, finishing second seven other times, thrice to a horse named Noor. Three days after Christmas 1950, Warren Wright died, and his widow, Lucille Parker Wright, decided to pursue her late husband's goal as a sort of tribute. Citation ran seven times as a six-year-old, closing out his career with four victories that brought him over the $1 million mark and recapturing some of his prestige with a decisive career-ending score in the Hollywood Gold Cup.

In 1952, Lucille Wright married Rear Admiral Gene Markey, a former movie producer, author (including such titles as *His Majesty's Pajamas* and *Women, Women, Everywhere*), and self-styled boulevardier who had been married to Joan Bennett, Myrna Loy, and Hedy Lamarr. Mrs. Wright had taken an active interest in the stable and Admiral Markey liked the game, so Calumet figured to continue thriving. The farm would win three more Derbies in the 1950s, but a decline had begun that would almost ruin the dynasty within a decade.

The problem was in the breeding shed. Calumet had failed to do what Arthur Hancock had done with Blenheim, and Bull Hancock did with Nasrullah: Seek out new blood to reinvigorate the farm and the breed. Instead, Mrs. Markey continued breeding to the Calumet stars who had come home to stud— Whirlaway, Citation, and Coaltown.

It was not a case, as it would be with Secretariat thirty years later, of horses doing well as stallions by any standards but their own as race horses. The three Calumet stars of the forties were utter failures at stud. Whirlaway sired only seventeen stakes-winners in seven crops before being packed off to France where he continued to toil in obscurity. Coaltown never sired a single stakes winner and eventually followed Whirlaway to France, and Citation managed only eleven stakes-winners before dying in 1959.

Their failures remain a bafflement of breeding history. Bull Lea had been so dominant a sire that Citation and Coaltown had figured to inherit his prepotency. Whirlaway, as Blenheim's best son, had looked like an outstanding prospect. The most widely accepted notion is simply that the Blenheim and Bull Lea influence ran only one generation and stopped with their Calumet sons, although some of their daughters fared better as producers. Whereas Bull Hancock had reached out for new blood to replace the aging Blenheim and struck gold with Nasrullah, Mrs. Markey had stuck with her homebred stallions.

This had been standard procedure in the brief history of American breeding, and the final results frequently had been the same. The Alexander brothers' Woodburn Stud dominated the nation's breeding rolls through its great sire, Lexington, from 1860 to 1880. Thereafter, it virtually disappeared. Similar fates befell other Kentucky farms such as Domino Stud and Hamburg Place. A dominant stallion sired numerous runners who made the farm's fortune, but those horses turned out to be poor sires and the dynasty faded. Calumet would be the last empire of its kind, a living lesson to breeders that diversification and renewal were the way to go.

The Markeys tried to adjust in the midst of Calumet's decline, but it was too late. The Calumet brood mare band had been weakened by the same kind of complacency, and nonproductive mares who should have been culled years earlier did no better when belatedly switched to outside stallions. Beginning in 1962, the farm fell out of the nation's top ten money-winning

stables for the first time in a generation and it stayed out for most of the decade. Jimmy Jones, who had taken over for father Ben in the mid-1950s, resigned in 1964 in a dispute over the farm's brood mare band. Forward Pass won Calumet its final Derby in 1968 but only on the disqualification of Peter Fuller's Dancer's Image.

The Markeys went through four trainers in the twelve years following Jimmy Jones's departure without much success. Then, in 1976, they took a chance with a young and unproven trainer who would give the devil's-red and blue a final run at glory.

He was John Veitch, whose father, Sylvester, had trained two Belmont Stakes winners. Born in Lexington and raised near Belmont Park, Veitch spent many of his summers working on the Kentucky farms owned by his father's clients. After being graduated from Bradley College, he worked his way up the racetrack hierarchy, and formed a small public stable in 1973. The following spring, he got a call from Melvin Cinnamon, Calumet's farm manager, asking him to meet the Markeys about a job offer. He said yes on April 15.

The Markeys liked Veitch and gave him a free hand to turn the stable around. He swept the stable clean, keeping only three of thirty-two horses in training. One of the keepers was a two-year-old filly named Our Mims, who would go on to become the champion three-year-old filly the following year. She had a younger brother on the farm, a colt the Markeys would name Alydar.

◆　　◆　　◆

Lucille Parker Wright Markey and Admiral Gene Markey in Calumet Farm study, 1971.

Alydar had been sired by Raise a Native, the most important purchase of Louis Wolfson's racing career. Wolfson, the
son of a Jacksonville, Florida scrap-metal dealer, had gone to
the University of Georgia on a football scholarship and hoped
to play and coach at the professional level, but suffered a career-
ending shoulder injury while trying to tackle Yale's All-Ameri-
can halfback Albie Booth in the 1931 Yale Bowl. He went home
to Jacksonville, borrowed $10,000 to start the Florida Pipe and
Supply Company, and over the next two decades parlayed
profits from one corporation to another and eventually gained
control of the Merritt-Chapman and Scott industrial complex.
By 1958, he was rich enough and ready to buy some horses.

He bought four yearlings in 1958 and turned them over to
Burley Parke, the Californian who had trained Noor to beat
Citation three times. Led by Francis S., a $31,000 yearling who
went on to win the Wood Memorial and the Dwyer Stakes,
Harbor View moved into third place on the nation's owner's
list in 1960, three spots ahead of the already declining Calumet
Farm.

In 1962, Wolfson bought Raise a Native for $39,000 at the
Saratoga yearling sales. The colt was a son of Native Dancer,
the "Gray Ghost," who was bred by Alfred Gwynne Vanderbilt's Sagamore Farm and became the most famous runner to
carry Vanderbilt's cerise and white silks. Native Dancer was
racing's first television hero, his career coinciding with the
early years of that medium and his gray coat making him easy
to spot in a crowded field. From 1952 to 1954, Native Dancer
won twenty-one of twenty-two starts, losing only when un-
lucky traffic problems cost him the 1953 Derby by a head to
Dark Star. Native Dancer was from the third key branch of the
Phalaris line. The first had led through Pharos, Nearco and
Nearctic to Northern Dancer; the second through Nearco and
Nasrullah to Bold Ruler; and the third through Sickle, Un-
breakable and Polynesian to Native Dancer.

Raise a Native, a muscular chestnut-colored colt, prompted

excited whispers as soon as he started training. He won his debut easily, set a track record of 57 ⅘ winning a five-furlong allowance race at Aqueduct next time out, equalled that winning the Juvenile Stakes in his third start, and then set a track record of 1:02 ⅗ for 5 ½ furlongs in the Great American Stakes, going more than a full second faster than the standard. In August, though, he took a bad step in a workout and damaged a tendon so badly that he was retired to stud at Harbor View Farm.

He had shown so much speed and potential that he was a hot stallion prospect, and his first crop of foals in 1966 brought a higher average than any new stallion. The following year, a Raise a Native colt fetched a world-record $250,000. The colt was named Majestic Prince, and he won the 1969 Kentucky Derby and Preakness. He broke down in the Belmont and entered stud at Spendthrift, joining his father, who had been moved to the more prestigious Kentucky operation in 1968.

Another son of Raise a Native was at Spendthrift by 1974, the year that Alydar and Affirmed were conceived. Wolfson had bred one of his mares, Exclusive, to Raise a Native in his first year at stud and gotten a big, chestnut colt he named Exclusive Native. The colt had his moments of brilliance, winning the Sanford Stakes in fast time at two, but a minor fracture laid him up through the spring classics and he was retired later in the year. He went to Spendthrift and stood for only $1,500 his first year, far less than his father, Raise a Native.

In March of 1974, at the height of the breeding season, two vans rolled into Spendthrift Farm for the matings that would produce the two best three-year-olds of 1978. One was from Calumet, bringing a mare named Sweet Tooth, the other from Wolfson's Harbor View Farm in Ocala, carrying a mare named Won't Tell You.

Sweet Tooth, a daughter of On-and-On, had by far been the better racehorse and had a better family tree. She had been second in a couple of stakes races and earned over $86,000, and was from a line of Calumet mares who were good producers. The year before, she had been bred to the Claiborne stallion Herbager, and the foal she had delivered a few weeks earlier would grow up to be Our Mims, the champion three-year-old filly of 1977. She now was being bred for the first time to Raise a Native, and the product of that union would be named Alydar.

Won't Tell You, a daughter of Crafty Admiral, had won five of twenty-three starts, mostly in claiming company, and earned just $21,210. Wolfson had purchased her in 1972 at a sale of brood mares in foal, at the urging of his second wife. Patrice Jacobs, daughter of the legendary trainer Hirsch Jacobs and a student of bloodlines, had decided there was a profitable "nick"—a combination of complementary factors—in crossing sons of Raise a Native with daughters of Crafty Admiral. So Wolfson bought Won't Tell You, who was in foal to Raise a Native, with the intention of breeding her to sons of that stallion. He began in 1972 by sending her to a stallion named Native Heritage. In 1973 she came up barren, and the next year Wolfson bred to her Exclusive Native. That second mating produced Affirmed.

♦   ♦   ♦

Affirmed began his racing career before Alydar, making his debut at Belmont Park on May 24, 1977, under the training of Lazaro Barrera. The Cuban-born trainer, one of six brothers who are successful horsemen in this country, had taken over the Harbor View string two years earlier and was coming off a year in which he had won awards for stretching the speed of Bold Forbes far enough to win the 1976 Derby and Belmont.

Wolfson and Barrera knew they had a fast one in Affirmed but managed to keep him a secret. They threw the bettors off by putting an unknown apprentice jockey named Bernie Gonzalez on him for his first start. Affirmed ran the mediocre time of 1:06 for 5 ½ furlongs, but that was good enough for a 4 ½ -length victory at odds of 14-1.

Alydar was no secret, having worked five furlongs in 58 seconds. Veitch started the colt out in a stakes race, the Youthful, which also was Affirmed's second start. Alydar, on reputation alone, was the 9–5 favorite and Affirmed went off the second choice at 3–1. Eddie Maple was on Alydar and Angel Cordero, Jr., had replaced Gonzalez on Affirmed. Alydar broke slowly, checked between horses on the turn, and closed furiously but could get no better than fifth. Affirmed had pressed the pace and hung on to win by a neck. It was the only one of the ten meetings between Affirmed and Alydar in which they did not run one–two in some order.

Alydar and Affirmed met for the second time, each making his third career start, in the Great American Stakes. Alydar was favored again, as he would be in exactly half of their ten meetings. Affirmed took the early lead but Alydar came and got him around the turn, blew past him and won by 3 ½ lengths. The comment in the Daily Racing Form chart was that Affirmed was "no match" for the winner. If the stretch-running Alydar could go by the front-running Affirmed at that short a distance, he figured only to beat him by more as the races got longer.

Kept out of each other's way, both colts ran off two easy victories. Affirmed picked up a new jockey along the way, a seventeen-year-old rider who had set the racing world on its head, a baby-faced Kentuckian known as "The Kid." Steve Cauthen, a quiet, self-contained son of a blacksmith, grew up around small Midwestern racetracks such as Latonia and River Downs and started climbing on horses almost before he could walk. He started riding regularly in New York late in 1976 and quickly rewrote most of the sport's records for apprentice jockeys. He twice won six races on a nine-race card at Aqueduct, something that had been done only four times in the history of the sport; with the aid of the five-pound weight allowance riders receive for their first year, he was named on every hot horse on the grounds. He developed a fervent following among the bettors, who backed everything he rode down to favoritism, and were often rewarded. Wolfson and Barrera wanted to tap into the Cauthen magic, and also knew they could count on the young rider's loyalty.

Following their two easy victories in each other's absence. Affirmed and Alydar now hooked up for the two-year-old championship and raced against each other in their next four starts.

The Hopeful Stakes was to set the tone for the rest of their rivalry. Affirmed stayed close to the early pace, took over at the top of the stretch, and then Alydar came flying at him. This time, Alydar got within a head with an eighth of a mile to go and looked like a cinch to win, but Affirmed would not let him by, digging back in and extending his narrow margin to half a length at the wire. Score: Affirmed 2, Alydar 1.

Two weeks later in the Futurity at Belmont, Maple moved Alydar earlier, getting within a head after half a mile, and the two were at each other from there on. Alydar got a head in front at the furlong pole, but again Affirmed held on and came back, winning by a nose. Score: Affirmed 3, Alydar 1.

Veitch decided to try a different rider and put up Jorge Velasquez, his regular jockey, who had been out with injuries. The two colts hooked up again in the Champagne, the one-mile race at Belmont in which Secretariat and Seattle Slew had set successive stakes records. Velasquez waited patiently, confident the extra distance would make a difference, and the plan worked. Affirmed moved to the lead after half a mile, but Alydar came at him in the stretch and drew clear to win by a length and a quarter. More impressively, he had been boxed in by other horses early, and had made several awkward turns to shake free. Score: Affirmed 3, Alydar 2.

Had Veitch stopped racing Alydar for the year, the colt probably would have been named the champion two-year-old, but the trainer wanted Alydar to get more experience at longer distances, and decided to run him two weeks later in Maryland's Laurel Futurity, a race on Affirmed's schedule.

Alydar was an overwhelming favorite, going off at 2–5. Affirmed had drawn the outside post, and Barrera and Cauthen devised a strategy; keep Alydar pinned on the deep, tiring inside rail to prevent the Calumet colt from making one of his wide, sweeping moves on the turn. The pace was extremely slow, and Velasquez had to keep Alydar close and then move him early. He was only a length behind Affirmed after a quarter mile, on even terms after half a mile, and once again they would run most of the race at each other's throats. Affirmed proved a neck the better, holding on to win in their longest and hardest drive against each other to date.

Affirmed was through for the year, the championship locked up with a 4–2 tally over Alydar, but Alydar started once more and ran into a buzzsaw in the Remsen November 26. Believe It took an early lead and forgot to stop, running the fastest time in the history of the race. Alydar, nine lengths back early, closed impressively but fell short by two lengths.

Affirmed headed west for the winter with the rest of Barrera's horses, and Alydar went south with Veitch. Neither trainer wanted to tangle again until the Triple Crown races, and each colt easily won his four Derby preps. Affirmed won an allowance race by five lengths, the San Felipe by two, the Santa Anita Derby by eight and the Hollywood Derby by two. Alydar, making his first start at three a month earlier than Affirmed, won an allowance race by two lengths, the Flamingo by 4 ½, the Florida Derby by two and the Blue Grass by 13.

Few horses had ever come into the Triple Crown off such decisive victories, and either by himself would have been among the heaviest favorites in Derby history. Both camps came to Louisville eager for the rematch, but also feeling some unfairness afoot. In almost any other year, either colt would have won the Triple Crown easily, and it seemed unjust that one might keep the other from a sweep.

Alydar had won his four Derby preps more impressively, running faster times over stronger company. Barrera, responding to the comparative criticism of Affirmed's races, invoked the old saw heard most recently from Billy Turner the year before—his horse would "only do what he has to do to win."

Alydar's superior performances would make him the Derby betting favorite. The Calumet connection and the deteriorating health of his owners had made him the nation's sentimental choice. Lucille Markey, now eighty-one, suffered from failing eyesight and arthritis, and she and the admiral were both confined to wheelchairs. The Blue Grass, Alydar's final Derby prep, could not have been scripted more mawkishly. Keeneland sent a station wagon to bring the Markeys to the track, where they were helped to the rail on the clubhouse turn. Velasquez swung their copper-colored colt out of the post parade and over to the owners, who were getting their first look at him since he had left the farm more than a year earlier. His thirteen-length romp at Keeneland, just down Versailles Road from Calumet, was the only one of his races they would ever attend.

Alydar was 6–5, Affirmed 9–5, in a field of eleven for the 104th Derby. Raymond Earl and Sensitive Prince, both speedballs, rushed for the lead around the first turn, and Affirmed settled into third place. Alydar was running choppily and seemed uncomfortable with the track, dropping seventeen lengths back. Affirmed advanced steadily and got the lead turning for home. Now only five lengths back, Alydar was in high gear, but he was moving too late. Affirmed spurted clear and Alydar got no closer than 1½ lengths at the finish.

Veitch and Velasquez said their colt had run a superior race since Alydar had not started moving well until too late and had not handled the Churchill Downs racing surface. Barrera testily responded that Affirmed "is just waiting for a horse that can make him run," and said the runner-up's only problem was that "he cannot get a hold of Affirmed. Alydar move early with him, we beat him. He move from the middle, we beat him. He move from the back, and we beat him. I don't want to hear no more excuses no more."

Alydar remained the popular favorite, and his personality helped. Affirmed was a phlegmatic sort who usually slept as much as possible before his races. Although he was about the same size as Alydar, he seemed smaller because he usually poked around with his head down.

"To tell you the truth, if you saw him come on to the track, you wouldn't want to bet on him," said Mrs. Wolfson, "but when he runs, that's a different story."

Alydar, Veitch and Velasquez frequently said, may have been as smart as racehorses get.

"You think Affirmed knows his name?" Veitch asked rhetorically one morning. "Hey, Alydar!" he called out. The colt, grazing nearby, dragged a groom over to Veitch and waited eagerly to play.

In the Preakness two weeks later, Affirmed took the lead earlier and got away with a slow pace of 47 ⅗ for the half-mile, but Alydar was never more than six lengths back and moved sooner than he had in the Derby. Alydar was at Affirmed's heels at the top of the stretch and began to inch closer. They raced together to the wire, the outcome in doubt with every stride in as close a Preakness as had ever been run. Alydar could not get by and Affirmed won by a neck, with Believe It 7½ lengths behind them.

The victory made Affirmed racing's youngest millionaire ever, and he was now a race away from becoming the eleventh winner of the Triple Crown after winning a Preakness that was being called the best Triple Crown race ever. That opinion took only three weeks to be revised.

The Belmont June 10 drew only five horses, and while Affirmed was of course favored, Alydar went off a closer second choice than he had been in the Preakness. Veitch wanted to beat Affirmed as much as Barrera and Wolfson wanted to win the Triple Crown, and he predicted that the 1½ miles would work to Alydar's favor. The more ground, he and many bettors reasoned, the better Alydar's chance of getting by his nemesis. Veitch also made an equipment change, taking the blinkers off Alydar in the hope that a clearer view of his rival would spur him on.

A crowd of more than sixty-five thousand jammed Belmont Park for the showdown. The three other colts in the race, entered to do battle for the honor of running third, all were taken back at the start, and Affirmed virtually walked through the early fractions. He was alone on the lead through a half-mile in 50 seconds, the fourth slowest fraction in the 110-year history of the race. Velasquez had to move or lose his chance and just before the halfway point he urged Alydar beside the leader. The pace quickened.

Turning for home, it was Affirmed by a head, but Alydar was inching up on the outside with each stride and Velasquez finally seemed to be getting a break. He skillfully had maneuvered Alydar so close beside Affirmed that Cauthen had no room to whip the colt right-handed. Cauthen had never whipped the colt on the left side but now he had no choice. The crowd was screaming for the final quarter mile, as no one in the stands could see who was in front. But at the wire, Cauthen raised his whip in triumph and the photo-finish proved him right. After racing together for the final six furlongs, Affirmed had beaten Alydar by a head. The time of 2:26 $\frac{4}{5}$ was the third fastest ever.

Affirmed had won the Triple Crown by a total of less than two lengths. Alydar would have won the three races by a combined margin of 21¾ lengths had Affirmed not been in them.

It had been the most dramatic Triple Crown ever, and even a third sweep in only six years was not dimming public enthusiasm. This time there was the duel of the two colts, and the crowd appeal of eighteen-year-old Steve Cauthen, to make it seem special.

Also, there was the prospect of a continuing Affirmed–

Alydar rivalry. Fans imagined them racing each other through the year and then as four-year-olds.

The two were widely proclaimed as champions, though their trainers had different outlooks on their quality. Barrera called Alydar "a great, great horse," leaving little question of where he ranked Affirmed. Veitch would go only so far as to call Affirmed a "damned fine racehorse," saying he had never seen a "great" horse. Secretariat, he said, came closest, "but since he didn't race as a four-year-old, he didn't have a chance to prove any greatness."

The question of whether Alydar could ever turn the tables again intrigued everyone and raised a question in the breeding world. Three times now, Alydar had not been able to get past Affirmed. Did that mean that Affirmed had an extraordinary will to win, a character trait that might be genetic, and did Alydar have some flaw? Would Affirmed's descendants always hold off Alydar's, and thus be the more desirable?

♦　　♦　　♦

Lou Wolfson had announced a week after the Belmont that he would not commit what he considered the mistakes made with the two other Triple Crown winners of the decade: Unlike Seattle Slew, Affirmed would not race for at least six weeks and would definitely pass the $300,000 Swaps at Hollywood. Unlike Secretariat, his colt would not be syndicated until the end of the year, guaranteeing that he would be able to race as a four-year-old and under Wolfson's control.

The two colts were headed for their next showdown in the Travers at Saratoga, the so-called Midsummer Derby and an unofficial fourth leg of the Triple Crown, though only Whirlaway had won all four races. Just as they had done going into the Kentucky Derby, the rivals took separate prep routes and were unbeatable apart. Alydar went to Chicago and won the Arlington Classic by 13 lengths. Two weeks later in the Whit-

Affirmed and Steve Cauthen nose out Alydar and Jorge Velasquez in the 1978 Belmont Stakes.

ney Stakes at Saratoga, he won by ten lengths with two interesting horses in his wake: Buckaroo, who would not be heard from again until his son Spend a Buck won the 1985 Kentucky Derby, and J. O. Tobin, who had beaten Seattle Slew in the Swaps Stakes the previous summer.

Affirmed got his eight weeks off and came back in the Jim Dandy at Saratoga three days after the Whitney. Seven lengths back with three furlongs to go, Cauthen went to the whip and the colt closed with a rush to beat Sensitive Prince by half a length in 1:47 ⅘, two fifths slower than Alydar had run in the Whitney.

The Travers August 19 drew a crowd of 50,359 to Saratoga,

Louis and Patrice Wolfson, owners of Affirmed.

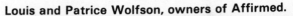

SUSAN RHODEMYRE

a wooden track built for half as many. The largest crowd in the track's 115-year history was expecting to see yet another Preakness or Belmont thriller.

A different scenario began to develop when Cauthen was spilled in a race the week before the Travers and suffered tendon damage in his right knee that would sideline him a month. Barrera decided to ride either Cordero or Laffit Pincay, Jr., a star California jockey, both of whom had ridden Affirmed earlier in his career. Barrera had been faced with the same choice when Cauthen missed the Santa Anita Derby because of a routine suspension, and had flipped a coin. Pincay won, and Cordero figured he would get the call if the situation arose again. Instead, Barrera stuck with Pincay.

Cordero's hurt feelings may have decided the Travers, an inglorious final chapter to the sport's greatest rivalry.

Only four horses were entered for the race: Affirmed, Alydar, Nasty and Bold, and Shake Shake Shake, a Puerto Rican import with skimpy credentials ridden by Cordero. When the gate opened, Cordero took Shake Shake Shake to the lead. Affirmed was second, and Alydar third on the rail. Moving into the far turn, Pincay began to move Affirmed to the leader, and Cordero steered Shake Shake Shake wide, forcing Affirmed to the outside. That opened up the rail for Alydar. Affirmed finally passed Shake Shake Shake, and Pincay then dropped him over to the rail, but the jockey did not see Alydar moving up there and Affirmed cut off Alydar so suddenly that Velasquez had to pull up his colt sharply. Alydar could not get going after that and Affirmed drew off to win by 1 3/4 lengths, but the track stewards immediately posted the "inquiry" sign, and summarily disqualified Affirmed, placing him second behind Alydar.

Barrera was enraged, saying Cordero and Velasquez had ganged up on Pincay. Both riders vehemently denied it.

"Alydar don't got no business to be in there on the rail if he didn't know Cordero was going to open the inside for him,"

Barrera said. "Cordero took my horse out to leave the rail for Alydar. This is the last meeting of the two or Affirmed will have another trainer because I don't plan to run no more against him."

Barrera rescinded that vow two days later, after Wolfson said that "we're not crybabies and we're not going to say anything more about this."

The disqualification made the boxscore 7–3 in Affirmed's favor. Affirmed had now won fifteen of eighteen career starts and finished second to Alydar the other three times. Alydar had now won twelve of twenty career starts, and seven of his eight defeats had been to Affirmed.

That was the way the rivalry would end. Alydar suffered a minor fracture a month after the Travers that put him out for the year, and when he returned as a four-year-old he was never the same. He had moments of his old brilliance but won only two of six starts in the first six months of the year, and a small fracture in an ankle was discovered in July. He was retired with fourteen victories in twenty-six starts and earnings of $957,195. He was vanned home to Calumet in July and slowly allowed to adjust to farm life. The following winter, he would be ready to take on Affirmed again, when their careers moved into the breeding shed.

◆   ◆   ◆

Affirmed's fortunes also took a turn for the worse after the Travers, the first of five consecutive defeats he would suffer. It was the worst losing streak by a Triple Crown winner.

The dark clouds that had begun to gather at Saratoga followed him to Belmont Park, where he lost twice to Seattle Slew. First he was flat outrun and outmaneuvered in the Marlboro Cup, running second virtually every step of the way and losing by three lengths. Cordero found the victory aboard Seattle Slew all the sweeter after the nastiness surrounding the

Travers. Cordero, who still denies any wrongdoing in that race, said the Marlboro proved that it took only one horse to beat Affirmed. Then came the Gold Cup debacle, when Affirmed's saddle slipped and he ended up finishing 19½ lengths behind Exceller and Seattle Slew.

Wolfson decided it was time to give his colt a break and also to hedge his investment against any further misfortunes. On November 2, the owner announced that Affirmed had been syndicated into thirty-six shares at $400,000 each for a record book value of $14.4 million, and that he was retaining sixteen of the shares as well as all control over the colt's racing career.

Wolfson had turned down several other offers, including one for over $20 million from Europeans, because he wanted to keep the colt in this country and to race him at four. Wolfson had put the deal together with his old friends at Spendthrift, already the home of Wolfson's two other stallions: Raise a Native, Affirmed's grandsire and Alydar's sire, and Exclusive Native, Affirmed's sire.

Barrera took Affirmed back to California, planning to run him in the series of rich winter handicap races at Santa Anita Park. Cauthen, who had returned from his spill to hit a cold streak in New York, decided to try California for the winter and stay near Affirmed.

Cauthen won two races on opening day at Santa Anita, but then turned even colder than he had been in New York. Although Cauthen to this day skirts the issue, other riders say privately that there was resentment of the eighteen-year-old, and that other eastern riders were ganging up on him at every opportunity.

"They chased him out mercilessly," a top California trainer would say three years later.

Affirmed made his debut as a four-year-old on January 7 in the seven-furlong Malibu Stakes at Santa Anita and ran third all the way, behind two locals named Little Reb and Radar Ahead. It was the first time in his career that anyone except

Alydar had finished in front of him.

His handlers threw out the race until he virtually repeated it thirteen days later in the San Fernando when Affirmed finished second, 2¾ lengths behind Radar Ahead and only a neck in front of Little Reb. The usually polite California crowd was disgusted. After years of listening to the quality of their local racing being belittled, they had seen two Triple Crown winners humiliated, first Seattle Slew in the 1977 Swaps, now Affirmed in two dull efforts. Affirmed was booed as he came back from the race and so was Cauthen, who had just lost his seventy-fifth straight race.

"He didn't run like himself," Cauthen said. "He only ran in spots. I don't know what's wrong."

Barrera was confused as well, saying "There's nothing wrong with him and he isn't hurting."

Cauthen's losing streak continued and eventually reached one hundred ten, but by then Barrera and the Wolfsons had decided to replace him. They said they felt bad about it but that their colt needed something to get him going and a rider mired in doubt and loss could not be helping. They said Cauthen might get the mount back someday, and said he would still get the breeding right they had promised him a year earlier. They again turned to Pincay, whom they had held blameless for the Travers fiasco.

Fifteen days after the San Fernando, Affirmed made his third start of the year in the Strub Stakes. He broke a bit slowly but then moved into a close second. Nearing the final turn, he went into overdrive, opened a two-length lead, and drew away to win by ten lengths under Pincay. It seemed unlikely that the jockey had made that much difference, but whatever the reason, Affirmed was back in top form and would reel off seven straight victories to close his career.

A month later, he carried 128 pounds to a 4½-length victory in the Santa Anita Handicap, setting a track record. After a two-month layoff, he carried 130 to a five-length romp in the

Californian, and a month later carried 132 to a narrow, driving three-quarter-length score in the Hollywood Gold Cup. He missed the track record by only a fifth of a second, and his victory moved him past Kelso, the veteran gelding of the 1960s, into first place on the sport's earnings list with career bankroll of $2,044,218.

After a summer off, he came to New York for the fall races, cast in the same role Seattle Slew had played in 1978: needing to beat a hot young three-year-old to reassert himself in the eyes of New Yorkers. This time, the role Affirmed had played the year before was being filled by Spectacular Bid, a dark gray grandson of Bold Ruler who had come within one race of becoming the third straight Triple Crown winner.

Purchased as a yearling by the Harry Meyerhoff family for just $37,500, Spectacular Bid had been a champion at two and had come into the 1979 spring classics a heavy favorite. After easy scores in the Derby and Preakness, he fell apart in the Belmont under a poor ride by Ronnie Franklin, a young apprentice that the colt's owners had nobly stuck with despite his almost having cost the Bid several victories.

The anticipated clash between Spectacular Bid and Affirmed did not materialize until the final leg of the Fall Championship Series at Belmont. Barrera held Affirmed out of the Marlboro Cup, and Spectacular Bid won by five lengths. Spectacular Bid was held out of the second leg, the Woodward, and Affirmed won it by two and a half lengths.

The stage was set for the Jockey Club Gold Cup, which promised to be as dramatic a showdown as the Seattle Slew–Affirmed Marlboro Cup of a year before, but unfolded in the same unsatisfactory way: the older horse stole the race by setting a slow pace. Affirmed got loose with a first quarter in an incredibly slow 25 seconds, and the race was over. Spectacular Bid ran gallantly and got to within a head of the lead but could gain no farther, losing by three quarters of a length.

Affirmed was retired in early November. He had won

twenty-two of twenty-nine starts and earned a record $2.39 million. He had won the Triple Crown and come back at four to win the major races on both coasts. He was one of the best ever, but still there was ambiguity about his place in the hierarchy of the best, his relationship to fellow Triple Crown winners Secretariat and Seattle Slew. His harshest critics maintained that he was lucky, having gotten the best of the pace and the breaks in all the Triple Crown races and in his Gold Cup showdown. His supporters, led by Barrera and Wolfson, said his record spoke for itself, that his heart and his courage were obvious, that his will to win had emerged on every important occasion, and would surface in his sons and daughters.

◆   ◆   ◆

Even before either colt had been sent to a single mare, the breeding world was predicting a narrow upset in the final round of the Affirmed–Alydar rivalry. It would be close, they said, but Alydar would emerge the better sire, despite having finished behind Affirmed in eight of their ten meetings.

The reasoning was pure pedigree. Raise a Native had been a more successful sire than his son, Exclusive Native, and Alydar's maternal pedigree was stronger. Sweet Tooth, his dam, had produced a champion in Our Mims, and a major stakeswinner in the filly Sugar and Spice. Won't Tell You, the cheap claiming mare who was Affirmed's dam, had produced little else of distinction. So if there was no more than a length's worth of difference between Affirmed and Alydar as racehorses, the reasoning went, the larger difference in pedigree could tilt things Alydar's way. A minority opinion held that since the two were from the same sire line and had so thoroughly proven their respective ability, they would come out evenly in the stud or Affirmed might again win by a bob of the head.

Their first crop of yearlings went through the sales ring in 1982, and the difference was more than slight. Nine Alydars sold for an average of $766,667, eleven Affirmeds for an average of $370,182. One Alydar colt went to Sheik Mohammed for $2.2 million, and another colt went to an American group for $1.7 million. The top-priced Affirmed yearling was sold to Robert Sangster for $1.5 million, but the colt probably fetched so high a price largely because of his dam—My Charmer, who had already produced Seattle Slew and would later produce the Nijinsky colt for which Sangster paid $13.1 million in 1985. The foreign buyers, who accounted for more than 55 percent of the gross receipts at the 1982 sales, obviously preferred Alydar's pedigree and rejected the verdict of the ten races between the two colts.

Alydar's success seemed to ensure Calumet's future. Mrs. Markey had sold a few seasons to the colt to outside breeders, but had planned to make him the foundation of the farm, as Bull Lea had been forty years earlier, and as Citation and Whirlaway had failed to be in the next generation. Her plans, however, died with her two weeks after the 1982 summer sales.

Admiral Markey had died two years earlier, and Calumet was without a leader. Mrs. Markey had only one child, Warren Wright, Jr., a geologist who had never taken much interest in racing and who had died in 1978. Wright's widow, Bertha, was still alive, so control of Calumet now passed to her and her four children, Lucille Parker Wright Lundy, Courtenay Marshall Wright Lancaster, Warren Wright III, and Thomas Cochran Wright. None of them knew or cared much about the horse business. The five heirs met in the fall of 1982 to consider the farm's future.

Before Alydar came along, Calumet's fortunes had been sagging and the heirs-to-be had assumed that the farm would be dissolved and sold after Mrs. Markey's death. The land was far too valuable to continue a marginally profitable breeding and racing enterprise in which they had little interest. There was talk of turning the land into the site of luxury housing development or a resort. But now, with Alydar a hot young sire capable of generating more money in stud fees each year than Calumet had ever earned as a racing stable, there was a reason to keep going. The heirs voted to keep the farm. They formed the Calumet Corporation and named as the president the only one with any horse experience, J. T. Lundy, husband of Bertha Wright's oldest daughter, Lucille.

From the start, Lundy could never have fit the breeding world's image of who should run Calumet Farm. Lundy was a working horseman, not a wealthy breeder. His passion was auto racing, and his best friends were drivers, mechanics, and farmers. Suddenly in charge of Calumet, Lundy made decisions that disturbed the farm's admirers in Lexington and the press and threatened its image as the quintessential old Kentucky home.

Lundy fired two of Calumet's oldest and most popular employees, farm secretary Margaret Glass and farm manager Melvin Cinnamon, saying that he wanted to clean house. He also announced that seasons to Alydar would be sold on the open market, with Calumet retaining fewer seasons each year. His plan for the racing stable was that Calumet would compete all over the country, in cheap as well as classy races, with divisions in California, Louisiana, Kentucky, and New York.

Other smart breeders and stable owners were undertaking similar approaches around the country. Lundy knew that it would be a mistake for the farm to rely on the sons and daughters of its own stallions to carry the operation. Such thinking had almost ruined Calumet once. But the public's charmed notion of what Calumet should be made Lundy's changes seem venal rather than practical.

Lundy also decided that each division of the Calumet runners would have a different trainer, with Veitch staying on in New York, but that all the trainers would be under the supervision of Lundy's old friend, Frank Whiteley. It was an intolerable proposition for Veitch, who had enjoyed free rein over the entire racing stable and a lot of influence in the breeding operation as well. The situation was made more awkward by the fact that Veitch's best friend was David Whiteley, Frank's son. The elder Whiteley was a revered trainer who had handled Damascus, Forego, and Ruffian, but Veitch could not live with what was clearly a stripping of his powers. He regarded the arrangement as an invitation to resign, and accepted quickly.

Veitch was disturbed by the change of events, for despite a somewhat antic youthfulness of manner, he had always been a stodgy traditionalist at heart. Once he ran a filly at The Meadowlands and refused to follow the track's practice of draping her in a Meadowlands blanket for the post parade; instead he sent her out in the devil's red and blue Calumet blanket. He was happy to pay a $25 fine. Veitch wore his loyalty on his license plates, ordering the vanity tags of ALYDAR–1 for his Jaguar.

Veitch also was stung by two acts surrounding his departure. Mrs. Markey had named a full brother to Alydar "John the Bald" in honor of her prematurely balding trainer. Lundy not only had the colt removed from Veitch's stable before the trainer's resignation was effective, but also officially renamed him Foyt in honor of Lundy's good friend A. J. Foyt. (One pundit suggested in print that Lundy should have chosen another racecar driver whose name was more appropriate to the gesture and renamed the colt Petty. Veitch whimsically announced he would change his name to John Foyt.) Lundy also declared that Mrs. Markey's bestowal of a traditional free breeding right to Alydar on his trainer was an informal contract voided by her death, and took the right away from Veitch. By contrast, the Wolfsons never rescinded the breeding season to Affirmed they promised to Steve Cauthen, an unusually generous gesture to a jockey, even after they removed him as Affirmed's rider.

Alydar's yearlings continued to sell better than Affirmed's.

From their second crops, twenty-five Alydars went under the hammer for an average of $478,600, while fifteen Affirmeds averaged $382,333.

In the following months, the first crop, now two-year-olds, began to race and the difference was dramatic. Two daughters of Alydar, Althea and Miss Oceana, emerged as the best two-year-old fillies in the country. From Alydar's second crop came Saratoga Six, who was undefeated before breaking down as a two-year-old and was syndicated for $16.6 million as a stallion, and Alydar's Best, one of Europe's top-rated two-year-olds the same year.

Affirmed, meanwhile, was getting only a few minor winners, few of them for Wolfson, who had kept sixteen of the shares. Unlike the Taylors and Hills with Seattle Slew, though, Wolfson had not set up foal-sharing arrangements with the owners of blue-chip mares, choosing instead to breed from his own Harbor View band. He was still pursuing the nicks with Exclusive Native. The difference in their appeal as stallions has become more pronounced each year. At the 1984 summer sales, Alydar's yearlings averaged $432,852 and Affirmed's hit a low average of $151,793.

Alydar had finally won, but to those who believe in poetic justice, the timing was all wrong. When Affirmed and Alydar were racing, it had seemed that Alydar somehow should be the winner more often than he was, partly for the sake of the Markeys, who were seeing their last Derby horse, partly because Alydar seemed to try so hard and so often to take the worst of the racing luck. Now, though, there was little reason to be rooting for an unrecognizable Calumet at which J. T. Lundy was sponsoring a devil's-red Calumet pace car for the Indianapolis 500, and raking in Alydar's huge stud fees. The racing stable had become an embarrassment. Calumet sent more than a dozen horses to the 1985 Saratoga racing meeting, all of them royally bred, the offspring of Alydar, the produce of such mares as Royal Entrance, Our Mims, and Sugar and

Spice. They all ran dismally. The New York division ran through three trainers in a year. When Calumet finally came up with a good-two-year-old, he had the undignified name of Judge Smells.

The roles of the two owners had been reversed and then twisted by irony. Calumet, the quintessential empire, had almost been ruined by its failure to change and the failure at stud of its champion runners. Now, it was being saved by a horse best remembered as a runner-up, and being transformed by an owner who was making changes at breakneck speed. Wolfson, the outsider and newcomer whose personal history was so far from the Calumet storybook, had done everything right in his management of Affirmed as a race horse, and shown his faith and loyalty in him as a stallion. His approach was closer to the one taken at Calumet in its glory days, and his reward was the most thorough flop at stud by a Triple Crown winner since Whirlaway and Citation had failed at Calumet thirty years earlier.

Nobody said the horse trading game was fair.

6

Woody and Wayne

Raise a Native, Alydar's sire and Affirmed's grandsire, had broken down so badly as a two-year-old that there was no chance of his ever racing again. Four starts in short races as a two-year-old were insufficient to prove anything other than that he was very fast and very promising, but that, and his being a son of Native Dancer, had been enough to make Louis Wolfson and other breeders gamble on him as a stallion.

The relationship between performance on the track and in the breeding shed is the constant riddle of the horse-trading game, and often hinges on the question of potential. While the outstanding colts of the 1970s—Secretariat, Seattle Slew, Alydar, Affirmed, and Spectacular Bid—had all verified their quality exhaustively before going to stud, they would have been just as fertile and potent had they broken down after one or two starts. All were lucky enough to stay sound for almost their entire careers and prove themselves beyond doubt as racehorses.

They were to be the last of their kind through the present. Over the next six years, no horse would win the Triple Crown or even repeat as a champion from two to three. Yet during that time, other colts would be syndicated for more than any of the best horses of the 1970s without proving half as much. After a decade of true champions, an era of flash was beginning, of guessing on potential rather than confirmed quality, and with more money than ever before at stake.

Three of the key horses of this new age would end up standing at Claiborne Farm, and Seth Hancock, again acting as a syndicator and not as an owner, would wield enormous power over their futures. But just as important a figure was Woody Stephens, the man who trained them all. Another trainer, D. Wayne Lukas, would emerge at the same time as a major influence on the market through his training of prospective sires and the offspring of valuable new stallions.

In an age when the investors and syndicators were becoming the dominant players in the game, Stephens and Lukas staked out new boundaries of power and influence as trainers. Their successes and failures, and particularly their methods, would raise new questions about performance and potential, value and worth, in the booming breeding market.

◆   ◆   ◆

Woodford Cefis Stephens was born to a tobacco-farming family near Midway, Kentucky, about thirty miles west of Lexington, in 1913. Aspiring to a richer life than the one he describes as "workin' from when you cain't see until you cain't see," he grabbed a boyhood opportunity to gallop horses at a neighboring farm, and went on to Chicago to become a jockey in 1932. He outgrew that profession physically and then became an assistant to various trainers in the Midwest, learning all he could about horses, keeping them sound and fast, and cashing a bet here and there.

He operated with a hustler's code of honor. In fifty years he has never run afoul of the rules of racing or been suspended for wrongdoing. As a rider, he was offered money more than once to hold back a horse but refused to do it.

As a trainer, he would take every edge that he could without breaking the rules, particularly in the supervision of morning workouts. He knew when to send out a horse to work just before the clockers arrived, or to instruct an exercise boy to work a horse "between poles," meaning that the horse would be clocked in a slower final time because the clockers were measuring its distance from different points of reference than the trainer. He also assimilated dozens of little home remedies and unorthodox treatments. He got one of his most successful horses over a foot problem in time for a big race by soaking the colt's hooves in gasoline-drenched sponges.

His favorite reminiscences are betting stories, of getting an unknown horse ready to win, and the punchlines invariably are "We got ALL the money" and "Our steaks sure tasted sweet that night."

In 1947, he took over as the trainer for Jule Fink, an owner and bettor who was known as the leader of the Speed Boys, a set of sophisticated handicappers who were using methods advanced for that era: privately clocking races and adjusting the final time for the condition of the track and the wind. The Speed Boys, whose handicapping methods would be commonplace a generation later, believed that they knew exactly where to spot a horse for a winning race, and they could calculate to the tenth of a second how good the competition was in each kind of race a track offered.

The Speed Boys also believed that speed won races, which sounds like a truism but is a more tactical idea than it seems. Many horses are ridden under orders to be restrained early and allowed to run free late. This makes sense for certain types of horses and in longer races, but for the relatively cheap sprints that comprise the majority of races run each day, early speed is the way to go: Gunning a horse to the front and making the others come get him wins more races than going slow and steady.

Stephens was the perfect trainer for such an outfit. His forte was training horses for early speed. With success came offers from other owners, and in the 1960s he was training for numerous society types and getting better horses. He meshed well with all kinds of owners, talking Kentucky with the hardboots and betting with the New Yorkers.

There was nothing deceptive about it. Stephens may be

Trainer Woody Stephens

FARA BUSHNELL

obsessive about scoring, putting one over and coming out the winner, and even his friends find his penchant for reciting his triumphs wearing. But he is sincere in his love for the game. He can not wait to get to his stable at five-thirty each morning. He and his wife, Lucille, have no children, and Stephens has no interests outside of the track.

"What would I do if I retired?" he once said. "Go into the middle of town, where nobody knows me and nobody talks about horses?"

He had just started training a few horses for Bull Hancock before Bull's death in 1972, and when Seth Hancock took over Claiborne at the age of twenty-three the next year, Stephens was one of the first people Seth called in. Bull's will had stipulated that Claiborne's racing stock be sold, leaving Seth to concentrate on breeding and selling at auction, but at the dispersal of Claiborne's horses of racing age in November of 1972 Seth purchased a yearling colt for $90,000 to run in his own name. He asked Stephens to handle the colt.

The following year, Stephens was training two prospects for the 1974 Kentucky Derby: Seth's colt, Judger, and Cannonade, owned by John M. Olin, a socially prominent financier. Judger was considered the more talented of the two colts by Stephens and fared better in the spring preps, but on Derby Day it was Cannonade who came through a crowded field of twenty-three to win the centennial Run for the Roses. Judger, mired in traffic all the way, finished seventh.

Aside from the homebred Judger, the first Stephens trainee to go to stud at Claiborne was Believe It, the colt who had beaten Alydar in the Remsen at two but would end up third behind Affirmed and Alydar from then on. Believe It had been owned by James and Alice DuPont Mills's Hickory Tree Farm, a Virginia stable that split its breeding stock between Claiborne and its Upperville, Virginia farm in the heart of the state's hunt country.

The next colt Stephens advised Claiborne to take was a

horse the trainer thought was as fast as any he had ever handled. His name was Danzig and he was by Northern Dancer.

Danzig had been bought as yearling for $310,000 by a new and flashy player, Henryk De Kwiatkowski, a Polish immigrant whose early life is as romantic as it is impossible to verify. He says his father was shot off his horse by Germans in 1939 as he attacked a German tank with a saber. Shortly thereafter, De Kwiatkowski was captured by the Germans and sent to a Siberian prison camp. In 1942, he says, he escaped and made his way to England via Iran and South Africa, and his adventures included being surrounded by sharks when a ship was torpedoed off the coast of Sierra Leone. Asked why he was not devoured, he replied that he had accidentally fallen into a barrel of oil on the way overboard, which repelled the sharks.

De Kwiatkowski is certain to have made his fortune in aircraft, starting with just $3,000 in 1962, buying used jets and renovating them for resale or acting as a broker between the buyer and seller, often dealing with the Arab world. His biggest score came in 1975 when he arranged the sale of nine 747's by cash-strapped Trans World Airlines to his friend, the Shah of Iran, for $150 million.

De Kwiatkowski's fee was $15 million, and he decided to buy some horses. His first purchase was Kennelot, a half-sister to Cannonade, the 1974 Derby winner. He wanted to build his own empire with top-class stock. He asked Stephens to guide him and gave him carte blanche in choosing and training the horses.

Danzig, one of their first purchases, made his debut at Belmont Park on June 25, 1979. Stephens knew he had an extraordinarily fast colt who was a cinch to win a maiden race. Danzig, let off at 3–1 in the mutuels, rocketed out of the gate and won by 8½ lengths. The trainer's steaks must have tasted sweet that night.

Danzig did not start again as a two-year-old. Ever since the colt had arrived in his barn, Stephens had known that he had a bone chip in his left knee. Some horses race successfully for years with knee chips, but Danzig was not one of them. He underwent surgery in which screws were inserted to stabilize the knee, then was sent to Florida, where his exercise for the next month consisted of swimming. Stephens knew the colt had the talent to be a major three-year-old the following year if he could overcome his physical problems, and when the stable headed north in the spring of 1980, Danzig went with them.

By May 14 Woody had him ready for a race at Aqueduct. The colt looked sensational, winning by 7½ lengths in 1:09 ⅖ for six furlongs. But Danzig was still favoring his knee, and his next start would be his last. He again was dazzling, winning a seven-furlong allowance race at Belmont in 1:22 by 5¾ lengths. But the colt came back even more gimpy than usual after the race, and Stephens sent some X rays to Dr. Robert Copelan, a veterinarian in Paris, Kentucky. The diagnosis was grim.

"Woody, if you run that colt again, you could destroy him," Copelan told him. The trainer reluctantly agreed to retire the colt.

Stephens called Seth Hancock in Kentucky and suggested that Claiborne take Danzig. Hancock agreed that the combination of the Northern Dancer pedigree and the colt's speed and precocity made him a good prospect, but he was undecided about whether he should make De Kwiatkowski an offer.

"I had heard a lot about Danzig and what other people were offering for him, and I thought it was a lot of money for a horse who had only run three times," he says. "I thought maybe it was best that I just stay out of it. I didn't want to make an offer that would embarass anyone. But Woody had a pretty nice filly of mine that was running in New York, and he had Henryk's filly De La Rose running on the same day—I think it was July 10—and he called me and said why didn't I come see my filly and De La Rose and talk to Henryk about Danzig."

Hancock flew to New York and met Stephens and De

Kwiatkowski for lunch in the Trustees Dining Room at Belmont. "Henryk said, 'What do you think he's worth?' " Hancock recalls. "And I said, 'I think about $80,000 a share.' And he said, 'If that's what you think he's worth and you can syndicate him for that amount, I'd like to have him stand at Claiborne.' And we shook hands and that was that."

Seth managed to sell only about three quarters of the shares in Danzig, at $80,000 apiece. De Kwiatkowski was disappointed to be stuck with ten shares in the colt.

Owner Henryk De Kwiatkowski (left)
with Seth Hancock, 1982.

♦   ♦   ♦

De Kwiatkowski left the picking and purchasing of yearlings to Stephens, and the two appeared to have a lucky charm
going from the start. At the 1978 Saratoga sale, they got Danzig. They came back the next year and left with a Nijinsky filly,
De La Rose, who would go on to be a grass champion. In 1981,
they came up with Sabin, a pretty chestnut daughter of the
Northern Dancer stallion Lyphard who would win more than
$1 million on the grass. But their most important Saratoga
purchase was a $150,000 Mr. Prospector colt that De Kwiat-
kowski named Conquistador Cielo, after a club of aviators
known as the Conquistadores del Cielo, the "conquerors of the
sky."

Mr. Prospector, like Alydar and Exclusive Native, was a
son of Raise a Native, and seemed even more like his sire than
the other stallions. Mr. Prospector himself had been brilliant at
six furlongs and never won beyond that distance, just as Raise
a Native had shown blazing speed in his brief career. Sons of
Mr. Prospector seemed to be blessed with lightning quickness
but short on stamina. Mr. Prospector, who stood at Claiborne,
was becoming a popular sire in the burgeoning yearling sales
market because his offspring developed early and won frequently as two-year-olds, earning quick returns.

Conquistador Cielo fit the pattern, and Stephens knew early
on he had a real speedball on his hands. Unfortunately, the
trainer feared he also might have another Danzig, in that Conquistador Cielo seemed brittle. As a two-year-old, he finished
third in his debut and then breezed to a fast and easy victory
in his second start. Stephens noticed a small knot on the colt's
left shin but decided it was not yet causing any soreness. Wanting to make the most of what he feared might be an injury-
shortened two-year-old campaign, he moved the colt into
stakes class, and he ran off with the Saratoga Special. Next time
out, in the Sanford, he ran into a traffic jam and finished fourth,

beaten just a head and two necks. The knot on his shin was getting bigger, and X rays revealed a small fracture that would sideline him until the winter.

He returned in February and ran a dull fourth in his comeback attempt, but ten days later posted a sizzling four-length victory in an allowance event, turning in a time of 1:22 $\frac{1}{5}$ for seven furlongs. He pulled up sore from the race, and X rays showed that the fracture was back. It was a minor injury but a volatile one. Called a "saucer fracture" because of its crescent shape, it was a small crack along the plane of the cannon bone, the long bone in the front leg extending from below the knee to above the ankle. It was something the colt could run on without apparent pain, but the catch was that the more pressure was put on, the greater the chance of aggravating the fracture, which would lead to soreness. One possibility was surgery; the other approach was to alternate rest with relatively brief campaigning, to make the most of the times when the fracture was better healed. Stephens and De Kwiatkowski could have turned him out for a year or more, but they reasoned that the colt would be three years old but once and that was when they wanted him at his best.

There also was a new device making the rounds of the stable area, and Stephens was willing to try anything to get his colt back to the races. Thus began a strange marriage between high technology and a sixty-nine-year-old trainer who had always relied on down home remedies and old stablehand tricks.

The gadget was called the Blue Boot Bi-Osteogen System, and was one of several electro-stimulation devices gaining popularity among horsemen. Originally developed to treat certain ailments in humans, it was approved by the Food and Drug Administration in 1979 and became available two years later as a treatment for horses. The unit cost about $2,000. The Blue Boot was strapped over the center of the injured area on the theory that mild electrical impulses would promote healing by accelerating cellular activity. It looked like a pair of shin guards, and its healing power came from a couple of plastic-covered coils within the pads, charged by a low-intensity battery. Stephens had heard good reports on the Blue Boot from some other trainers, and though it had not been tried with a stakes-class horse, he wanted the fracture to heal up in time to make at least one or two of the Triple Crown races.

The program called for daily treatments of up to three and a half hours with the blue boot. Stephens also used more traditional remedies, such as soaking the leg in ice, and tried a training regimen of seven days of walking alternated with five days of slow gallops, but no fast workouts. By April, the fracture was healing up again, and about twice as quickly as it had without the boot between the previous August and January.

Conquistador Cielo came back north with the Stephens stable in April at the end of the Florida season, and began training sharply. Stephens knew that the colt could win a major stakes if he stayed sound. The Kentucky Derby was too long and too soon, and it was decided to consider pointing the colt for the Preakness, the shortest of the Triple Crown races and the one where early speed had always been thought to do best.

The management of Pimlico Race Course, home of the Preakness, called Stephens and encouraged him to bring Conquistador Cielo for the Preakness Prep, a 1 $\frac{1}{16}$-mile allowance race the Saturday before the classic. They were having trouble attracting starters, told the trainer it would be an easy spot, and suggested that it would be a help for the colt to have raced over the track if he were going to run back a week later.

Conquistador Cielo won the Preakness Prep against a poor field by just three lengths, handling the Pimlico track well and covering two turns competently if not impressively. Off the performance, he looked like a legitimate contender for the Preakness, and the track wanted him because suddenly the 1982 Preakness needed all the contenders it could get.

It had been a dismal year for the three-year-olds. The two leaders of the class had already been knocked out of the classic picture, Timely Writer by a severe stomach virus and Deputy Minister by a wrenched ankle. In their absence, a 21–1 shot named Gato Del Sol had come from last place in a slow and strangely run Derby to win the roses, but now was passing the Preakness. A big, plodding gray colt who did best when given plenty of time between his races, he figured to run poorly over the shorter Preakness distance and the speed-favoring Pimlico track. Gato Del Sol's trainer, a young Californian named Eddie Gregson, did not want to run the colt in the Preakness, meaning that he was voluntarily foregoing a chance for the Triple Crown, a virtually unprecedented decision. Gregson, though, was thoroughly backed by the colt's owners: Leone J. Peters, a real estate executive from New York, and Arthur B. Hancock III—Seth's brother and Bull's elder son, who had left Claiborne a decade earlier after Seth was chosen to run the farm. Now Arthur had won the Derby that had always eluded Claiborne but knew he did not have a colt of Triple Crown caliber.

With Gato Del Sol out of the Preakness, the heavy favorite was Linkage, who had thrashed Gato Del Sol in the Blue Grass but then skipped the Derby because his handlers thought he lacked seasoning. While Stephens did not fear that colt, he was not happy with Conquistador Cielo's performance in the Preakness Prep. He decided on a new goal, the Metropolitan Handicap at Belmont, a prestigious mile race against older horses on Memorial Day. He thought the colt would prefer that distance, and figured that Conquistador would achieve more value by beating older horses in the historic Metropolitan than perhaps lasting to win a Preakness that had not even attracted the Derby winner.

Stephens put Conquistador Cielo into a one-mile allowance race at Belmont May 19 to give the colt a prep over the track for the Metropolitan. He rocketed away to win by eleven lengths, covering the mile in 1:34 $\frac{1}{5}$, just one second slower than the track record. Off that performance, he was made the slight favorite in the Metropolitan twelve days later, but even his backers could not have predicted the race that followed. Running against a fast group of milers, Conquistador Cielo dueled for the lead for a half-mile after breaking from an outside post in a field of fourteen, then spurted free from the pack and opened a three-length lead. After battling head and head through six furlongs in 1:09 flat, he figured to tire, but he just kept going, extending his lead to 7¼ lengths and stopping the timer in 1:33 flat. The three-year-old had broken the track record by one-fifth of a second.

Stephens was jubilant in the winner's circle, and laughed as fans half-seriously yelled to him, "Run him back in the Belmont, Woody!" The Belmont Stakes was just five days off, and it seemed like a shame that the race was coming up so soon for a colt who now looked like much the best three-year-old in the country.

"I can't see running him back off four days' rest," Stephens said. "He'd be picking up fifteen pounds and going a mile and a half. You'd have to be crazy to run him back."

Stephens went home that night thinking that way, but the voices in the winner's circle had planted an idea. His three-year-old had pasted the best older horses in the country, by 7 ¼ lengths and in track-record time. The colt had taken on that otherwordly dimension, done something horses just aren't supposed to do. Whatever the reason, Stephens says it came to him the next morning.

"He looked like he hadn't even run," the trainer said. "And I began to think, why not? The thing about the distance never bothered me. If they can win a mile, they can win a mile and a half, and I was getting the feeling that this colt could do anything as long as he stayed sound."

The idea was a wild one, surprisingly so for a successful and established trainer. Inexperienced owners and trainers often put horribly overmatched horses in the Belmont for all the wrong reasons, and the notion that a colt who can win at a mile can win at a mile and a half has ruined many horses who were never the same after trying the Belmont's demanding route. But the impulse and the instinct to run this freakish colt in the Belmont Stakes had taken hold of Stephens.

There was little need or opportunity for any workout going into the Belmont, considering that Conquistador had run a mile five days before the race. Stephens decided to fool the colt, not give him any indication there was another race coming up.

"He walked the morning after the Metropolitan. The next day I walked him under saddle and didn't take him to the track. The third morning I let him gallop the wrong way beside the pony. I didn't want his mind working at all about what he was going to do. The next morning I did the same thing."

Racetrackers were split on whether Stephens was taking a daring shot or merely a stupid one. Seth Hancock offered his opinion that Conquistador Cielo would walk home, exhausted after a mile.

A true verdict was washed away the next morning, when the skies opened and began to pelt Belmont Park with heavy rain that would last through the day and turn the track into a quagmire. Stephens was delighted. Sprinters often carry their speed farther on soft and wet tracks, and those chasing them become discouraged by having mud kicked into their faces.

As post time approached, Stephens gave explicit instructions to a jockey who had never ridden the colt before. Eddie Maple, who had been aboard Conquistador Cielo in all nine of his career starts, had gone down in a spill the previous afternoon when a filly he was riding fractured a leg and pitched him to the track. Maple suffered three broken ribs and would watch the Belmont from a Long Island hospital bed. Stephens had called in Laffit Pincay, who flew in from California the morning of the race.

In the paddock, Stephens told him about a race he had once won with a filly who probably had not been a true mile-and-a-halfer.

"I told the rider that day to just take her out into the middle of the track, don't even cross the reins, just relax her and let her take the turns easy like she's just galloping along," he said to Pincay. "You do that. Take this colt out off the rail and let him cruise. He'll take you."

A 44–1 shot named Anemal, whose owners had entered him because one of them had a vision in his sleep about winning the Belmont, gunned to the lead on the inside when the gates opened. Conquistador Cielo was just behind him, and took over when Anemal virtually stopped after half a mile. Pincay was riding well out in the center of the track and hardly moving at all, keeping the colt restrained and relaxed. Another longshot named High Ascent came up to challenge for the lead, again on the inside, and Conquistador Cielo was a head in front of him after a slow first mile in 1:37 $\frac{2}{5}$.

High Ascent was through quickly, but Conquistador Cielo was rolling along at the same steady clip. Those who had been expected to challenge made brief bids behind him but could get no closer than four lengths turning for home. The result was now foregone, but the margin began to widen dramatically, from five lengths at the top of the stretch to 14 $\frac{1}{2}$ over Gato Del Sol at the finish.

The crowd was roaring and reporters were rushing to the record books. Only three horses had ever won the Belmont by larger margins: Secretariat by 31 lengths in 1973, Triple Crown winner Count Fleet by 25 in 1943, and the legendary Man o' War by 20 in 1920. Only four colts had ever run the distance faster, none of them on sloppy tracks.

Racing fans and press, hungry for a star, acclaimed Conquistador Cielo a superhorse. Winning the Metropolitan in track-record time and then the Belmont by 14 $\frac{1}{2}$ lengths five days later added up to a spectacular week. But the Belmont had really proven only one thing: A front-runner who gets an easy lead on a sloppy track can run 1 $\frac{1}{2}$ miles in good time. It was hardly the confirmation of greatness Secretariat had shown in the Belmont, but the juxtaposition of the two disparate accomplishments seemed to overpower any moderation of praise.

The breeding world was perhaps even more impressed. Typically unconcerned with the actual conditions of a victory, the students of bloodlines marveled over the fact that a son of Mr. Prospector had won at 1 ½ miles. That was not supposed to happen, suggesting that this colt represented a genetic milestone, perhaps embodying the combination of speed and stamina the breeders are always seeking to blend.

De Kwiatkowski, who was already boarding all his breeding stock at Claiborne, began to discuss a syndication with Seth Hancock. They knew they could get a lot of money for this

Conquistador Cielo winning the 1982 Belmont Stakes.

colt, and Seth was privately putting Conquistador's value at about $750,000 a share, a total of $30 million.

A month later Conquistador posted his sixth straight victory, trouncing five third-rate three-year-olds in the Dwyer Stakes. He ran his first six furlongs in a blistering 1:08 ⅗ and then finished up in a respectable 1:46 ⅕ for 1 ⅛ miles, scoring by four lengths. What again looked so impressive was the blazing early speed coupled with the ability to keep going and cover a longer distance.

It was time for the racing world to move upstate to Saratoga, where two years earlier de Kwiatkowski had paid $150,000 for a leggy bay colt who was now worth millions. Negotiations between Hancock and de Kwiatkowski began in earnest, but things did not go as smoothly as they had when Seth syndicated Danzig in 1980. It had taken the two men about thirty seconds to reach an agreement on the terms of that deal; this one would take three days.

Windfields Farm in Maryland, home of Northern Dancer, was also bidding for Conquistador, and that gave De Kwiatkowski the leverage to demand more than Seth thought the colt was worth. Henryk curtly dismissed Seth's initial suggestion of $750,000 per share, saying that it was "meager" compared to Windfields's offer. Seth was taken aback, and contemplated telling Henryk to go ahead and sell his horse to Windfields, but the prevailing atmosphere of Saratoga convinced him not to. The small town was burning up with talk of racing's newest superstar, and people were constantly stopping Hancock and telling him they wanted in on the syndication. Seth wanted this horse, even at an inflated price. He was surrendering to the madness of the market.

He went back to De Kwiatkowski with another offer, and after some wrangling about the schedule of payments and the computation of interest, they settled on a price just under the forbidding threshold of $1 million per share. Seth was asking more than six times what he had a decade earlier for Secretariat, and three times as much as Seattle Slew had commanded just three years earlier. Those colts had won the Triple Crown, Conquistador Cielo just one leg of it, but Stephens had almost changed the rules. The combination of the Metropolitan and the Belmont, the major tests of speed and stamina, was suddenly as attractive as the Triple Crown itself. Now that unraced yearlings were selling for $4 million and up, $900,000 for a lifetime share in the new American wonderhorse did not seem like that much of a gamble.

On August 11, Claiborne announced that Conquistador had been syndicated in 40 shares for a total of $36.4 million, $910,-000 per share with the extra $10,000 per share for insurance premiums. The timing was pegged to De Kwiatkowski's tax situation. He had bought the colt two Augusts earlier, and had to keep the horse in his name for twenty-four months to realize the most favorable capital gains situation.

The tax benefits of owning a race horse are threefold. The IRS looks kindly on the horse's initial cost, operating expenses such as feed and training, and the profits received from its sale. Under the heading of Accelerated Cost Recovery, the horse buyer may depreciate the purchase price, and thus deduct it from his taxes, over three or five years, depending on the age of the horse when it is put into service. Thereafter the new owner may deduct operating expenses as they occur; most business owners must calculate, and thus defer, their expense deductions over a long period. When the time comes to sell the horse, the profits may be counted as long-term capital gains, and up to 60 percent of the net gain will be free of any tax.

De Kwiatkowski's timing also worked out well because the announcement came between Conquistador Cielo's last victory and his final career start.

After the Dwyer, the next step would be the Travers at Saratoga and Stephens as usual wanted his horse to have a race over the track. He entered the colt in the traditional Travers prep, the Jim Dandy, the race in which Affirmed had come from way back to nail Sensitive Prince four years earlier. Again, no one of quality ran against him, and he won at odds of 1–10. This time, though, he scored by only one length over a nonentity named Lejoli. Stephens downplayed the slim margin, saying somewhat accurately that Maple, recovered and back on the colt since the Dwyer, had barely urged him. But there was more to it than that, and this time it was not just the same old fracture.

Running on the fracture had apparently caused some complications, because now the colt's left front ankle was bothering him too. The ankle had been worrying Stephens for months, and he had switched from high tech to home remedies, discontinuing the Blue Boot and soaking the ankle in hot water, then immersing it in a tub of ice, and finally wrapping it in a mud poultice. The regimen had worked so far, but now the problem was much worse than it had ever been.

Conquistador Cielo may have injured the ankle in the Jim Dandy, because he came out of the race with sprained ligaments. There was now heat and swelling there, and the tendon sheath was filled with fluid. The colt's last two workouts had been uncharacteristically dull, and Dr. Robert Fritz, his veterinarian, told Woody he had two choices: give the colt a long rest and let the injury heal itself, or drain the fluid out of the ankle to relieve the pressure and pain. The trainer decided to try to hold Conquistador together for one more race. Five days before the Travers, he told Fritz to "tap" the ankle.

At 8:30 that night, after everyone else had left the barn area, Fritz, Stephens and an assistant trainer gathered under the shedrow. Inserting a hollow needle into the tendon sheath, Fritz gently squeezed the ankle, withdrawing the fluid. He finished by injecting the area with a mixture of steroids and antibiotics and wrapping the ankle in a clean cotton bandage.

Stephens did not tell De Kwiatkowski or Hancock about tapping the ankle. He wanted to guard against the news spreading, which might attract more starters to the Travers. But word leaked out around the backstretch and Seth heard about it a couple of days later. Hancock had suspected for a long time that something new was wrong with Conquistador, and now all he could do was hope for the best and wait for the colt to come home to Claiborne.

Stephens and Hancock had decided going into the Travers that it would be the colt's last race, and despite Conquistador's problem ankle they thought there was enough left for a winning finale. The colt came onto the track wearing front bandages for the first time, to give him some extra support. A few sharpies noticed the equipment change and ran off to bet against him, but the rest of the crowd made him the 2–5 favorite in a race that had drawn just five horses.

The event was a milestone of sorts, the first time the Travers had served as a rubber match among three colts who had carved up the Triple Crown. The field consisted of Derby winner Gato Del Sol, Preakness winner Aloma's Ruler, Belmont winner Conquistador Cielo, and two outsiders: Lejoli, second in the Jim Dandy, and Runaway Groom, a Canadian colt of moderate talent whose owner had grown up near Saratoga and had always dreamed of running a horse in the Travers.

Aloma's Ruler, who had won the Preakness by leading every step of the way, was in post five, Conquistador just inside him. The favorite was the quicker of the two, but Stephens suspected that if he told Maple to gun the horse early, Cordero would send Aloma's Ruler right with him, knowing it would be dangerous to let Conquistador get loose. So Stephens told Maple to take it easy the first part of the race, let Cordero send Aloma's Ruler in front of him early if necessary, and just stay close.

He might as well have given the same instructions to Cordero, because Cordero was determined to ride Aloma's Ruler the same way—stay close or even and try to save something for the stretch. So when the gates opened, neither rider went rushing for the lead, but began watching the other, both letting their colts run freely side by side through moderate early fractions. Midway down the backstretch, Maple eased Conquistador Cielo back on the rail, and Aloma's Ruler opened a lead of almost a length. As they bent into the far turn, it was still way back to the others, and now both riders went into a drive. The two colts were less than fresh after running side by side for a mile and now they were being asked for their all. Both were tiring at the top of the stretch, and suddenly a big gray colt was looming up on the outside and about to overtake them—not the expected one, Gato Del Sol, who was later found to have a bone chip in his knee, but Runaway Groom, the impossible outsider in the field. Midway through the stretch, Conquistador Cielo cracked first, falling back into third, then Aloma's Ruler gave way, and it was Runaway Groom the winner.

Stephens was not delighted with Maple's ride, but could only blame himself for not having told the jockey to gun the colt away from Aloma's Ruler early. "I made a big mistake," he said later. Aloma's Ruler's trainer, Butch Lenzini, was frustrated that his colt had dueled with Conquistador Cielo all the way around, instead of either sprinting free or being taken back, but was happy to have beaten the $36.4 million colt. Runaway Groom's people were as amazed as they were delighted that they had beaten the Kentucky Derby, Preakness, and Belmont Stakes winners.

Stephens wasted little time announcing the inevitable. Conquistador Cielo was officially retired the next day.

"I rolled the dice one time too many," he would later say, meaning that he had gambled and lost by running the colt in the Travers instead of retiring him the day the syndication was announced.

At the time, Stephens and De Kwiatkowski painted the retirement as a matter of an unfortunate injury tragically cutting down a great horse's career. In fact, the colt had been unsound for a year and his triumphs on the track were Stephens's as a stage manager. In the mere nine weeks between the

Metropolitan and the syndication announcement, the trainer had won four races with a colt who had previously won just one stakes race, and made him worth $36 million.

What had the victories really said about Conquistador's quality? The Metropolitan was the one unassailable triumph, a brilliantly fast race that proved the colt to be a dazzling miler and a worthwhile stallion prospect. But it was the subsequent, far less meaningful victories that had made him worth ten times what he would have been after the Metropolitan alone.

The Belmont had been run on such a sloppy track that those behind him failed to produce anything close to their best races, while Conquistador sailed along in a sea of mud. Had the colt covered the 1½-mile distance in the same time in a morning workout, he would not have tripled in value overnight, but that was really what the Belmont amounted to. The Dwyer and the Jim Dandy were widely perceived as confirming the Belmont, sloppy track or no, but in fact did not. In both races, he got loose on the lead and downed the mediocre colts entered against him. He ran fast times, but was not tested for character or fortitude the way that Seattle Slew or Affirmed were. In the one race where he faced such a test, the Travers, he cracked.

The Travers defeat, John Finney guessed, dropped the colt's value by about $125,000 a share. Some of the breeders who had bought in were angry after the defeat, since it burst the superhorse bubble surrounding the colt. Suddenly they were wondering what they had gotten so excited about, what had made him worth $910,000 a share.

Seth Hancock was so embarrassed by the defeat that he left the track at once, hearing the grandstand bettors laughing about the stupid fat cats who had paid $36 million for the colt.

"It was the lowest moment of my career," Hancock said later. "When Secretariat got beat in the Wood, I felt there was a chance for him to redeem himself. Hell, he was a sound horse, and you knew he was going to run again. I felt much worse when Conquistador finished third in the Travers, because I knew that was his last race. He had been syndicated for a lot of money, maybe more than what he was worth, and I felt just terrible about all those people who had paid that much for shares in him. But nobody will know what was right until his foals start running. If they turn out good, everything'll be great, and if they turn out bad, it'll look just as stupid to have paid $910,000 a share as it would to have paid $410,000."

Surely no trainer ever more deserved a breeding right than the one De Kwiatkowski gave Stephens in Conquistador Cielo. The crucial decision had been to try the colt in the Belmont, and the plain luck of the weather made it in retrospect a brilliant choice. Had the track stayed dry, would Conquistador have won? Had he lost, would he have had to run against only the same terrible fields that were subsequently entered in the Dwyer and Jim Dandy? Would he even have made it as far as the Travers?

With Conquistador Cielo out of action and out of mind in mid-August, it seemed unlikely that he would win any year-end honors except for the three-year-old championship, given that he had missed all the big fall races. But it was to be a confusing fall in which no older horse emerged as the dominant one and the other divisions failed to yield a star. When the votes were counted, Conquistador Cielo was a narrow winner in the balloting for Horse of the Year. It was hard not to think that the $36.4 million syndication price had been as persuasive a statistic as any, and equally hard not to marvel that he had achieved that value, and the sport's highest honor, for winning four races in eight weeks.

Once done, it was a precedent the sport would follow. The next year, a French filly named All Along would emerge from obscurity to win four of the world's top grass races in three countries over six weeks, and she was named Horse of the Year. In 1984, John Henry, the popular nine-year-old gelding, would defy age one more time, win three major races in six weeks toward the end of the year, and be voted the Horse of the Year award over rivals who had won more often and over longer spans.

Conquistador Cielo had set not only a new level for stallion syndication prices but a new set of criteria for excellence, ones that favored short, dramatic bursts of brilliance rather than longer and truer tests of quality. Only a few years earlier, the old guard would have sniffed at the colt's accomplishments. Now, he had been syndicated for more money than any other horse.

◆   ◆   ◆

Conquistador Cielo's victory in the 1982 Belmont Stakes was the first of four straight triumphs in the race for Stephens, an unprecedented and, for several reasons, a flatly incredible accomplishment. Despite the quality of horses being sent to Stephens by a select group of clients—and each of his four Belmont winners raced for a different owner—the chances of the one Belmont winner from each year's crop of more than 35,000 foals landing in Stephens's barn were astronomical. Second, Stephens had always been a speed man, getting his horses ready to run fast early, and consecutive victories in the longest of the American classics did not suit that style. Finally, his next three winners were all colts who had not even begun as the best three-year-old within the Stephens stable.

In 1983, Stephens had two Triple Crown prospects, Chumming and Caveat. Chumming, a $1 million son of Alleged belonging to the Millses of Hickory Tree Farm, looked all winter like the better of the two. After he rallied to finish second in the Flamingo under Maple, the rider and trainer decided Chumming was their number one colt, and Maple opted to stick with him. Stephens called in Pincay to ride Caveat, a son of Stephens's 1974 Derby winner, Cannonade.

In the Derby, Caveat ran into traffic and closed well but could only finish third behind winner Sunny's Halo. Chumming, who bruised a foot during the race, wound up twelfth and would never compete again. Caveat skipped the Preakness, where Sunny's Halo finished a poor sixth over a sloppy track in a race won by a local mudlark named Deputed Testamony. In the Belmont, though, Pincay gunned Caveat through a narrow opening on the rail as Cordero, on Slew o' Gold, tried to close the hole. Caveat bounced off the rail and ran down Slew o' Gold to win the race, but the roughhousing on the turn for home cost him his career, as he came down with a bowed tendon that prompted his retirement two months later. Caveat had not won a race of significance other than the Belmont, and was syndicated for a "mere" $7 million by Windfields Farm.

Stephens was not all that upset to see Caveat go, considering what else he had down the shedrow. He was just beginning to crank up his two-year-olds, and there were half a dozen he thought had the potential to be as good as Caveat had been, and a couple who might be as good as Conquistador Cielo.

Those two colts were named Swale and Devil's Bag. They were born a week apart in that order, but for the rest of their careers the question of who was first would change back and forth as often as they ran.

Swale was the product of a two-year foal-sharing arrangement between Seth Hancock and the Hills and Taylors, Seattle Slew's owners. In 1980, the Hills and Taylors had their pick of two colts and chose a Seattle Slew–Alluvial colt who would be named Slew o' Gold and go on to be voted a champion twice. In 1981, the Hills and Taylors picked a full brother to Slew o' Gold, a colt who died the following year. Claiborne got a Seattle Slew–Tuerta colt and named him Swale.

Swale was from the first crop of colts since Bull Hancock's death in 1972 that Claiborne raced rather than sold. Seth Hancock, angered by what he considered the poor prices the Claiborne yearlings were fetching at Keeneland, had decided to break the intent of his father's will and start racing again.

"People were just buying fashion and publicity and not the

best horses and not our horses," he said. "Our horses were better than what the market was bringing, and I thought we could do better with them by racing them because if one turned out well he'd be worth more as a stallion than we were getting for the whole lot of yearlings."

Seth had never been comfortable with selling yearlings anyway, especially in an era of fancy salesmanship in which it was commonplace for breeders such as Leslie Combs at Spendthrift and Tom Gentry to court potential buyers and stage lavish presales parties. Gentry's annual summer sales bash, a glitzy invitation-only affair, featured entertainment by Las Vegas headliners, circus animals, and hot-air balloon rides. Gentry's promotions included numerous giveaways of such trinkets as inexpensive wristwatches, yardsticks, and pens—all emblazoned with his name and his farm's blue and gold colors.

Such antics would be completely foreign to Hancock, who seldom lets down his guard in public and, despite his position in the industry, still seems uncomfortable in the limelight. He is a stickler for punctuality among his staff, and his own rigorous self discipline includes recording the times of all his morning jogs in a log book. He can be courteous and deferential to those he respects, but he can cut an unwanted interruption short with an icy look and a curt reply.

"I guess selling is a 365-day-a-year business, and I've never really cared for it. It's just not part of my personality, and I always wanted to get back to racing anyway," he says.

"Seth's approach to selling," says his younger sister, Dell, "was just something like, 'Well, here's the horse. We like him.' "

Arthur Hancock had been the true salesman of the family, relishing the competition of the auction ring. Bull Hancock had preferred the racing game, and in 1954 he had turned away from the sales end of the business, racing the Claiborne horses by himself and in partnerships. Twenty-seven years later, his younger son followed the same route.

Seth got the farm's lawyers to approve the following plan: He and several Claiborne partners, breeders who boarded their stock there, would form a new racing entity called Raceland Stable. Each year, Raceland would buy Claiborne's yearling colts, then the partners would meet the Sunday before the Keeneland summer sale and draw lots to see which horse would run in whose name, though all would be owned equally by Raceland.

The partners were Edward A. Cox, a Chicago commodities trader who struck up a friendship with Seth a few years earlier and started boarding some mares at Claiborne; William Haggin Perry, a longtime partner of Bull's whose Coastal, a half-brother to Slew o' Gold, had won the 1979 Belmont and was now a Claiborne stallion; Peter Brant, an ambitious young newcomer to the game who had made a fortune in newsprint and whom Seth liked personally; Cherry Valley Farm, the stable name for Seth's personal racing interests; Seth's sister, Dell; and Claiborne Farm, represented by Seth's and Dell's mother, Mrs. Waddell Hancock.

In 1982, the first year of the drawing, Claiborne got fifth choice. Three sons of Nijinsky had already been snapped up, followed by a son of 1967 Horse of the Year Damascus. The five remaining yearlings were by Seattle Slew, Silent Screen, Avatar, Honest Pleasure, and Believe It. Seth, on behalf of his mother, picked the Seattle Slew–Tuerta colt to carry the farm's golden-orange colors. Seattle Slew's two-year-old daughter Landaluce was already a sensation in California, but Seth's choice was partly sentimental. On the night Tuerta was born, Bull Hancock had been hoping for a colt to represent Claiborne in the Derby. When he learned the new foal was a filly, and born with only one eye to boot, he was furious, but Tuerta became the last stakes winner to carry the Claiborne silks during Bull's lifetime.

Her colt was precocious in his early training, and Stephens tabbed him as the quickest youngster in the barn. Making his debut three weeks after Caveat won the Belmont, Swale finished second as the heavy favorite, but won his next start and then the Saratoga Special, which had been Conquistador Cielo's first stakes victory. He was not running fast times, but looked like he was going to be one of the leading two-year-olds.

By the Saratoga Special, though, Stephens knew that Swale was not even going to be the best two-year-old in his own barn. Devil's Bag, a striking bay colt, had been bred at E. P. Taylor's Windfields Farm and purchased at Keeneland for $325,000 by the Millses' Hickory Tree Farm. The son of Halo and the Herbager mare Ballade made his first start as a two-year-old toward the end of the Saratoga meeting and won by seven lengths in 1:10 ⅗, faster time than Swale had ever run. Eight days later, he covered the same distance in the same time over a slower track, and when he made his stakes debut in the Cowdin a month later, he was the heavy favorite. Even Stephens did not expect what followed. Devil's Bag broke smoothly, opened an early lead, and finished the seven furlongs in 1:21 ⅖. It was the fastest Cowdin time in history, faster than a two-year-old had ever covered the distance in New York. Stephens could not contain himself.

"I've been around the racetrack fifty-one years and I never seen a colt run that fast, twenty one-and-two for a two-year-old," he said after the race.

Two weeks later, in the Champagne, the one-mile race that had certified beyond doubt the excellence of Secretariat, Seattle Slew, and Affirmed, Devil's Bag continued to exceed his predecessors. He drew out to win by six lengths and his time of 1:34 ⅕ was one fifth of a second faster than Seattle Slew's stakes record and four fifths faster than Secretariat had run.

Seth Hancock had reached James Mills at Hickory Tree after the Cowdin.

"I'm sure you're going to be getting a lot of calls and people are going to be wanting to syndicate the colt," Hancock told him. "I won't call you again, but keep us in mind. We'd sure like to have your colt."

After the Champagne, Mills returned the call. Go ahead, Mills told Hancock, I want to enjoy the colt without the worry and the risk. Syndicate him if you can.

No one had syndicated a top colt who had yet to run as a three-year-old since Seth Hancock had handled the sale of Secretariat ten years earlier, but everyone wanted in now on Devil's Bag.

"I just used the list of potential buyers from when I syndicated Conquistador," Hancock explained. "I sold out Devil's Bag before I got to the bottom."

Devil's Bag's pedigree was a hot one. His dam, Ballade, had already produced a champion, Glorious Song, a full sister to Devil's Bag. Halo, his sire, had fathered Sunny's Halo, that year's Derby winner. He came from yet another branch of the Nearco line, through Hail to Reason, and his dam, Cosmah, was a half sister to Natalma, the dam of Northern Dancer.

In the volatile thoroughbred market, the successes of Sunny's Halo and Devil's Bag were enough to cause a stampede toward Halo. A few months later, a syndicate of Texans bought the stallion from Windfields and moved him to Arthur Hancock's Stone Farm.

Seth, meanwhile, had syndicated Devil's Bag for the same price that the Texans had paid for Halo: $36 million. That was overall $400,000 less than Conquistador, but Devil's Bag was syndicated into only thirty-six shares, so they sold for $1 million apiece, tying the record price that Sheik Mohammed had gotten for Shareef Dancer earlier that year. More important, Devil's Bag had yet to run around two full turns, much less win a race like the Irish Derby, as Shareef Dancer had, or the Belmont, as Conquistador had.

Swale had gone through the rest of his two-year-old season quietly winning major races but by small margins in mediocre time. Stephens flatly said that Swale "would never beat Devil's

Bag" and planned to keep them apart until the Derby. Devil's Bag received 191 of the 192 votes for champion two-year-old, and came within a few votes of becoming the first two-year-old to be named Horse of the Year since Secretariat.

The syndication was not announced until December, by which time Devil's Bag had won his final start of the season, the Laurel Futurity. He headed to Florida for the winter as the star of a Murderers' Row of newly turned three-year-olds: Devil's Bag; Swale; the top-ranked three-year-old filly, Miss Oceana; and four other colts who would have been the top Derby contender from virtually any other stable in the country. But Devil's Bag was the pampered star of the show, and the center of more media attention than any colt since Secretariat.

Stephens proclaimed at every opportunity that Devil's Bag was the best horse he had ever been around, Conquistador Cielo, Caveat, and Danzig included. The only question was whether Devil's Bag would make the normal leap from two to three and cover longer distances as easily. His pedigree and disposition said he would, but Stephens wanted to be extra sure. He began training the colt differently, ordering him to be restrained in the early part of workouts and then come on strong at the end. It seemed to be working perfectly. In his first start as a three-year-old, Devil's Bag relaxed nicely and came from off the pace to win by seven lengths. The time was good though not spectacular, but Stephens was exhilarated by the colt's easy change of styles and figured he was a cinch to win the Triple Crown.

Two weeks later, Devil's Bag was the 1–2 favorite for the Flamingo despite the presence of two other exceptionally talented three-year-olds in what was looking like a crop of tigers, Frances A. Genter's Dr. Carter and Ogden Mills Phipps's Time for a Change. The 1984 Flamingo provided Stephens with a chance to replay the 1982 Travers, and this time he gave Maple the orders that he wished he had given the rider for Conquistador Cielo: Go to the front, Stephens told him, confident that

Devil's Bag could outsprint the field and draw away like the wonder horse he was supposed to be.

Devil's Bag had drawn the outside post and the front-running Time for a Change was on the rail, so Devil's Bag could have relaxed off the speedy Damascus colt and been in control, as Aloma's Ruler was against Conquistador. Instead, Maple gunned his colt in a diagonal path over to the rail, and Time for a Change moved up outside of him. Devil's Bag could not shake free. The two colts dueled for six furlongs in 1:09 ⅖, a full second faster than Aloma's Ruler and Conquistador Cielo had gone in the Travers. Turning for home, it was Devil's Bag who began to flounder. Dr. Carter came swooping by the tiring favorite, and looked like the winner, but Time for a Change dug in courageously and won by a neck. It was six lengths back to Rexson's Hope, a second-rater who had passed the weary Devil's Bag in midstretch, the latter checking in fourth after winning his first six races.

The racing world was as stunned as Stephens. He hid out from the press in the Turf Club bar, consoling himself with stories of past triumphs and the vagaries of the sport. The next morning, though, he faced the world and took the blame squarely on himself, saying he had been overconfident and perhaps had mistrained the colt. Devil's Bag would be back, he assured everyone, and in the meantime, there was another colt to whom people should start paying attention.

Swale made his first start as a three-year-old four days later, and while he was still no Devil's Bag, he had become a much better colt than he had been at two. He won the Hutcheson Stakes at Gulfstream Park by eight lengths, drawing away instead of barely winning as he had the year before. He lost his next start but then beat Dr. Carter in the Florida Derby.

By then, Stephens had taken off for New York with Devil's Bag, planning to run him in the Gotham and the Wood Memorial, leaving Swale in Florida with his assistants. Seth Hancock did not like the idea of Claiborne's Derby hope being handled by Stephens's deputies, and called in a man of his own from the farm, Mike Griffin, a former trainer who now was in charge of breaking yearlings at Claiborne. Hancock was beginning to wonder how firm a grip on things Stephens had, considering the Flamingo outcome.

Stephens made his preference clear as to who was the top colt by heading to New York with Devil's Bag. Eddie Maple had been riding both colts, and also appeared to be showing faith by sticking with Devil's Bag. Actually, he had little choice.

"Eddie wanted to give the colt another chance, and I told him he had to stay with him whether he wanted to or not," Stephens would say a year later. "How would it look, Seth syndicating the horse for $36 million and then Eddie getting off him to ride Seth's own colt?"

Storms washed out the Gotham Stakes, wrecking Devil's Bag's training schedule, and Stephens made another change of plans, to take the colt to Kentucky and prep him for the Derby in two sprint races. Devil's Bag made his first start since the Flamingo in the Forerunner Purse at Keeneland and blew away a poor field by 15 lengths. He did not seem quite as brilliant as he had been at two, but considering he had been off five weeks, the race was encouraging. Two days later, Swale made his final pre-Derby start, over a muddy track in the Lexington Stakes, and ran poorly, finishing a distant second to an obscure gelding named He Is a Great Deal who was not even being considered for the Derby. Devil's Bag was back on top once more as the two colts headed for Churchill Downs.

Stephens, though, was sick and growing worse by the day. The seventy-year-old trainer had broken three ribs in a household fall in Florida and now was beginning to cough a lot during an unusually rainy and cold April. Two days after Swale's defeat, Stephens was checked into a Louisville hospital and diagnosed as having pneumonia. Devil's Bag won his final scheduled Derby tuneup, the one-mile Derby Trial Stakes at Churchill Downs, by 2 ½ lengths, but little about the race was encouraging. He had labored to beat a bad field, tired in the stretch, and weaved to the wire as if trying to get off a sore leg. X rays were taken the next afternoon when the press was gone from the stable area, and they revealed an ambiguous cloudy area around the knee, perhaps nothing, perhaps a serious problem.

Devil's Bag winning the 1984 Flamingo Prep.

JIM RAFTERY/TURFOTOS

Before getting a second set taken, Hancock went to visit Stephens in the hospital the Tuesday after the race. His mission was to convince the trainer not to run Devil's Bag in the Derby. He had received no pressure from members of the syndicate, but feared in his gut that the colt would be beaten badly and might never recover. Stephens had lost control and agreed. They would pass the Derby, take another set of X rays, and decide if the colt should ever run again.

Stephens was hoping that he could get out of the hospital and salvage something with Devil's Bag in the coming weeks. He even talked about "doing a Conquistador," getting the speedy colt ready for the Metropolitan. But Seth Hancock had pretty much decided that the colt's career was over. The official story was that he would be pointed for the Preakness, but the decision to retire him had been made even before a second set of X rays revealed a small bone chip in the colt's right knee.

The chip could have been surgically removed or given time to heal and Devil's Bag could have been racing again by late fall. But the syndication agreement had called for him to be retired by the end of his three-year-old season, and no one was eager to take any chances bringing him back. His retirement was announced two days after the Kentucky Derby.

Harsh reaction followed the retirement announcement, even from the trade publications that usually support the breeders. Devil's Bag had a career record of eight-for-nine and was coming off victories in two Derby preps. Even the knee chip, described by one skeptical columnist as history's first chip transplant, failed to sway public opinion that the colt was being retired to protect his value as much as his health.

Two days earlier, Claiborne had won its first Kentucky Derby. Swale, sent off as the second choice to the Alydar filly Althea, had run a solid race from just off the pace to win the 110th Derby by 3 ¼ lengths. There was not much behind him, with Devil's Bag injured and Time for a Change and Dr. Carter sidelined with viruses, but the victory was sweet for Seth Hancock. He dedicated the triumph to his father, Bull, who had always hungered for the roses.

Swale went on to Baltimore for the Preakness. The colt had fallen into a pattern of alternating good and bad races and his two Preakness workouts were too fast. Even though he was the 4–5 favorite in the race, his own handlers thought he would run poorly. Seth Hancock was so sure of it that he stayed home in Kentucky, using the excuse of having to attend a friend's wedding. Swale, dull after his overly fast workouts, came up empty when called upon. Pincay did not pressure him, and the colt finished a poor seventh.

Back in New York, preparing for the Belmont, Swale began to thrive again. Stephens was on his home turf, and the race was shaping up in his colt's favor. Swale had been just off the pace in the Derby and won, but had gotten trapped in a five-way fight for the lead in the Preakness that sealed his fate there. None of the Preakness speedballs would be trying the 1 ½ miles of the Belmont and it appeared likely that Swale, the lone front-runner, would control the pace. Sent away the favorite, he did exactly that, running smooth and even fractions all the way around the track to score by an easy four lengths and record the fourth-fastest Belmont time in history.

As a Derby and Belmont winner and a son of the red-hot Seattle Slew, Swale's value was now conservatively estimated at $30 million. It figured only to grow. Considering the way that Slew o' Gold had slowly matured and continued to improve, Swale seemed likely to get better, just as he had from two to three. Hancock announced that the colt would race at four. The plan was to rest him for the summer and bring him back for the big fall races.

Eight days after the Belmont, Swale went to the track for a typical light morning gallop. He went well, returned to the stable in good spirits, and was standing outside the barn waiting for a spongebath when he suddenly fell backwards and began to flail. Three minutes later, he was dead. The initial diagnosis was a heart attack, but an autopsy found nothing to substantiate that. After two months of tests, a microscopic bit of heart fiber showed scar tissue suggesting some kind of heart irregularity, but after hundreds of hours of research that hypothesis was the best that anyone could come up with. There was no evidence or logical scenario to suggest foul play. The colt had simply died.

It was a mysteriously tragic ending to the year of Stephens's two colts. They had been expected to end up together at Claiborne, stablemates again as stallions, but now just Devil's Bag was roaming the fields while Swale's remains lay buried in the farm cemetery, close to those of his great-great-grandsire, Bold Ruler, and Bold Ruler's sire, Nasrullah.

Devil's Bag was bred to a blue-chip book of mares his first season, including Natalma, the dam of Northern Dancer. The breeders remained convinced that his brilliance as a two-year-old had been genuine and would be passed on in his genes. Yet his reversal of form at three remained a mystery to the breeders and fans alike. Had Devil's Bag been that good in the first place? The empirical evidence, his times and his margins, said yes. Stephens still calls him the fastest two-year-old he has ever seen. But if the knee injury had been to blame for his loss in the Flamingo and his dull victory in the Derby Trial, why hadn't it shown up earlier? And, had that been all that was stopping him, why hadn't the syndicate allowed him to come back and race again after a recovery?

The key point was that the colt was withdrawn from the Derby before there was any proof that there was anything wrong with him. Stephens still believes that had he run, he would have been "no worse than second and he might have won because he always was a better horse than Swale." Hancock, on the other hand, was sure that "he would have gotten beat the length of the stretch."

In effect, the colt's career had peaked at the close of his two-year-old season with his syndication. It had been fated to end the second anything went wrong. He was retired coming off a victory and with a record of eight triumphs in nine career starts. Still, the $36 million pricetag was simply too high to let him run again. The last time Hancock had let that happen, Conquistador Cielo had cracked in the Travers.

♦   ♦   ♦

Hancock, stung by the Devil's Bag experience, said he would never syndicate another two-year-old. He said it was time to reverse the trend of early syndications and retirements, and let horses instead prove themselves first. That pronouncement did not stop others from trying to capitalize on the syndication market with a glamorous two-year-old. One of those who did was D. Wayne Lukas, the California-based trainer who would become Stephens's West Coast counterpart as a stallion-maker and set some new standards of his own.

Lukas grew up on a small farm near Antigo, Wisconsin, and began hustling horses even in his childhood. By the time he was in high school, he and a friend named Clyde Rice, who would later become one of the shrewdest horse trainers and sellers on the leaky-roof circuit of small tracks, were spending their weekends traveling to midwestern auctions, buying and reselling farm horses. They would buy a horse, clean him up, and resell him the same afternoon. It was an enterprising boyhood that taught him as much about salesmanship as horsemanship.

The factor that would eventually make Lukas a success on a massively greater scale came when he was coaching high school and college basketball in the 1960s. He began to study and espouse motivational techniques and a self-help philosophy that seemed equal parts Dale Carnegie and Werner Erhard. His basketball players not only took an extra hour of practice, they also received lessons in grooming and manners from local Holiday Inn hostesses and speeches from Lukas about character and success.

On the wall of Lukas's stable office hangs a sign listing a trainer's "daily dozen" of ideals, reflecting his tidy universe of values: "1. The value of time. 2. The success of perseverence.

3. The pleasure of working. 4. The dignity of simplicity. 5. The worth of character. 6. The power of kindness. 7. The influence of example. 8. The obligation of duty. 9. The wisdom of economy. 10. The virtue of patience. 11. The improvement of talent. 12. The joy of originating."

While assistant coaching at the University of Wisconsin, he had begun training quarter horses part time, driving sixty miles to and from a ranch before school each day and then spending off days running his horses at the informal race meets where these Western-bred sprinters compete. In 1967, he turned to it full time.

By 1976, he had set new records and standards for the quarter horse sport. No one before had ever trained more than two champions a year, but in 1975 Lukas had eight in his barn. He had charged into a languid game populated with part-time cowboys and set up a stable operation with the cold efficiency of any Fortune 500 corporation. As much a part of his success as his hard work and quasi-religious philosophy of achievement was his eye for a horse, the sixth sense he had developed in childhood.

It had taken him just eight years to master and outgrow the quarter horses, and now he turned to thoroughbreds. Several of the owners he had made rich followed him to the new sport, put up their money, and Lukas was off and running. Within two years he was among the top five trainers in California, and new clients were begging him to take their money and horses. He began to attend the Keeneland sales, picking out expensive youngsters by physical appearance first and pedigree second. His eye went to blocky and muscular horses, the kind that could develop quickly into precocious speedballs.

Like Stephens, his strength as a trainer was in getting young fast horses ready to race early. Quarter horse racing, where sprinters must be sharpened to cover short distances in dashes over straightaways, was a perfect training ground.

In 1978, Lukas took a two-year-old filly from Secretariat's

second crop named Terlingua and had her so ready to go that she beat males in the Hollywood Juvenile Championship in July, two days before the yearling auctions at which Secretariat's third crop would sell.

A trainer who could do that was extremely useful to the major breeders, and they began seeking out Lukas. Claiborne already had Stephens, so Spendthrift went after Lukas, sending him their own youngsters as well as some of their clients, especially those who were buying expensive yearlings sired by Spendthrift stallions.

Stephens and Lukas had gained an unprecedented star quality as trainers, and both were getting more offers than they could possibly handle. This in turn made them succeed even more because they had an unparalleled choice of young horses to pick from. Stephens each year looks over more than 200 yearlings or two-year-olds owned by his clients and picks the twenty or thirty best-looking and best bred. Lukas, who acquires most of his horses from his clients' yearling purchases, has a similar range of choice by recommending virtually all the purchases.

Lukas and Stephens had raised the ancient question of how much difference a trainer makes. Although there is a wide range of talent and competence at any track, the top trainers agree there is very little difference in the actual methods of conditioning horses among the very best trainers.

"We all buy our feed at the same place, and use the same veterinarians," says David Whiteley, who has trained three champions. "It's all the horses. All we can do is screw up."

What Lukas and Stephens had done was to gain superior access to the best horses. While their specific talents would have made them successful under any circumstances, having so many top horses to pick from and work with made them look like magicians. The access to so large a pool of expensive and talented horses snowballed from their success as stallion makers.

Their popularity gave them such power that the standard owner-trainer relationship, in which the trainer is usually an employee subject to the whims and orders of the owner, now often seemed reversed. Stephens was able to juggle offers from clients and receive far more than the usual 10 percent commission on earnings.

"A woman called me the other day and asked me to take a two-year-old filly of hers," Stephens mentioned casually one morning. "She said she'd give me an extra $25,000 if I got her stakes-placed, $50,000 if she won a stakes. It looks like a nice filly but I had to tell her I just don't have the room."

Another time, one of Stephens's most prominent owners threw a small tantrum at Saratoga after watching one of his horses run dead last in her debut.

"Get your horses out of my barn," Stephens said. The owner spent the next four days begging Stephens to reconsider, and the trainer did on the condition that the owner visit the stables less.

Even at Stephens's lowest point, when he was hospitalized amid uncertainty about both Swale and Devil's Bag and Mike Griffin was sent in to take over for him, the trainer was able to flex his power. Hancock was having his doubts about Stephens's ability to continue on the job, and there was similar talk among other owners.

"Anyone who's not happy with the job I'm doing can pick up their horses and leave tomorrow," Stephens said. Nobody took him up on the offer.

Stephens and Lukas both used their power to gain a personal stake in the breeding market as well. Both receive the usual complimentary breeding rights in the stallions they develop as well as a 10 percent commission on the sale of mares. Lukas also frequently has been given an ownership interest in the horses he purchases for his clients. He used the Hollywood Lassie in 1982 to help do for Spendthrift's Seattle Slew what Terlingua did for Claiborne's Secretariat. When Landaluce, from Seattle Slew's first crop, won the race by an astounding 21 lengths in brilliant time, it sent prices for Seattle Slew's second-crop yearlings, and his stud fee for the following season, soaring.

The next year, Affirmed's and Alydar's first offspring were two-year-olds, and Lukas had an Alydar filly, Althea. Her first race was too late to plump the price of Alydar yearlings at Keeneland, but four days after that sale she won the Juvenile and, like Terlingua, beat colts. At Saratoga two weeks later, the auctioneer reminded the buyers of Althea's smashing victory every time an Alydar yearling went through the ring.

Lukas's barn each year seemed to have one crack two-year-old after another, and the trainer was finding ways to win purses and boost the breeding value of all of them. He capitalized on the possibilities of flying and vanning horses around the country as no trainer before had done. Frequently he had horses running in three or four stakes races over the same weekend at three or four different tracks. He sent his horses into spots he thought they could win.

"I have owners who don't mind spending the $25,000 it costs to fly a horse across the country for a big race," Lukas said. "They know they'll usually make more than that by running."

Late in 1984, he split his stable between California and New York, sending the latter division out with his son, Jeff, a capable, twenty-seven-year-old carbon copy of his father. Campaigning horses on both coasts allowed Lukas to increase his rate of success, since he could match his horses to the most advantageous conditions prevailing in either of the nation's two racing centers.

In 1985, Lukas shattered most of the sport's training standards, winning seventy stakes races to break the record of fifty-four stakes victories in one year that Jimmy Jones had set with Calumet Farm, and running up record purse earnings of over $11 million.

In addition to shipping around to find soft spots, Lukas had begun to exploit the weaknesses of the racing calendar and to tailor each of his horses' careers to best advantage. In 1985, he had a very moderate two-year-old named Sovereign Don rated as about the sixth best juvenile in his stable.

"By the end of the year, he'll be running in Omaha," Lukas said.

But rather than relegate Sovereign Don to a second-level career of mediocrity, Lukas cracked him out for New York's earliest stakes races for two-year-olds, when the fields are weak because most trainers are handling their top two-year-olds patiently and delicately, waiting for longer and more prestigious stakes events later in the year. Sovereign Don was able to win three straight stakes events against moderate fields in unimpressive time. As Lukas had predicted, by the time the better two-year-olds in the country emerged, Sovereign Don could not keep up. But Lukas had won almost $200,000 with the colt and earned him an eventual career at stud.

The trainer's surroundings reflect his methodical ambition. The barn at his Santa Anita headquarters is a landscaper's delight, replete with neatly trimmed hedges and wrought-iron lawn jockeys. His stable help, who earn better pay than most through a profit-sharing system, are required to rake the dirt in the barn in a particular herringbone pattern.

"That kind of attention to detail instills pride and discipline," he says.

Lukas himself is as impeccably manicured as his stables, with a dazzling set of teeth and a good tailor. Whereas Woody Stephens attracts affection with his down-home informality and crinkly charm, Lukas wins admiration through his articulateness and his infectious confidence. He is a master at dealing with the press, frequently using accessible sports metaphors and carefully remembering everyone's name. He knows how to play to a television camera. Other trainers come off looking dull by comparison.

Lukas's master job of salesmanship involved his top two-year-old of 1984, an Alydar colt named Saratoga Six because Lukas and five clients were partners in paying $2.2 million for him at the Saratoga sales the previous year. Saratoga Six won his debut by two lengths, then the Hollywood Juvenile by four, the Balboa by a half and the Del Mar Futurity by three lengths. The colt was solid but not spectacular. His times were nothing special. But Lukas was talking him up as the best two-year-old he had ever trained, and much of the racing world took him at his word.

Saratoga Six seemed headed for a showdown with the east's top colt, Chief's Crown, a youngster from the first crop of none other than Danzig, the Northern Dancer colt of De Kwiatkow-ski's that had entered stud at Claiborne in 1981. Chief's Crown's handlers were eager for a confrontation and sent their colt West, since he was supposed to make his last start of the year in a rich new race for two-year-olds at Hollywood Park. He was scheduled to clash with Saratoga Six once before that, in the Norfolk at Santa Anita. But a few days before that race, Saratoga Six broke down in a morning workout, fracturing the sesamoids in his right front ankle.

Saratoga Six underwent surgery and was saved for stud duty, but his racing days were over. He was the latest casualty in a series of Lukas-trained horses which had suffered career-ending injuries or sudden declines. No one knew whether it was horrendous luck, hard training, or a little of both, but Lukas's top young horses had displayed an uncanny tendency toward illness, injury, and form reversal after their triumphs. In 1980, he had sent out Codex to win the Preakness Stakes, but the colt never raced again after turning in a bad showing in the Belmont. Marfa never won a race of significance after being beaten in the Derby. Lukas's top two-year-old of 1981, Stalwart, had broken down early in his three-year-old season.

All three of these colts were quietly syndicated and retired at healthy sums ranging from $1 million to $6 million. All of them won more races and more money, and did it more impressively, than Saratoga Six. But this colt was a son of Alydar, whose popularity was due in large part to Lukas's early success with Althea and Woody Stephens's with Miss Oceana. Between the fashionable pedigree and Lukas's salesmanship, the syndication of Saratoga Six went quickly and for an astounding $14 million—for a colt who had made just four starts, all as a two-year-old, all in the state of California against second-rate competition. No other trainer, except perhaps for Stephens, could have talked up half as large a price for so young and untested a horse.

It was not to be the last, or the most lucrative syndication of a two-year-old in 1984. Chief's Crown went on to win the Norfolk and Carl Rosen's heirs decided the time was right and the market atmosphere perfect to protect themselves and syndicate their colt. Before his final start of the year, the Rosens announced that a group of breeders headed by Robert Clay of Three Chimneys Farm in Lexington had purchased a half-interest in the son of Danzig for $10 million, making him worth $20 million on paper.

Though Chief's Crown would go on to be beaten in all the Triple Crown races, no one who bought into him had any regrets. Danzig's first crop included both Chief's Crown and Stephan's Odyssey, and between them those two colts would account for second and third place in both the Derby and the Belmont, and victories in the Travers and the Marlboro Cup.

Danzig was suddenly hot, a son of Northern Dancer siring top dirt colts, not European grass runners, and getting two of them from his very first crop. The breeding world as usual was quick to pounce on early results. Late in 1985, a share in the young stallion was sold for $2.725 million. De Kwiatkowski, who had been "stuck" with ten shares that could not be sold for $80,000 apiece five years earlier, and Hancock, who had doubts about the colt's soundness but took him because he was a son of Northern Dancer, suddenly had another gold mine on their hands.

Ironically, the same month that the Danzig share went for over $2 million, a share in Devil's Bag, whose first foals had yet to be born, was sold for $700,000. On the basis of one crop, Danzig's value had increased almost 4,000 percent, while Devil's Bag's disappointing three-year-old season had dropped his stock by 30 percent.

Chief's Crown and Saratoga Six had been syndicated as two-year-olds less than six months after Devil's Bag had been sent home to stud without winning a major race as a three-year-old. The optimism of the market had triumphed, along with the blood of Northern Dancer and Alydar, and the magic of Woody Stephens and D. Wayne Lukas.

7

The Breeders' Cup

Chief's Crown had been sent to California for the Norfolk, instead of running in the traditional year-end races in New York, so that he could close out his two-year-old campaign in a richer and more important event: the inaugural running of the Breeders' Cup Juvenile, one of seven lucrative, new championship races that were all scheduled to be run at Hollywood Park on November 10, 1984. As the name implied, these were races dreamt up and staged by the breeders, not by track operators or promoters. After a decade of changing just about everything else in the sport, the horse traders now even had their name on its richest races.

The man behind the Breeders' Cup was John Gaines, the owner of Gainesway Farm near Lexington. At first, no one took him too seriously. When he pitched the Breeders' Cup idea to John Galbreath at Darby Dan Farm one afternoon early in 1982, the eighty-five-year-old Galbreath replied, "Why, John, I didn't know you smoked pot."

The first the public heard of it was the day after a crudely mimeographed press release was passed out in the Keeneland press box on April 23, 1982. A few reporters called Gainesway to make sure it wasn't a practical joke. A year earlier, some prankster had dropped a stack of press releases in the Santa Anita press box saying that a star mare worth $4 million had been retired and was being bred to Elephant Walk. A few reporters went ahead and ran the story only to find that Elephant Walk is an obscure stallion who stands for $1,500.

Gaines's announcement sounded just as preposterous. He stated that the nation's most prominent breeders had agreed to fund and administer a program called the Breeders' Cup Ltd., which would culminate in seven races worth a total of at least $13 million to be run at one track at the end of 1984.

Many newspapers ignored the story, and even the *Daily Racing Form* viewed it cautiously. To anyone familiar with racing in America, the idea sounded impossible. How would the race tracks, always competing with one another to attract top horses, agree to cooperate with such a plan? Where would the money come from? How could a seven-race card, spanning four hours, possibly be televised and promoted? Why would trainers and owners agree to run their best horses against one another instead of dividing and conquering the existing banquet of American stakes races?

The proposal was quickly forgotten amid Derby Week and the subsequent clamor over Gato Del Sol's skipping the Preakness and then the hoopla over Conquistador Cielo's Belmont. Soon after, though, lush four-page advertisements began to appear in trade magazines such as *The Thoroughbred Record* and *The Blood-Horse,* and for two reasons they made it sound as if the thing might really come off. First, the ads explained that the funds would be raised by having the owner of every stallion in America pay in the equivalent of that stallion's stud fee each year to make all of his offspring eligible to compete in the series. Also, the owner of each newborn foal would make a small one-time payment. These fees would amount to about $20 million.

Second, and perhaps more assuringly, the ads presented the nation's breeders as a happily united front, working together for the dramatic new program. The published roster of officers covered all the big bases. Gaines, the master of Gainesway Farm, was president. The two vice-presidents were Seth Hancock of Claiborne and Brownell Combs II of Spendthrift. Charles P. Taylor, now managing his ailing father's Windfields Farm, was secretary, and Brereton C. Jones, whose Airdrie Stud in Lexington was building a fat roster of new stallions, was treasurer. The twenty-three listed members of the Board of Directors included Robert Sangster, Louis Wolfson, Penny Chenery, Arthur B. Hancock III, Nelson Bunker Hunt, Stavros Niarchos, and Vincent O'Brien. The eleven "Honorary Directors," several of whom were presumably too aged to take an active role or attend board meetings, included Leslie Combs II, John Galbreath, William Haggin Perry, E. P. Taylor, and C. V. Whitney.

The roster was overwhelming and, in a way, overly comprehensive. John Gaines had assembled a list of every famous and influential horse breeder in the business, to impress the industry with the seriousness of the Breeders' Cup. Each of the big names, though, was used to acting independently, and each had his own ideas about how the Cup should operate. At times Gaines found that he had stacked the board of directors against himself.

To achieve his goal, he would finally depend on the compelling necessity of the Cup. The breeders needed to do something grand and drastic or their market was in danger of collapsing.

There would be no stallion syndications or skyrocketing yearling prices, no breeding industry at all, if ordinary citizens did not attend the races every day and bet their money. The money to operate the tracks and pay purses to the owners of horses comes directly from the track's cut of the daily betting handle. Without tracks and purses, there would be no need for race horses of any price or pedigree.

Amid the explosive growth of blue-chip breeding, the dirty secret of the sport was that the racing end of the game was in trouble.

◆   ◆   ◆

While the numbers being generated by the top end of the breeding industry had been escalating for the past decade, the figures being turned out in those same years by the one hundred and five tracks in North America had been discouraging. The same dwindling crowd was attending the races, and their betting was just barely keeping pace with inflation. Although thoroughbred racing technically was still outdrawing every professional sport in the country, these numbers had always been phony. Most of the figures came from the same core of daily racegoers at each track, not a broad base of casual fans. Worse yet, demographic studies said that the steady fans, while representing the widest possible socioeconomic range, had one thing in common: their average age was increasing every year because racing had been unable to attract younger fans.

The sport had been stretched about as far as it would go. In the 1970s, racing had changed from a seasonal to a perpetual game as revenue-hungry states, particularly in the northeast, started running year round. In New York, the tracks had previously shut down in December, January, and February, but now there was racing six days a week even during snowstorms. The sport also devised an array of new betting temptations, adding numerous exotic wagers each day. Fans now could shoot for higher payoffs by betting on the first two finishers in an exacta or the first three finishers in a trifecta. Nothing seemed to help. Attendance and handle were essentially stagnant, and it wasn't just the demographics that were making the future look bleak. State lotteries were springing up nationwide to compete for the American gambling dollar. In 1976 New Jersey legalized casino gambling and made Atlantic City a gambling magnet for the 16 million people living within 200 miles of the decrepit beach resort.

Much of the sport's trouble had its roots in the ascendance of television a generation earlier. Racetrack operators had made a great mistake in the early days of the medium by resisting most efforts to put their sport on the air. They feared that if fans could watch races at home, they would find ways to get their bets down without going to the tracks. It was a shortsighted view, sacrificing the chance to give their sport exposure in a medium that would have flattered it. Racing lends itself perfectly to television, with its pageantry of color and short bursts of drama. Even today, many print advertisements for television sets use a horse race as the on-screen image.

The sport's early resistance to television would cost it dearly. The price was not merely that other athletic contests, especially football, soared in popularity through television exposure in the 1960s and 1970s while racing became increasingly invisible. More damaging was that an entire generation of sports and news-media power brokers matured with the perception that racing was out of the mainstream of popular sports and entertainment. It was not on a par with baseball, football, basketball, tennis, or hockey. Instead, it was something that had to be acknowledged three times a year, with the Triple Crown races, but otherwise was a disreputable pastime for gamblers and a hobby for the idle rich.

Secretariat stirred widespread interest and stimulated investment, but by the next year racing had fallen out of public awareness again. New developments in the sport proved less attractive. One move in particular that might have revolutionized the industry was tried in the nation's largest city and instead became a civic embarassment that continues to blight the sport.

Off Track Betting (O.T.B.) in New York was supposed to be a model for the future of the industry. In England and France, numerous shops are available where fans can bet as easily as buying a newspaper. Countless casual fans have been created this way, and the shops and parlors make the fact of racing visible in everyday life. On-track attendance has decreased, but track operators share betting revenues with the offtrack operators. In New York, the motive for O.T.B. was to meet a quick $300 million revenue gap in 1970. The public was told that O.T.B. would replenish state coffers and wipe out illegal bookmaking by offering a legal alternative.

Instead, neither objective was met. The New York tracks fought rather than cooperated. They resented sharing the betting take with O.T.B., and losing admission and concession revenues. The state made a joke of its intention to wipe out bookmakers by slapping an outrageous surtax on winning bets that effectively imposed a penalty for complying with the law. To this day, O.T.B. bettors receive lower payoffs than on-track patrons. The difference is supposed to be 5 percent but can go as high as 50 percent. A bettor who wagers with a bookmaker receives the track payoff, more than he collects at the O.T.B. outlet.

O.T.B., as a new state agency, quickly became the New York government's biggest dumping ground for political patronage jobs, resulting in mind-boggling inefficiency and waste that had it on the verge of actually losing money by 1984. Most visibly, the city's approximately one hundred fifty so-called parlors, offering neither seats nor rest rooms, much less refreshments or other comforts, quickly developed the same social standing as peep shows. Many would-be patrons understandably avoided the shops and continued betting with bookmakers or, worse, forgot about racing. In the fifteen years since O.T.B. began, no other state has wanted to follow such a disastrous example, and the possibilities of offtrack betting have been generally abandoned. A limited version called simulcasting, which involves patrons at one track betting on races telecast from another, began to accelerate beginning in 1982, but will never account for more than 10 percent of any major track's revenues and is a tiny expansion compared to the possibilities of a network of offtrack shops in major cities.

Having missed the boat on television and rejected the New York experience with offtrack betting, the racing industry was facing no significant avenues of growth amid the breeding boom of the 1980s. It was beginning to occur to some of the breeders that this meant an inevitable downturn in the market: With more stallions being sent off to stud each year, there would be a larger foal crop but no more purse money or places to race the offspring. Supply would soon outstrip demand.

The very fact that the breeders took action, and had the influence to effect it, proved that power was shifting significantly in the sport. The breeders had in the past had little to do or say about the actual operation of racing or the publicizing and promotion of the sport. Although many of the breeders were powerful enough to hold influential positions at individual tracks, it was the race tracks' job to run the game. Now, though, the breeders were saying that it was time for them to take charge.

♦   ♦   ♦

Their new involvement was of course prompted by self-interest, which extended to the specifics of the initially proposed Cup program. While many breeders independently were voicing the kinds of complaints that moved Gaines to conceive the program, his proposal also stemmed from the specific nature of his own breeding operation.

Gaines grew up in upstate New York, where his family was involved in the animal feed and ration business that would eventually grow into the Gaines Dog Food empire. Gaines's father began buying standardbreds in 1939, and Gaines himself was fascinated early by breeding and genetic theory. The first horse he bought, the standardbred Demon Hanover, turned into a champion and Gaines syndicated him—back in 1953— for $500,000. After numerous successes as an owner, including two victories in the Hambletonian, he sold the Kentucky standardbred farm he had developed and decided to try something new, switching to thoroughbreds in 1963.

The first mare he bought was a stakes winner named Oil Royalty. He was in Chicago for one of her races in 1964 when he met Fred Hooper, a pioneer in Florida racing and breeding who was then campaigning a colt named Crozier that Gaines admired. Hooper asked him what he thought Crozier could be syndicated for, and Gaines opined that the colt could command $25,000 a share.

"Do it and you're a prince," Hooper said. Gaines sold the horse easily, and unwittingly was off on a career of stallion syndications. His next major purchase, with partners John Hanes and John Olin, was Bold Bidder, a son of Bold Ruler, who would go on to sire Derby winners Cannonade and Spectacular Bid.

In the 1970s, Gaines went quickly and heavily for the European bloodlines and the Northern Dancer influence, carving out a spot for his Gainesway Farm as one of the Big Three stallion plants along with Claiborne and Spendthrift by building an enormous roster of sires, many of them European in origin or appeal. By 1982, he had forty-five stallions at Gainesway, many of whom had the grass-favoring pedigrees the Europeans were snapping up at the summer sales, including Vaguely Noble, Lyphard, and Riverman.

Gaines remained a student of genetics and a patron of tradition. His tastes in stallions sometimes seemed eccentric but were grounded in careful research. Gainesway itself, the fussiest of the big three plants, is lavishly decorated with Renaissance art and Gaines's own study is built from the wooden stall walls of the stallion Mahmoud, the Epsom Derby winner whose granddaughter, Natalma, produced Northern Dancer.

His European investments and interests had much to do with the impetus for the Breeders' Cup. Virtually all American racing fans and most owners and breeders pay little attention to the results of even Europe's biggest races, which disturbed the man whose farm stood the sires of many of those major stakes-winners.

Wanting to attract top European horses was just one of the factors that led to Gaines's conception of the Cup. His primary one was the stagnation of the racing industry and what he perceived as a flood of negative publicity in the 1970s.

The institution of exotic bets such as the trifecta, where picking the first three finishers in a race in exact order could return thousands for a $2 wager, had spawned a race-fixing scandal at Eastern tracks. Over a three-year period in the mid-seventies, a ring of gamblers backed by organized crime systematically bribed jockeys to hold back favored horses in tri-

John Gaines (right), **founder of the Breeders' Cup.**

fecta races, yielding high payoffs on unlikely combinations held by the crooked gamblers. The scheme resulted in the suspension of more than two dozen jockeys but, typically, no significant convictions among the masterminds.

Another unsavory development was the institution of "controlled medication programs" in every major racing state except New York, where the old-line purists resisted. The strain of year-round racing was wearing down horses and creating a demand for more runners to fill the programs. Horsemen demanded, and were granted, permission to use painkillers and other drugs that would allow their horses to race more often. Ironically, the analgesic that caused Peter Fuller's Dancer's Image to be disqualified in the 1968 Kentucky Derby was legal for any race in Kentucky a decade later. The daily use of these medications prompted numerous exposés, many of them as sensational and inaccurate as they were compelling to outsiders, which unfairly portrayed the sport as one that was dangerous and cruel to animals.

Amid this extensive negative publicity, Gaines began to search for a single bold idea to present the sport in a more favorable light while also creating a new event that might showcase an international field.

"The Breeders' Cup was founded on two fundamental convictions that I held," he said. "One: The conditions of racing will determine the shape of the breed. Two: The sport of racing has only one thing to sell, only one appeal to the public—who has the best horse."

His experience in harness racing shaped his next steps. He chose the Hambletonian Society, which owns the race of that name and other important fixtures in the standardbred sport, as a model for Breeders' Cup Ltd., a nonprofit, privately-owned corporation. Gaines next began to canvass the likes of Hancock, Combs, and Taylor, to create a coalition of all the sport's power brokers.

That was where things got sticky. The major breeders were

not used to working as anything but masters of their own empires, and Cup board meetings became argumentative and divisive. There were disagreements over virtually every detail of the program, particularly over how much of the money raised should go to the seven big races, and how much should be given out in hundreds of other existing major stakes races during the year. Gaines wanted at least $13 million, almost 75 percent, paid out in the seven races. Within three months, five board members had resigned.

"I regret to say that I do not believe that the Breeders' Cup, in its present form, will be acceptable to the vast majority of our industry," Brereton C. Jones of Airdrie Stud wrote to Gaines. "I am extremely disappointed that I have been unable to convince you that it is unhealthy to collect all this money from thousands of people in our industry and give nearly 75 percent of it . . . to a handful of people on one day."

William duPont III told Gaines that "there are too many loose ends, too many unanswered questions, too many egos, and too much money."

The Hancocks resigned because of the division of money and possibly over a subtler issue of bias, toward grass racing, toward Europeanization, and toward California as the likely site of the first Cup. Their ties had always been to the East, to dirt racing and dirt pedigrees, and they sensed an attempt to legislate a new set of priorities.

The entire Cup program was in danger of going under. Press skeptics began to question the fundamental idea of the program. Couldn't racing publicize itself more effectively with a $10 million advertising campaign than with a single four-hour telecast? Wouldn't it be bad for the sport to put so much emphasis on one race instead of a season-long campaign? Wouldn't the Cup races diminish the importance of existing races? Wouldn't horses be raced more sparingly, pointed only toward the one big race a year?

The answer was yes to each of these questions, but Gaines,

his allies, and the trade press rallied around the Cup idea by insisting it was needed to save the sport from its slide. Gaines finally made some concessions, and brought the board members who had resigned back into the fold. He agreed that the money would be split fifty–fifty between supplementing existing race purses and the Cup Day purses. Gaines also decided it was best to step down as president to avoid personality and power conflicts with the other major breeders. His successor was C. Gibson Downing, Jr., a fifty-two-year-old lawyer and former state senator who owned a moderate-sized breeding operation called Winfield Farm and had earned a reputation as a skillful negotiator and down-home diplomat.

The Cup was in full swing again, though more hostility was engendered when California was officially chosen as the site for the inaugural Cup races. The New York establishment reacted haughtily, since the sport's titles had always been settled at Belmont Park in the fall, and those championship events were now being made into prep races for something in California. The board's explanation was that the weather was likely to be better in California in early November and that the proximity to Hollywood meant a greater chance for a television extravaganza replete with celebrities.

Another reason was that Hollywood Park had pitched itself more enthusiastically than the New York tracks, but the Cup suffered another blow when word got out that this encouragement had included the promise of a $200,000 contribution by Marjorie L. Everett, the president of Hollywood. Cup officials and Mrs. Everett insisted the contribution had made no difference in selecting the track and that her gesture had been purely charitable and meant to help promotion of the Cup, wherever it was held. Some journalists remained skeptical.

Another problem began to surface a year later, as horsemen started thinking realistically about the Cup and trying to run their best horses in it. Amid the confusion over the program and whether it would come off, many breeders had missed the deadline for paying their stallions' stud fees and owners had failed to nominate their horses at the one-time $500 nominating fee. By mid-1984, more than half the top horses in every division were not eligible to run in the Cup without being supplemented at exorbitant fees that amounted to as much as 12 percent of the purse—up to $360,000 for the $3 million centerpiece race.

As it became apparent that confusion and ignorance rather than cheapness or hostility had kept many horses from being nominated, Cup officials began to leak word to the press that the board was considering a one-time deadline extension. It seemed the fair thing to do and consistent with the breeders' insistence that the industry work together to make the Cup a success. Not all of the breeders, though, were willing to extend that spirit of cooperation to their own personal disadvantage.

"Why in hell should I let in some owner who wasn't smart enough to read and play by the rules so he can beat my horse?" said John Nerud, the retired trainer who was now president of Tartan Farm and a high-ranking Cup official.

Despite the urgings of the press and some Cup officials who were not owners and breeders, the board voted not to reopen nominations. Anyone who wanted to run could pay the supplemental fees. Unlike most races, where such fees are added to the purse so that an owner has a chance at getting some of them back, these fees would kick into the Cup coffers for future years' purses.

The $3 million race, at 1 ¼ miles on the dirt for three-year-olds and up, had finally been called the Breeders' Cup Classic, the most expressive of the names finally chosen for the events. Names of great horses had been considered, but the feeling was that this would yield confusion, since there was already a Secretariat Stakes at Arlington Park, a Man o' War at Belmont and a Citation at Hollywood. So the Cup board went for generics, with of course the key words Breeders' Cup thrown in at every turn.

In order, the seven races to be run would be the $1 million Breeders' Cup Juvenile, a mile for two-year-old males; the $1 million Breeders' Cup Juvenile Fillies, a mile for two-year-old fillies; the $1 million Breeders' Cup Sprint, six furlongs for three-year-olds and up; the $1 million Breeders' Cup Mile, at one mile on the grass for three-year-olds and up; the $1 million Breeders' Cup Distaff, 1 ¼ miles on the dirt for fillies and mares three years old and up; the $2 million Breeders' Cup Turf at 1 ½ miles on the grass for three-year-olds and up, and the Classic.

Gaines had initially envisioned the 1 ½-mile grass race, which figured to draw plenty of Europeans, as the richest and climactic race, but was overruled by the American breeders who reminded him that the vast majority of good old American racing was still conducted on the dirt. A race patterned on the Kentucky Derby, not the Epsom Derby, should be the high-light.

Nineteen eighty-four was beginning to look like a bad year for an international equine olympics of racing because the crop of available athletes was weak and ragged. There was Chief's Crown but not much else among the two-year-old colts; nothing of quality among the two-year-old fillies; no compelling three-year-olds following the retirement of Devil's Bag, the death of Swale, and the illnesses suffered by Dr. Carter and Time for a Change; the sprinting division was weak, and among the older horses Slew o' Gold was running away from every field he met despite a chronic problem with cracked hooves.

Then, in September, along came the nation's most famous and popular racehorse with a final age-defying burst. John Henry, an obscurely bred gelding, had become the sport's best story and richest runner over the past five years and now was going strong again at the age of nine. Purchased privately as a three-year-old for $25,000 by Sam Rubin, a bicycle importer and horseplayer, John Henry had blossomed when tried on the grass and proved to be an iron horse, coming back year after year to post increasingly improbable and impressive triumphs.

In 1981, as a six-year-old, he had won the sport's first $1 million race, the inaugural running of the Arlington Million in Chicago. Later that fall he took the Jockey Club Gold Cup on the dirt, and was a unanimous selection as Horse of the Year. Sidelined during much of 1982 and 1983, he nevertheless was named the grass champion in 1983 at the age of eight.

Now, as a nine-year-old, he was staging a final campaign for glory. The Turf Classic on September 22 was the setting for a ballyhooed first meeting with All Along, the French filly who had stormed America in 1983 and was named Horse of the Year over Slew o' Gold and Devil's Bag after winning three major grass races against males. John Henry scored a narrow victory over a popular local horse named Win while Majesty's Prince beat All Along for third. Seizing on John Henry's popularity and trying to guarantee his appearance at a race they were already sponsoring in New Jersey, the promoters of Ballantine's Scotch offered a $500,000 bonus to any horse who could win the Turf Classic and the Ballantine's Classic. They were delighted to hand Rubin a check for that amount after John Henry swept to a victory that gave the event and the scotch a lot more than $500,000 worth of publicity.

After the race, everyone wanted to know what Rubin would do about John Henry and the Breeders' Cup. Rubin had not nominated the gelding the previous year because it had looked like he was nearing retirement. The owners of John Henry's sire, Ole Bob Bowers, had not paid the $1,000 equivalent of his stud fee to the Breeders' Cup because no other offspring of Ole Bob Bowers were Breeders' Cup material.

The question put to Rubin was whether he would supplement John Henry to the $2 million Breeders' Cup Turf, a race the old gelding would be the favorite to win, even though it would cost Rubin $240,000 to do so. The answer everyone expected was yes, but Rubin was not ready to give it.

"I don't like the way the Breeders' Cup people have acted," said Rubin. "They don't seem to want John Henry in the race. It's outrageous they didn't reopen the nominations. I don't think I want to put up that kind of money to be in their race."

Rubin was hoping to bargain down the entry fee, and while the breeders were not going to accommodate him on that score, they were chagrined at the slap at the Cup and reassured him how much they wanted John Henry in the race. Their backers did the dirtier work of going after Rubin publicly, piously suggesting that Rubin owed it to the sport to supplement John Henry.

Rubin has never forgiven those critics, but was swayed by the breeders and announced he would pay the $240,000. Half of it was due twelve days before the race, and Rubin had a check delivered. The next morning, John Henry came up with a swelling in his ankle and he was never entered for the Cup Turf. Rubin forfeited his $120,000. The race had lost a star, but the Cup had won a more important symbolic victory. By the following summer's select yearling sales, 95 percent of the catalogued horses had been fully nominated to the Cup for future years. Everyone was playing by the rules now, the rules set by the breeders and their Breeders' Cup.

♦   ♦   ♦

Cup officials devised a system to select the fields for the Cup races, which the breeders had assumed would attract an over-flow of entries and have to be limited. Under the scheme finally agreed to, horses would receive points for first-, second-, and third-place finishes in important American stakes races. Two thirds of each field, or nine of the maximum fourteen starters, would be admitted by points. Five others who did not qualify on this basis would be invited by a panel of American and European racing officials.

This latter provision was designed partially so as not to

exclude a late-blooming American horse who lacked points but clearly belonged in a race, but mostly to ensure broad European participation. For the first Cup, though, the Europeans were not even interested in this free ride. All Along, already over here for the fall grass races, would accept an invitation, and the big international players wanted token representation. Sangster, the Aga Khan, Sheik Mohammed, and Khaled Abdullah of Saudi Arabia all would enter one horse, though in each case it was not the best horse in their stables. The top Europeans were staying home. Why risk flying halfway around the world for a new and unproven series of races?

Secreto, the Epsom Derby winner, was the lone possibility as a glamour representative, and arrived in the United States in October, ostensibly to run in the Washington, D.C. International and the Cup Turf. This announced plan may have been less than sincere. A half-interest in the colt, yet another son of Northern Dancer, had been purchased by the new J. T. Lundy–run Calumet Farm, and Secreto was scheduled to take up stud duty in Kentucky the following season. Shortly after his arrival, he came up with an unspecified foot injury and was vanned to Calumet for examinations that would determine whether he was fit to run in the Cup. He never left the farm.

All the concerns about point systems and how many Europeans to invite became moot when preliminary entries were taken for the Cup races nine days before post time. Not one of the events drew the maximum fourteen entrants. The 1 ½ -mile Cup Turf drew the most, twelve, but that included the already-injured John Henry. Seven of the horses had raced in Europe that year, but none was considered among even the top ten of the European season. Lashkari, the Aga Khan's entry, had won just three of seven starts and earned only $56,594 in his entire career.

The horses, horsemen, and press began to arrive at Hollywood Park a week before Cup Day and found a starkly different atmosphere from Derby Week at Churchill Downs. The two

Derby barns at Churchill are open-air facilities where trainers and reporters mill around in the morning drinking coffee from plastic foam cups and watching the Derby horses graze. The Breeders' Cup stakes barn was a concrete fortress sealed off from the press by high wire fences and determined security guards. The Derby Week social events are loose but well-stocked nightly parties centered on the sport, with one dinner honoring owners, another trainers, another given by the writers for the Derby participants. The main event of Cup Week was a formal ball at the Twentieth Century Fox Studios, with tickets going for $250 apiece.

The breeders had hired slick Madison Avenue outfits to handle marketing and promotion and leaned heavily on Marge Everett's Hollywood acquaintances. The celebrities dotting the week's festivities came not from racing but from the soundstages. The cast of *Dynasty* was involved in one function, and the timing neatly coincided with the release of a "Dynasty" line of apparel and cosmetics. On Cup Day, Hollywood's special guests included Elizabeth Taylor, Gregory Peck, Cary Grant, and Fred Astaire.

Most of them spent the day in the open-air Turf Club restaurant instead of the facility that consumed most of the $10 million Hollywood Park had spent on improvements for the Cup, a five-story glass-and-steel tower named the Pavilion of the Stars. Not quite finished on time, and built with $100 seats that offered partially obscured views, the pavilion resembled a huge parking garage.

The days leading up to the races offered little racing news beyond Slew o' Gold's ongoing foot problems. The colt, now four years old, was coming off an unprecedented sweep of the Woodward, Marlboro Cup, and Jockey Club Gold Cup, the series his father had missed winning by the length of Exceller's nose in the 1978 Gold Cup. Despite his triumphs, Slew o' Gold had been running with various hoof cracks that Jim Hill and the colt's veterinarians were constantly examining and patching up. Had it been any other race, the Hills and Taylors would have scratched him and sent him home to Three Chimneys Farm, where he was scheduled to begin stud duty in 1985, but they wanted to be represented in the Cup and the race looked like a virtual walkover. They also remembered how both Seattle Slew in 1978 and Slew o' Gold in 1983 had narrowly missed Horse of the Year honors. A Cup victory, capping an undefeated season that included the sweep of Belmont's Fall Championship Series, would make Slew o' Gold an automatic choice.

Cup Day came up perfect weather-wise, and a crowd that would reportedly reach 64,254 began arriving much earlier than normal, not out of anticipation but because of the unusual scheduling. NBC television had bought the rights to the Cup and had planned a four-hour network telecast. They had insisted on a Saturday rather than Sunday running, so as to avoid conflict with pro football, and had mandated an 11 A.M. start, California time, so that the telecast would run from 2 P.M. to 6 P.M. in the East.

The breeders had also lined up corporate sponsorship for all seven races, with each sponsor agreeing to buy commercial air time for one segment of the show. North American racing had attracted only a few corporate sponsors to fund race purses before, all of them tobacco or alcohol concerns: Philip Morris for the Marlboro Cup, Rothmans for the Rothmans International, Anheuser-Busch for the Budweiser-Arlington Million, 21 Brands for the Ballantine's Scotch Classic. The breeders had sought and gotten broader support this time, such as Robert Brennan's First Jersey Securities for the Juvenile, Mobil Oil for the Distaff, DeBeers Diamonds for the Turf, and Chrysler Corporation for the Classic.

Only as the colts for the Juvenile, the first race on the card, arrived at the paddock did it finally seem that the Cup was going to happen. It suddenly dawned on everyone that seven races would be run in rapid succession, showcasing most of the top available horses in the country. It was almost a glut of quality, but exactly what John Gaines had in mind all along. The day went rapidly, almost giddily, for everyone.

One frequent fear had been that the Cup races might end with meaningless upsets, defying their purpose as definitive championship events by offering up winners who clearly were not deserving of divisional titles but happened to be feeling good that day on a new track. The Juvenile immediately set a different tone. Chief's Crown, far back early, made his usual sweeping rush on the outside to catch the early leader, Spend a Buck, and then hold off Tank's Prospect, D. Wayne Lukas's top two-year-old now that Saratoga Six was retired. The outcome certified Chief's Crown's already strong claim to the two-year-old championship.

The Juvenile Fillies, a race short on talent with weak favorites, added some quick drama to the proceedings. Fran's Valentine, a 74–1 shot, beat Outstandingly, a 23–1 shot, by half a length, but the inquiry sign immediately began to flash. Tapes clearly showed that Fran's Valentine had banged into a filly named Pirate's Glow on the stretch turn, and she had to be disqualified and placed next-to-last. Outstandingly, an Exclusive Native filly owned by Louis and Patrice Wolfson's Harbor View Farm, was placed first. The Cup was two races old and there had already been a disqualification and a longshot winner.

The Sprint, a race which had seemed likely to produce a longshot winner who might then be voted an Eclipse Award on the basis of one victory, instead narrowly went to the deserving favorite, Eillo. The son of Mr. Prospector opened a long early lead and then just lasted over Commemorate and Fighting Fit. Among the happiest spectators was Seth Hancock, since two of the first three Cup races had now been won by sons of Claiborne stallions.

The Mile, a race designed for Europeans since few grass races at that distance are run in this country, went to an Irish-bred filly who had been running here all year. Royal Heroine snaked her way through the field to score by 1 ½ lengths over the longshot Star Choice. In the winner's circle to receive the trophy for the richest purse he had ever won as an owner was Robert Sangster. The winning trainer, John Gosden, had been Vincent O'Brien's assistant in Ireland for six years.

Royal Heroine had been sired by Lypheor, a son of Lyphard, making her a great-granddaughter of Northern Dancer. Previous triumphs by Royal Heroine and the Lypheor colt Tolomeo, who edged John Henry in the 1983 Arlington Million, had resulted in the stallion being repatriated from stud duty in Japan, and in 1984 Lypheor had joined Lyphard at Gainesway. So after four races, the sire standings were two for Claiborne, one each for Spendthrift and Gainesway, and a sweep for the Big Three.

The Distaff again went to a favorite and the day's most impressive winner. Princess Rooney, a four-year-old gray, drew off by seven lengths over Life's Magic, a three-year-old filly trained by Lukas. It was a dispiriting race for Woody Stephens, whose lone Cup Day entry, Miss Oceana, ran last, and lost all chance of beating Life's Magic for the three-year-old filly championship. Princess Rooney was sired by Verbatim, who stands at Elmendorf Farm, an old-line Lexington nursery.

The two richest races now remained, and before they were run, a telegram to John Gaines was displayed on the brand-new color matrix board in the infield. It sent good wishes to Gaines and the Breeders' Cup from an old horseman named Ronald Reagan.

The Turf, in John Henry's absence, proved an utter triumph of Europeanism. Eight of the eleven starters had raced abroad at some point in their careers, and the first five finishers had all competed in Europe in 1984. Even the running style was continental in flavor, with a slow early pace and a furious run to the wire. At the finish, it was the longest shot in the race on top, Lashkari at 53–1, with All Along just a neck behind in second. Finishing third was Raami, a British colt who had been bought the month before by Robert Brennan, who wanted to be represented on Cup Day.

The Aga Khan, hardly expecting a victory, was not present, so Elizabeth Taylor gave the trophy to the colt's trainer and the manager of the owner's stud farm. Even the European experts on hand had dismissed Lashkari's chances before the race. His victory, following a pattern of mediocre European horses coming to life the first time they ran in this country, had to have been exasperating for a lot of the Europeans who kept their top horses at home. It was an oversight they would not commit again.

All that was left was the Classic, with Slew o' Gold the heaviest favorite of the day. After an afternoon which could hardly have been scripted better for drama, combining favorites and longshots, squeakers and runaways, the Classic shaped up as a sedate finish, a virtually certain crowning of Slew o' Gold as the Horse of the Year in the richest race in the sport's history.

It still looked that way at the top of the stretch. A 31–1 shot named Wild Again had been leading all the way and now seemed ready to call it a day. Slew o' Gold, who had been reserved off the early pace, was making his move, and Gate Dancer, who had won the Preakness but finished behind Swale in the Derby and Belmont, was only starting to gain ground on the outside. Slew o' Gold drew even with Wild Again, but then surprisingly could not go by him, and Gate Dancer was gaining on the outside. With a furlong to go, it was a tired Wild Again at the rail, Slew o' Gold next to him but not gaining, and Gate Dancer drawing even in midstretch. The three colts were heads apart, and began to bump in tight quarters. Wild Again was wobbling to his outside and Gate Dancer was bearing in, the two of them making a bit of a sandwich out of Slew o' Gold. It was anybody's race in the final strides, but at the wire it was still Wild Again on top by a head, with Gate Dancer second, and Slew o' Gold, with Angel Cordero now standing up in protest, third between them.

It took less than a minute for the inquiry sign to go up and for NBC to show head-on shots of the stretch run to the public. Unfortunately, the network's camera was not the same one used by the track and the stewards, and its placement made a questionable foul look flagrant. It looked on the NBC tapes as if Wild Again had steadily veered out from the rail, impeding Slew o' Gold, with Gate Dancer contributing to a lesser extent from the outside. The stewards studied their own films for the next seven minutes.

Wild Again's owners paced and clenched their fists in the winner's circle. No one had put up more to be there, and almost everyone had scoffed at them. Their colt, an erratic sort who had alternated good and bad races in major events outside of New York, was coming off a dull third in a race at Bay Meadows, a second-rate track near San Francisco. Despite his apparently hopeless chances against a colt like Slew o' Gold, his owners had supplemented him for $360,000. The gesture fit their style. A group of Texans, they called themselves the Black Chip Stable, after the color of the $100 denomination of casino chips.

Finally, the lights on the board stopped blinking, and the numbers were quickly rearranged. It took the Wild Again crew a moment to realize that their horse was still the winner, and then they began jumping and whooping. The stewards had decided that Gate Dancer was the culprit, and disqualified him from second to third for lugging in through the stretch. (Six months earlier, Gate Dancer had become the first horse ever disqualified for interference in the Derby and was knocked back by the stewards from fourth to fifth place.)

It only seemed fitting that Gaines should be involved with the Classic finish. Wild Again had been sired by Icecapade, a Nearctic stallion standing at Gainesway.

Everyone left Hollywood Park with good feelings about Cup Day, and the numbers backing that impression confirmed it as an instant success. The Hollywood fans had wagered $11.5

million on the card, a California record and a world record for any day other than the Kentucky Derby. The NBC telecast had drawn a 4.9 Nielsen rating, below the annual 1 ½ -hour Derby telecast but impressive for a four-hour show. Also, the NBC telecast, which had wisely used racing specialists instead of the usual generalist sports announcers, had been a surprisingly tasteful and intelligent production, laced with frequent Breeders' Cup–sponsored ads selling the sport and encouraging track attendance.

The Eclipse Awards three months later reflected the instant importance of the Cup. John Henry and Swale were the only divisional titlists who had not raced on Cup Day. Chief's Crown, Outstandingly, Eillo, Princess Rooney, and Royal

Wild Again (#2) beats Gate Dancer and Slew o' Gold in the inaugural Breeders' Cup Classic.

HOLLYWOOD PARK

Heroine had clinched their respective championships by winning Cup races, as had Life's Magic by finishing second in the Distaff. Slew o' Gold had already accomplished more than enough to be named best older dirt horse. Gaines was given a special award of merit, and NBC's telecast won the television award.

The only close call was for Horse of the Year, between John Henry and Slew o' Gold. Had Slew o' Gold won the Classic, he would have been a unanimous selection, and had he skipped the race he probably would have won it. But in the narrowest vote in the award's history, John Henry proved the popular choice, having lost less in absence than Slew o' Gold had in defeat.

The one clear negative effect the Cup had, as predicted, was to diminish the significance of other major races on the calendar. This did not much bother the breeders, though, for transparently self-interested reasons. The Cup races had forced many tracks to rearrange their stakes schedules, running traditional year-end fixtures sooner in their new role as Cup preps. This had led to races within the same division at different tracks, especially for the two-year-olds and the grass horses, being run on the same days or weekends.

In 1983, Devil's Bag had run in the Cowdin and Laurel Futurity a month apart, but a year later those two races were on the same day. All Along had run in the Turf Classic, the Rothmans, and the Washington, D.C. International, and now the latter two races were on the same weekend. As a result, the quality of these divisions was spread thin, and inferior horses were able to win or place in previously major events. The breeders hardly minded this, since it resulted in more opportunities for their horses to pick up stakes credentials and money.

The results, though, could be embarassing. The Champagne, the race that Secretariat, Seattle Slew, Affirmed, Spectacular Bid, and Devil's Bag had won, in 1984 was moved to

Aqueduct and lengthened to 1 ⅛ miles to accommodate the timing of the Cup. It drew a poor field and was won by a gelding named For Certain Doc, who not only failed to win in his next ten starts but was beaten by a total of 236 ½ lengths in those races. New York racing officials were so mortified that they restored the Champagne to Belmont and its original distance.

◆　　◆　　◆

The second running of the Cup was held at Aqueduct Race Track on November 2, 1985, and many of the season's developments leading up to it reflected the immediate changes the breeders had effected on the game. Horses were being raced more sparingly now, their campaigns designed to have them peaking in November. Several trainers stopped on their top horses in late summer to give them a freshening before the fall.

Gaines's desire to internationalize the sport also seemed to be working, thanks largely to Lashkari. Beginning as early as June, European turf horses were being sent over to compete in major grass stakes, and a fresh wave started coming in October for the Cup, including some of the top runners from the Continent. This time, five of the races drew more than the maximum fourteen entries, so the point system and committee selections had to be invoked. Sharp trainers had anticipated this and chosen starts for their horses throughout the season based on where they had the best chances to rack up points. Lukas, as usual, was the master of this kind of shopping and shipping. Nearing the end of a season in which his trainees had won record earnings and stakes races, Lukas had gotten five different two-year-olds in his barn to accumulate enough points in graded stakes races to qualify for the Cup events. He started a total of ten horses in five Cup Day races.

There was plenty of apprehension surrounding the second Cup. Aqueduct, the relatively dingy home of New York's winter racing, would not have the sparkle of Hollywood, and perhaps the whole program would suffer from a lack of novelty now.

On a cool day for which rain had been predicted but never came, 42,131 fans showed up at the Big A, approximately as many as had come for the Belmont Stakes in June though 22,000 fewer than had attended the inaugural Cup at Hollywood a year earlier. But many New York fans bet the races at O.T.B. and then watched the four-hour telecast instead of standing around in nippy weather. The ten thousand reserved seats had all been sold by July.

The Juvenile lacked the two top two-year-old colts and prospects for the 1986 Triple Crown races, Ogygian and Meadowlake, both out for the year with sore shins. In their absence, the race went to Tasso, a California-based son of Fappiano, a son of Mr. Prospector standing at Tartan Farm. The runner-up, beaten a nose, was Storm Cat, a son of Storm Bird and grandson of Northern Dancer. Storm Bird had been purchased by Robert Sangster for $1 million at the 1979 Keeneland sales.

Lukas sent out the first two finishers in the Juvenile Fillies, both owned by Eugene Klein: Twilight Ridge, a daughter of the Claiborne stallion Cox's Ridge, and Family Style, a filly by the Spendthrift stallion State Dinner. The sprint went to Precisionist, Fred Hooper's homebred son of Crozier, the first thoroughbred John Gaines had syndicated. The Mile, which attracted Europe's top three milers, went to Cozzene, a Tartan homebred and a son of the Spendthrift stallion Caro.

Lukas and Klein ran one-two again in the Distaff, with their four-year-old Life's Magic beating their three-year-old Lady's Secret. Life's Magic, like Twilight Ridge, is a daughter of Cox's Ridge, meaning Claiborne stallions had sired two Cup race winners in each of the first two years. Lady's Secret, the runner-up, is a daughter of Secretariat. The Turf again had a heavily Continental flavor with the popular British filly Pebbles, a daughter of the Gainesway stallion Sharpen Up, leading an all-foreign charge to the wire.

The races had again proved the definitive championship events in most divisions, with Tasso, Precisionist, Life's Magic, Cozzene, and Pebbles all on their way to Eclipse Awards. Once again, the winners had come from the blue-chip nurseries, with each of the Big Three again accounting for at least one sire of a Cup race winner. The breeders, having put their official imprint on the racing calendar, had also consolidated the power of the top end of the market.

It had been a great show on the track, but the ratings for the telecast were a major disappointment, down 20 percent from the first year. The slippage had almost all been on the West Coast, where the telecast ran from 9:30 A.M. to 1:30 P.M., two hours earlier than the previous year and out of the prime afternoon sports-watching slot. It had been impossible to run the races any later in the east because of early darkness in November and the lack of lights at the major tracks, which run during the day.

Cup officials worried that NBC might drop its commitment to the series if the trend reappeared in 1987, when the Cup races were scheduled to be held at Churchill Downs, again in the eastern time zone. So they readily acceded to the network's suggestion that the races be run in California that year as well as in 1986. The Cup officials also cast doubt on whether the races would still be held as scheduled in Florida in 1988.

The decision was surprisingly quick and exploded the principle of moving the series around the country. Now three of the first four Cups would be run in California, where eastern horses often fail to run their best and where permissive medication programs cloud the significance of results. Once again, though, the industry and the trade press rallied around the decision. Keeping the telecast was more important than the integrity of the series.

The final race of the second Cup Day fit the championship purpose of the Cup program perfectly. The champion three-year-old, champion older horse, and Horse of the Year titles were all on the line.

The outcome of the race and those titles involved the three colts who had been favored in the Kentucky Derby the previous May: Chief's Crown, Spend a Buck, and Proud Truth. It had been an eventful six months, much of it hinging on Dennis Diaz's decision on whether to run Spend a Buck in the Preakness or the Jersey Derby. His choice, and its aftermath, said as much about the power of the breeders in horse racing as the fact that the year's most important race was no longer the Kentucky Derby or the Jockey Club Gold Cup, but the Breeders' Cup Classic.

8

To Make a Buck

The Breeders' Cup, Robert Brennan was saying to Dennis Diaz three days after the 1985 Kentucky Derby, was exactly the kind of bold new step that racing needed, and it was just the beginning. Look down below you, Brennan urged, it's a whole new world down there and you can do anything you want.

Brennan and Diaz were flying in one of Brennan's private helicopters from Manhattan to Garden State Park in Cherry Hill, New Jersey. The owner of Garden State was telling the owner of the 111th Kentucky Derby winner about the brand-new world of horse racing, in which running the winner of the Kentucky Derby in the Preakness Stakes was no longer an automatic move. Diaz had not announced his decision on Spend a Buck's next start, though as he listened to Brennan he had already made up his mind. The old rules were gone, Brennan was saying, and the new order had begun, with possibilities as vast as the country below them.

A dozen years earlier, before Secretariat had won the Triple Crown and begun an era in which horses were raced to be bred more than bred to be raced, there would have been little place for a Robert Brennan in the sport. Even now, he was the brashest of outsiders and regarded suspiciously throughout the industry. But in the racing world of 1985, he was trying to alter the game and he was succeeding. He was going after the Triple Crown, the most fundamental and seemingly inviolable pillar of the sport. Whether or not he would succeed in convincing Dennis Diaz, he had already proved that nothing in the game was sacred anymore.

◆   ◆   ◆

The fifth of nine children growing up in a five-room apartment in Newark, New Jersey, Brennan had gotten his first taste of the track as a teenager, riding the bus into New York on Saturdays for the races at Aqueduct, Belmont, or old Jamaica Park. As he watched the society types who filled the paddock to see their horses being saddled up for the Saturday stakes races, Brennan knew he wanted to be on the inside one day, collecting purse money instead of betting his last few dollars.

Brennan grew up revering his father, a small-time salesman who always provided for the family by selling neckties, turkeys, or whatever else he could buy cheaply in quantity. Brennan was convinced that his father, with a different education and connections, could have been a captain of industry anywhere, and Brennan resolved to live the unfulfilled scenario himself.

His entrepreneurial skills emerged early, as he became the local king of newspaper routes and selling candy out of shopping bags. While still in high school he got a job as an ad-taker for the *Newark News*, and by graduation he was managing the department. He then went to Seton Hall University, where he majored in accounting and was graduated in two years by attending classes night and day.

His accounting work gave him a taste of the stock market, and again he felt like the little boy looking in from the grandstand side of the paddock. He saw Wall Street controlled by nepotism and clubbiness, rather than rewarding hard work, and began to dream of working his way inside. In 1974, with money borrowed from friends, the thirty-one-year-old Brennan formed his own company, First Jersey Securities, starting with five brokers who sought customers to invest in what Brennan called "emerging companies," small unlisted low-price shares in companies that Brennan saw as having potential for the future. His critics would maintain that Brennan was running a boiler-room operation, getting unsophisticated customers to invest in highly speculative issues, often ones in which Brennan himself had already bought shares, thus inflating the price of his own holdings. Within five years, First Jersey had grown to thirty branches with 12,000 employees.

Brennan was still going to the races occasionally, and in March 1980 he bought a couple of horses at a sale of two-year-olds in training. Four months later, he was waiting for them to make their first starts when he went to Monmouth Park with a boyhood friend, Tony Palletiri, the part-owner of a 24–1 shot named Thanks to Tony who was running in the Monmouth Invitational Handicap. The colt pulled off an upset and Brennan found himself part of the winner's circle celebration. The charge, even as a hanger-on, was electric. Brennan couldn't wait to get in on the game himself.

That September, he took $1 million to the Keeneland fall sales and bought eighteen yearlings. The night the sales ended, he headed back to New Jersey for the debut of one of his two-year-olds, who was running at The Meadowlands. Brennan had hired one of the sport's few black trainers, a Cuban named Reynaldo Nobles, and Nobles told him that the filly probably would not run too well. But Brennan wanted to make a big bet on his first starter, and put $2,000 to win on the horse he had prophetically named Newkidontheblock. The filly got up in the final strides and Brennan won over $60,000.

He was off and running as an owner, and his own stable would begin to grow and include top stakes horses and expensive breeding stock. But he had another and more lucrative idea ahead. It came straight from Brennan's brokering experience:

Raise money to do what you want by selling lots of small pieces to lots of small people.

In 1981, Brennan announced an initial offering of three million units, at $1 per share, in his newly formed International Thoroughbred Breeders, Inc., a new stock offering through First Jersey. Within two months, that issue and two subsequent offerings of a million units each had sold out, and Brennan had enough of a bankroll to play the 1981 summer yearling sales.

"Leslie Combs, the old gentleman who owns Spendthrift Farm, introduced himself to me," Brennan recalls. " 'You did a bad thing, young man,' he tells me. 'You didn't check with us.' Well, I knew I was doing something right."

The kicker Brennan enjoys so much is that three years later, Spendthrift had gone public and was being traded on the American Stock Exchange. It is Brennan's favorite anecdote and captures the spirit of his approach to both racing and Wall Street. His first whiff of the market was just like his first view of the owners at Belmont Park, only more painful.

"Wall Street fifteen years ago was dominated by great-grandsons," Brennan says. "They all went to Harvard or Yale and the attitude was, 'Let's start drinking together at four o'-clock and, oh, if you see anyone on the horizon trying to break into our club, squash him.' "

Brennan blames his self-perceived role as an outsider for a decade of problems with the Securities and Exchange Commission, which pursued allegations of impropriety and fraud until Brennan signed a consent decree in 1984.

Amid these problems, First Jersey continued to expand, and Brennan was soon the country's best-known securities dealer. The star of seemingly incessant television ads in the New York and New Jersey area, Brennan became a familiar face. An

Robert Brennan

immaculately groomed man with a wiry build, neatly trimmed blond hair, a chipmunkish smile and a penchant for talking with his hands, Brennan made buying First Jersey securities sound like a patriotic duty. Summoning the spirit of the American Revolution and the frontier, he took subtle shots at the S.E.C. while praising unbounded free enterprise and urging the public to "come grow with us." (His horses race in the name of Due Process Stable, a reminder of the principle he felt was lacking in his dealings with the S.E.C.)

Further issues of I.T.B. shares gave Brennan the funds to invest heavily in blue-chip brood mares and stallion shares, though these racing and breeding interests seemed almost secondary to his holdings of I.T.B. stock. He claimed the original issue of $1 shares were worth $35 each by 1985, and Brennan remained the principal stockholder. He now controlled the company and had a racing stable and two breeding farms, but there was one other aspect of the game he was waiting to attack.

Garden State Park, for forty years part of the New Jersey circuit, had been shuttered since a 1977 electrical fire virtually leveled the grandstand. The track's operators had neither the funds nor the interest to rebuild it, and sold it to developers who had a shopping mall in mind. That project never got off the ground, and in 1982 the matter was placed under the authority of a circuit judge, who announced he would accept proposals and bids for the property. Brennan pounced. After receiving assurances from state legislators that Garden State would be treated favorably if reopened as a track, Brennan blew into the courtroom with a thoroughly researched proposal and a cashier's check. He walked out as the new owner, through I.T.B., of Garden State Park, at a final price of $15.5 million.

His purchase came at a time when small tracks on the Eastern seaboard were struggling to stay in business. Delaware Park had already slashed its dates, Atlantic City Race Course was begging for tax relief, and Maryland racing was on the verge of a reorganization that would shut two of the state's four tracks for good. Brennan's response was to forge ahead, confident that his salesmanship and enthusiasm could turn the situation around. A year after buying Garden State, he purchased the Philadelphia area's other thoroughbred plant, Keystone, for $33 million, to corner the local market. He began talking of a New Jersey–Delaware Valley circuit with all of the tracks, he hoped, someday owned by I.T.B.

Much of his confidence about reviving Garden State stemmed from his having convinced state legislators to give him the same sweet deal that the state was giving itself at The Meadowlands Race Track, a public facility that was part of the New Jersey Sports and Exposition Authority. Under that arrangement, the state took only one half of one percent of the mutuel handle, as opposed to the four percent taken at New York tracks.

Brennan used The Meadowlands as the model for his vision of a "Racetrack of the 21st Century," a glittering modernistic facility that could be adapted for the changes he envisioned in the sport, specifically the simulcasting of out-of-state races. Brennan's prevailing conviction was that the game could and should be opened up to new segments of the population, just as he had done with securities. The way to do it, he decided, was to put up a track that was as far as possible from the traditional notions that novices held about the game.

"I want to destroy the two myths about racing that I think have kept ninety percent of the public from ever attending," he said a few weeks before opening the track in April 1985. "First, that racing is an elite sport dominated by fourth-generation snobs who think fans are an intrusion. Second, that racing is a sport that attracts unemployed degenerates and creepy old men who have nothing better to do with their time."

He needed a gimmick to get Garden State on the racing map and into the national consciousness quickly, and for a track slated to open in the spring, Kentucky Derby preps were the way to go. Brennan thought the New York series of Triple

Crown preps—the Bay Shore, Gotham, and Wood Memorial —was vulnerable to competition, because these races offered relatively low purse money in the absence of any competing events in the Northeast. He also wanted a way to ensure that the winner of his first Derby prep would not then run off to the Wood. The simple solution was the bonus arrangement that now had succeeded beyond his highest hopes. Spend a Buck, having won Garden State's Cherry Hill Mile and Garden State Stakes, and then the Kentucky Derby, could earn a $2 million bonus if he ran in, and won, the Jersey Derby.

Dennis Diaz was hit from all sides in the two days between the Derby and his decision. First came the argument most compellingly put to him by a surprise visitor the morning after the Derby. A Cadillac pulled up outside the barn where Spend a Buck was stabled, and the driver got out and asked for Diaz.

"There's someone to see you," the driver told Diaz. "Mr. Jimmy Jones, who used to be with Calumet Farm, would like to congratulate you."

Diaz was tickled, and hurried over to the passenger side of the car, where the legendary trainer was waiting to talk to him. He told Jones how honored he was to meet him, how flattered he was that Jones had sought him out. He meant it.

The two men chatted for about five minutes. Diaz did not know that Jones had been encouraged to talk to him by Chick Lang, the general manager of Pimlico, home of the Preakness, and by at least one official of the *Daily Racing Form*. Jones was speaking sincerely, though, when he told Diaz how thrilling it had been to be associated with Triple Crown winners, Whirlaway in 1941 and Citation in 1948, and encouraged the young owner to go for the glory at Pimlico and not the gold at Garden State. Diaz thanked him for his advice, told him he had not made a decision, and was still shaking his head in disbelief that Jimmy Jones had come to congratulate him as the Cadillac pulled away.

Later that morning Chick Lang himself dropped by. Lang

had spent the week dreading a Derby victory by Spend a Buck, the only horse who would not automatically be coming to Baltimore. Lang had cornered Diaz the night before in the Churchill Downs press box after the race, where the owner had gone to grant interviews and watch a replay of Spend a Buck's victory. Lang acted as if he expected the colt to come to Baltimore, and told Diaz of the fun he could expect to have as the owner of the Derby winner. He told Diaz that Spend a Buck would be housed in the same stall Secretariat, Seattle Slew, Affirmed, and Spectacular Bid had been given, the one reserved for the Derby winner, the only colt with a chance to win the Crown.

The next morning, Lang was a bit more desperate. Diaz had yet to announce he was going to the Preakness and all Louisville was talking about the very real possibility that he would not. Now Lang told Diaz that the $2.6 million awaiting him at Garden State was really only $1 million, after taxes and commissions to the jockey and trainer. Diaz, who had brokered enough real estate and insurance deals to retire a wealthy man at thirty-eight, did not appreciate the lecture.

"The guy was talking to me like I was an idiot," he would say later.

Another point Lang stressed was the value of recent Preakness winners. He showed Diaz an advertisement Pimlico had been running in trade publications that spring, a full page divided into nine squares with a photograph of a recent Preakness winner in each box, and the horse's syndication price superimposed in white lettering.

Lang's point to Diaz was that those syndication prices, ranging from $3 million to $22 million, were more than Brennan was giving away.

The ad struck a sour note with Diaz, who was trying to sort out the issues of money and tradition.

"Nowhere on that page did I see a word about tradition," Diaz said. "People keep saying I have to honor tradition and you owe this to racing and you owe that to racing. But then in the same breath I hear that the point of the tradition is to make more money. Are we talking about money or tradition? People say to do the right thing by your horse, and then you realize they're saying make the most money."

The lines indeed were blurred. Had Seth Hancock and Woody Stephens done the right thing by their horse in withdrawing Devil's Bag before the previous year's Derby and retiring him? Had the Rosen heirs done the right thing by their horse in announcing six months before the Triple Crown that Chief's Crown would be retired at the end of his three-year-old season? Both of those colts had been syndicated for a fortune. Was that now the real mark of success? If so, Diaz reasoned, he should base his decision on which race would make his colt more valuable.

For that advice, he could not turn to Robert Brennan, Chick Lang, or Jimmy Jones, and ultimately it was not one of their voices that swayed him. The push he needed came not from a trainer or a track operator, but from a breeder, a stallion maker: the man who had shown interest in his colt as a stallion even before the Kentucky Derby victory, William S. Farish III.

◆　　◆　　◆

Farish, frequently described as one of the nicest rich guys you could want to meet, looks and acts as if he has always been a Kentucky breeder, but he came to the Bluegrass by way of Texas. He is the president of his own Houston-based Fluorex Corporation, which is involved in international mining and exploration. His grandfather, William Farish I, was a founder of Humble Oil and raced horses in the name of Lazy F Ranch, and his aunt, Martha Farish Gerry, campaigned three-time Horse of the Year Forego. However, Farish himself was initially more interested in the polo ponies he bred at his 1,200-acre ranch, Houisache, fifty miles north of Houston.

Through polo, Farish became friends with various thoroughbred owners and breeders, and in the mid-1960s began to race a few horses in partnership with his father-in-law, Bayard Sharp, owner of Sharp Farm near Middletown, Delaware.

Farish's first major success was something of a fluke. In 1972, he entered a mediocre colt named Bee Bee Bee in the Preakness, where he was 19–1 in a race that Penny Chenery's Riva Ridge was heavily favored to win. The Pimlico track came up very sloppy on a rainy Preakness Day, though, and Farish's mudlark splashed to an upset victory. Bee Bee Bee never won another important race after the Preakness, but Farish had enjoyed being so close to the top of the sport and increased his involvement in the coming years.

Amid the stallion boom of the late 1970s, Farish formed partnerships with several other wealthy owners and began buying yearlings and breeding stock. He emerged in the Sangster-and-Sheik years as one of the few Americans still in the bidding when it came down to those two, and also was selling a few of those pricey yearlings. Farish began to be recognized as a leadership figure, and was named a steward of The Jockey Club, a largely honorary position but one that reflected his ascendance in the game. When Queen Elizabeth II made a royal visit to the Kentucky horse farms in 1984, the Farishes were her hosts.

As Farish had become more involved in the sport, he wanted a substantial Kentucky spread of his own, and in 1980 purchased a farm called Lane's End in Versailles, just west of Lexington. He wanted to build it slowly and carefully, and rather than plunge ahead amid the glut of available stallions, waited four years before bringing any to Lane's End. His first choices were extremely solid and tinged with a high tone. In 1984, he announced that Lane's End would stand two stallions for Paul Mellon's Rokeby Stables: Fit to Fight, a widely admired son of Cutlass, and Hero's Honor, a son of Northern Dancer and a blueblooded Rokeby female family. A third arrival was Dixieland Band, a Northern Dancer colt his father-in-law, Bayard Sharp, had raced.

He would not go after another stallion until Spend a Buck. Farish went to Garden State to see him race in the Garden State Stakes, and the colt's runaway victory sent Farish home full of enthusiasm.

"The thing that attracted me most about Spend a Buck was his brilliant speed and his outstanding conformation," he said. "He is just a beautiful horse, and he had that tremendous speed and the ability to carry it any distance."

Farish characterized Spend a Buck's pedigree as only "very acceptable," noting that his sire, Buckaroo, was a promising young son of Buckpasser. Spend a Buck thus represented yet another branch of the Phalaris line, which went through Pharamond II and Menow to Tom Fool, Buckpasser's sire and Spend a Buck's great grandsire.

Farish visited the colt and his owners at the Churchill Downs stables several times during Derby Week, and told them of his interest in standing the colt. Diaz said he did not want to make any deals before the Derby, but both sides went into the race figuring they would be partners eventually, regardless of the outcome.

Before Spend a Buck won the Derby Farish had not given much thought to where the colt might run next. "At that time of year the Derby is the only thing anyone is thinking about, and nothing beyond that has much importance until it's over," he said. Diaz himself had planned to skip the Preakness and go for the $1-million bonus in the Jersey Derby if his colt did not win the Kentucky Derby. Spend a Buck's victory left him with a tougher decision.

Diaz expected that Farish, like the sport's other traditionalists and old-liners, would tell him to run in the Preakness. Surely, Farish would want a Triple Crown winner at his farm. Spendthrift, with Seattle Slew and Affirmed, and Claiborne, with Secretariat, had that market cornered. Diaz also suspected that Farish might have a sentimental attachment to the Preakness, because of Bee Bee Bee's triumph there thirteen years earlier. Diaz was ready to consider passing up the chance for $2 million if his new friend and imminent partner strongly advised it.

"There's no question," Farish told him. "Run him in the Jersey Derby."

Diaz would later say, a few days after Bob Brennan led him into the press conference at Garden State's glitzy Phoenix dining terrace to make it formal, that "Will Farish is the one that convinced me. I figured if a man that important in the sport, with that much knowledge and influence and tradition behind him, felt that way, it was good enough for me."

For Farish, the decision had been straightforward, the logical business choice of a stallion maker.

"If Dennis didn't feel strongly about running in the Preakness, and he didn't, I thought this was the way to go," he said. "Other horses had won the Triple Crown, and there was no guarantee that Spend a Buck would. But Dennis had a chance to do something different."

Six months later, Farish and Diaz would say that the dominant factor in skipping the Preakness—outweighing career earnings, bonuses, prestige, tradition, loyalty to Bob Brennan and his track, and syndication values—was the welfare of the colt himself. They both pointed to the fact that Spend a Buck had undergone surgery the previous November to remove a bone chip in his right knee, and stressed that waiting to run in the Jersey Derby would give the colt an extra nine days of rest.

"Our horse was starting to show some signs of wear and tear," Diaz claimed. "We think we could have won the Preakness, but then we would have been locked into going in the Belmont, and that would have been too much to ask. If he had an easy race in the Jersey Derby, we were still hoping to go to the Belmont."

Farish echoed Diaz's contention. "For a horse coming off

a hard race in the Kentucky Derby, the Jersey Derby made a great deal more sense," he said. "I've got tremendous respect for the Triple Crown, but when you're campaigning your horse you have to consider what's best for him."

Diaz and Farish undoubtedly were sincere in their concern for the colt's welfare, but this belated explanation had a hollow ring. Many Derby winners had been raced much harder than Spend a Buck and had not needed an extra nine days to get over the race and ready for the Preakness. Those horses worthy of winning the Triple Crown had managed to get through the series in five weeks. The argument also seems shaky considering Diaz's contention that he was hoping to run the colt in the Belmont Stakes only twelve days after the Jersey Derby. That would have subjected the colt to just as hard and perhaps a slightly harder schedule than the Triple Crown.

A likelier explanation is that Farish believed winning the Triple Crown was a shaky proposition for Spend a Buck. The two previous living Kentucky Derby winners, Gato Del Sol in 1982 and Sunny's Halo in 1983, had failed to win another Triple Crown race and had rocky careers thereafter. Both were syndicated for under $8 million.

Spend a Buck, with only an "acceptable" pedigree, could have suffered a similar fate with a Preakness defeat. But a victory in the Jersey Derby alone would make the colt worth at least $10 million as a stallion prospect and give him credentials that would look good on paper. A victory in that one race would ensure that when he retired he would be the leading earner among stallions with a career bankroll of at least $3.9 million.

Owners and breeders had always shopped for soft spots for their horses, since the name of the game is winning races. Diaz's decision to skip the Preakness, though, was unique. He was passing up what had been the sport's greatest prize for what had become the sport's dominant goal: He would not try for the Triple Crown because another route offered better odds of increasing Spend a Buck's worth in the breeding shed.

◆   ◆   ◆

Considering the way that the Preakness unfolded in Spend a Buck's absence, he would have had a tough time winning the race. Eternal Prince broke the way he should have in the Derby, when he was expected to duel with Spend a Buck instead of letting his rival get out to an easy lead. Eternal Prince set a blistering pace, then Chief's Crown, the even-money favorite despite his third-place finish in the Derby, uncorked a powerful middle move and caught Eternal Prince on the far turn. Chief's Crown looked home free in midstretch, but a horse in yellow and blue silks was suddenly flying at him from far back. It was Tank's Prospect, the Lukas trainee who had been second to Chief's Crown in the Breeders' Cup Juvenile the previous November, the race in which Spend a Buck had been third. These two were going to finish one-two again, and at the wire, the photo-finish confirmed that this time the order would be reversed. Tank's Prospect had gotten up by a head in 1:53 ⅖, breaking the official track record by one-fifth of a second and tying Secretariat's unofficial time in the 1973 Preakness.

Both colts were scheduled to make their next starts in the Belmont, along with all the other top Derby and Preakness finishers. No trainer was eager to run his colt back on nine days' rest or to go up against Spend a Buck on his home court, the speed-favoring Garden State track over which he had won the Cherry Hill by 10 ½ lengths and the Garden State by 9 ½. The Jersey Derby was beginning to look like a virtual walkover for Spend a Buck, with a bunch of third-raters fighting it out for the rich second- and third-place prizes. In addition to the $2 million bonus that only Spend a Buck could win, the race purse was $1 million, with $600,000 going to the winner, $200,000 to the runner-up, and $120,000 for third.

That kind of money was attractive to stables deep enough to spare a second-stringer, and it drew horses from the two strongest benches around, those of Woody Stephens and D. Wayne Lukas. They brought very different horses and for different reasons. Lukas entered Huddle Up, a sprinter who figured to want no part of 1 ¼ miles but might well give Spend a Buck some early trouble, setting it up for some other horse to run down the Derby winner in the stretch. Lukas clearly was out to beat Spend a Buck, which would enhance Tank's Prospect's Preakness victory and chances to emerge as the top three-year-old by year's end. As for Stephens, the Jersey Derby looked like a good spot to get second or third money with Creme Fraiche, a durable gelding he considered second-best in his own stable to Kentucky Derby runner-up Stephan's Odyssey, who was awaiting the Belmont. Creme Fraiche had won the Derby Trial a week before the Derby but Stephens thought him not good enough for the main event and he had not raced since.

Jersey Derby Day at Garden State was everything Robert Brennan could have hoped for when he began drawing up the bonus scheme almost a year earlier. A season-high crowd of more than 35,000 streamed in, many of them the newcomers Brennan was seeking to attract. People who had obviously never been to the races were wandering around gawking at the futuristic betting palace and snapping up Spend a Buck souvenirs. Brennan also had succeeded in drawing the traveling circle of racing society that turns up at only the most important races, and the sporting press from around the country. If the Breeders' Cup had joined the Triple Crown races the previous fall as one of the premier events of the season, the Jersey Derby seemed to have reached that level too.

Spend a Buck was sent off as the 1–20 favorite, the lowest price possible and a reflection of the amateurish composition of the crowd. No serious gambler takes such short odds, and obviously there were thousands of bettors who did not understand that they would make only a dime for each $2 they wagered if Spend a Buck won. They all just wanted to bet on the famous horse.

Spend a Buck stumbled at the start, banging into the gate and cutting his tongue, but recovered quickly and went to the front. Huddle Up was at him almost immediately. The two were head-and-head into the first turn and through a fast first six furlongs in 1:09. Creme Fraiche had gotten through on the rail and was gaining quickly, and an upset seemed on its way. Spend a Buck had finally disposed of Huddle Up, but he had to be exhausted from the duel.

Rounding the stretch turn, Creme Fraiche drew abreast on the inside, got a head in front, and looked ready to draw off as he pleased. Spend a Buck was weaving a bit and drifting wide, usually a clear sign of fatigue. But just as he seemed beaten, he started to fight back, getting his nose in front once more and refusing to give an inch. The two of them raced down the stretch together, and then a new threat, El Basco, came loping up on the outside and looked as if he would get them both. The three went for the wire together, but Spend a Buck's determination had gotten him home a neck in front of Creme Fraiche, with El Basco just a head back in third.

The winning margin had been tiny, the time of 2:02 ⅕ mediocre at best, but Spend a Buck had shown remarkable courage and resolution, the intangibles that say a horse is truly extraordinary and has an added dimension. It confirmed what Farish had sensed about the colt.

In the winner's circle, Diaz was presented with a huge mock check for $2.6 million in lieu of the real one Brennan would hand over the next day, and the giver looked as happy as the receiver. It was one of the longest winner's circle ceremonies ever, with even the governor making a speech. Spend a Buck had run a wonderful race, Diaz had made his $2.6 million, Brennan had put on a better show than the Preakness while luring a horse out of the Triple Crown and into his new racetrack, and Will Farish was going to be standing the highest earner ever to go to stud.

◆   ◆   ◆

Spend a Buck's victory over Creme Fraiche, and the wisdom of running him in the Jersey Derby, looked even better twelve days later after the Belmont Stakes. There was a blistering early pace that almost surely would have prevented the front-running Spend a Buck from winning at 1 ½ miles. At the wire, the race was an intramural contest that had to end in a record fourth straight victory for Woody Stephens. Creme Fraiche and Stephan's Odyssey were dueling to the finish, five lengths in front of a sapped Chief's Crown, and at the wire Stephens's gelding beat his colt. He would have preferred it the other way around, since a Belmont victory would have boosted Stephan's Odyssey's value as a stallion prospect—a career not open to Creme Fraiche—but the trainer had so wanted to win the race a fourth time that he gave himself twice as many chances. Lukas, meanwhile, suffered yet another casualty as Tank's Prospect sustained a career-ending ankle injury.

It was tough to knock Spend a Buck's Jersey Derby score now, and after a Triple Crown series he had largely skipped he had emerged as clearly the best three-year-old in the country.

He was getting a needed rest now, and the plan was to bring him back in the Haskell Handicap at Monmouth July 27. The race seemed to fit perfectly as a prep for the Travers, and it also was part of yet another bonus series, one that had been conceived solely to attract him to other New Jersey tracks. Called the New Jersey Challenge, it offered a $1 million prize if Spend a Buck could sweep the Jersey Derby, which he had already done, the Haskell and then the Pegasus at The Meadowlands in September. Diaz and Farish liked the idea since it raised the possibility that by year's end Spend a Buck could exceed even John Henry's career earnings of over $6.5 million, and not only be the richest horse ever to go to stud but the richest horse ever, period.

The colt's stud plans were made official a month after the Jersey Derby when Diaz announced that Farish had purchased half of Spend a Buck and was in the process of syndicating him.

The price was never officially announced but Farish confirmed privately that the colt's total paper value was between $12 and $20 million, or $300,000 to $500,000 per share. That was only about half what Conquistador Cielo and Devil's Bag had fetched, and neither one of them had won the Kentucky Derby or earned almost $4 million, but Spend a Buck's pedigree was uninspiring. Farish called it a realistic price and predicted that it would one day be seen as a bargain.

"Buckaroo is a stallion we'll be hearing a lot more about," Farish predicted. "The most interesting thing about Spend a Buck is his heart."

Buckaroo, incidentally, was no longer standing at Greentree. Six months before Spend a Buck's Derby victory he had been purchased privately by a syndicate of Florida breeders which included Dennis Diaz and Steve and Gary Wolfson, whose father, Louis, had raced Affirmed. The younger Wolfsons, devoted pedigree students, had shared Farish's enthusiasm for the Buckpasser line and were impressed with Spend a Buck even as a two-year-old. Buckaroo now stands at their Happy Valley Farm in Ocala, Florida, where his stud fee has risen from the $5,000 Greentree was charging to $25,000.

The Haskell drew a field of seven, led by Spend a Buck and Creme Fraiche, who had followed up his Belmont score with an easy victory in Chicago. Spend a Buck was the heavy favorite, but two hours before post time, Farish was trying to convince Diaz and his trainer, Cam Gambolati, not to start the colt.

A combination of factors suggested he might not run well. He had missed a day of training a week earlier after wrenching an ankle in a morning workout. The conditions of the Haskell called for him to carry 127 pounds, one more than Creme

Fraiche and up to 13 more than the others in the field. Finally, the track had come up a bit muddy and was favoring come-from-behind horses instead of front-runners.

"Will wanted to scratch the horse and Cam was fifty–fifty," Diaz said. "It came down to me. I came within thirty seconds of scratching him. It was a hard decision. The people at Monmouth had been so good to us. I just hoped the horse would be fit enough to win. I was wrong."

Spend a Buck made the lead easily, and opened a clear advantage nearing the far turn. When he straightened away in the stretch, though, he was clearly tired. Creme Fraiche was not firing either, but a longshot named Skip Trial, who had been ninth in the Preakness and then won the minor Ohio Derby on a sloppy track, was gaining quickly. Spend a Buck was passed in midstretch and settled for second, 3 ¾ lengths behind Skip Trial.

After the race, Spend a Buck bled a little bit from his left nostril, which revived a topic his handlers had tried to downplay, and now would compromise his career and reputation.

Almost all horses, and people, experience some degree of hemorrhaging from the lungs under the exertion of racing, usually a tiny amount of blood that can be found in the windpipe. With some horses, for reasons that continue to baffle equine science, the problem is so severe that a horse will bleed heavily from the nostrils after a race.

The cure for the condition once had been extended rest and, if the problem failed to clear up, retirement, because a horse who bleeds three times is barred from further racing. But several medications had been found to control the problem, and they were legalized with the advent of year-round racing and permissive medication programs in the 1970s. The chief medication used to control bleeding was furosemide, a diuretic.

The medication has proved troublesome, however, for two reasons. Before more sophisticated drug-testing programs were instituted, furosemide could be used to mask other drugs. Additionally, experience proved that furosemide not only controlled hemorrhaging but also improved overall performance. Horses who chronically tired seemed to get a second wind, especially the first time they were treated with the drug.

Kentucky and Maryland both permit the use of furosemide by horses who are certified as bleeders. Sunny's Halo had won the 1983 Derby and Gate Dancer the 1984 Preakness with the aid of it. This revelation had tarnished their victories in the eyes of purists, particularly in New York, the only major racing state that does not permit the drug. When both of these horses failed to win a race in New York without furosemide, their critics and those of medication programs claimed victory for the purity and importance of New York racing. Wild Again had won the inaugural Breeders' Cup Classic with at least three medications that would have been banned in New York.

Spend a Buck had bled very slightly after winning the Garden State Stakes in April, his final prep for the Kentucky Derby, and his handlers had taken advantage of Kentucky's wide-open medication policy by giving him what they called a "small" and "purely precautionary" dosage of furosemide for the Derby. Gambolati said the dosage was half or less than what confirmed bleeders are given, and said he thought it had made no difference at all in the outcome of the race. The colt did not bleed after the Derby and was given no furosemide before the Jersey Derby, which his handlers cited as proof that the medication had made no difference.

Now, though, there was a case to be made that it had. What if Spend a Buck had enjoyed the improvement shown by so many first-time furosemide users? After all, in his two subsequent starts without it he had just held on at odds of 1–20 over a track where his average winning margin had been ten lengths, and then he had been beaten in the Haskell.

The theory that the colt needed the medication got a big boost when Diaz announced three days after the Haskell that Spend a Buck now would skip the Travers, where he would

not be able to get furosemide. Instead, he would run at Monmouth again, against older horses in the Monmouth Handicap
on the same day as the Travers, and he would race with furosemide.

Spend a Buck ran a race that otherwise would have earned
him unmitigated praise in the Monmouth Handicap, setting a
fast pace, and then battling courageously to hold off the good
older horse Carr de Naskra by a nose while setting a new track
record of 1:46 $\frac{4}{5}$ for 1⅛ miles. But now his absence from the
Travers and his racing with furosemide clouded the whole issue
of his quality.

In his absence, a revivified Chief's Crown, looking better
than ever after a summer freshening, was an easy and impressive winner of the Travers, and four weeks later won the Marlboro Cup, beating the best field of older horses that had been
assembled all year. Spend a Buck, meanwhile, had wrenched an
ankle in a workout, muddying a future that already was in
jeopardy. Publicly, his owners were saying he still might race
again in New York without furosemide in the Breeders' Cup,
but privately Farish was urging the colt's retirement. On the
morning of the Marlboro, Diaz made it official, and a week later
Spend a Buck was vanned to Farish's farm.

He had ended his career with a record-setting victory but
was going home under a cloud. A few months earlier he had
looked like a shoo-in for Horse of the Year, but now it appeared
that Chief's Crown had wrested both the three-year-old championship and that title away from him. Spend a Buck was
hardly being slighted for a lack of success in the Triple Crown
series since he was now being rated behind a colt who had lost
all three of those races, each time as the favorite.

The Breeders' Cup Classic on November 2 figured to offer
a final verdict. Chief's Crown was the heavy favorite at 9–5 in
a field of eight, and a victory would make him a virtually
unanimous Horse of the Year choice. At the top of the stretch,
he was making his usual middle move and surging to the lead.

An instant later, though, he was being passed, and he would end up finishing fourth, beaten almost ten lengths in the final and worst race of his career.

The race was between the four-year-old Gate Dancer, who had been second in several major races during the fall, and Proud Truth, a forgotten horse on the comeback trail. Proud Truth, after finishing fifth in the Derby, had won the Peter Pan Stakes, a major Belmont Stakes prep, but then was found to have a small saucer fracture in his left front leg. He underwent surgery and was given the summer off to rest and recuperate, then came back with two straight victories, but was a 7–1 longshot in the Classic. Now, though, he was surging on the outside, and nearing the wire got a neck in front of Gate Dancer and kept it there.

Proud Truth's victory in the $3 million race was wonderful vindication for trainer John Veitch, who had been second so often, first with Alydar behind Affirmed, then with Dr. Carter behind Devil's Bag, Time for a Change and Swale. It was the richest victory ever for eighty-eight-year-old owner John Galbreath, who now had a Breeders' Cup to go along with his two Kentucky Derby trophies, an Epsom Derby cup, and his World Series ring.

Another big winner was Spend a Buck, who was suddenly back in the running for everything. How could Proud Truth be Horse of the Year off one major victory? How could it be Chief's Crown, the most consistent campaigner of the bunch but now a loser in all three Triple Crown races and the Breeders' Cup as well?

It was an ironic outcome for the Breeders' Cup, which had been designed to provide a definitive year-end championship. Instead, it had shifted attention, and championship titles by default, to a colt who had been held out of the race.

A few days later, Lane's End began buying huge breeding advertisements for Spend a Buck in the *Daily Racing Form* and the trade weeklies. The odd thing about them was that there was no mention of Garden State Park or the Jersey Derby. Instead, there were numerous photographs of Spend a Buck winning the Kentucky Derby, and a blow-up of the chart of that race. And to help the Eclipse Award voters with their selections was the statement that Spend a Buck had beaten Proud Truth, Chief's Crown, and Creme Fraiche in every one of their meetings that year. His campaign had come full circle. Instead of being the colt whose owners had rejected the Triple Crown, he was now being portrayed as the classic winner, draped in roses after winning America's race.

It was hard not to think of Conquistador Cielo, who had backed into the Horse of the Year title after being retired when a chaotic fall season failed to yield a superior candidate. Both colts had enjoyed bursts of success, winning four races in eight weeks and being syndicated as stallions. That was enough to make the breeders gamble that the brilliance was in the genes and would come out in their sons and daughters, enough to certify them as successes in the new world of racing.

◆   ◆   ◆

In August 1985, an unusual auction was held at Saratoga. The merchandise was not horseflesh at a yearling sale but an old barn on the Saratoga backstretch. The wooden structure, part of the original track that had opened in 1863, was going to be demolished until the local historic preservation society stepped in. They could not get it designated a historic landmark, but convinced track officials to let them raffle it off for charity in the hope that the winning bidder would reconstruct and preserve it somewhere.

Unbeknownst to each other, the two bidders were Penny Chenery and Bob Brennan, bookends on the dozen years in which the breeding industry had transformed the sport.

When Penny Chenery had decided to syndicate Secretariat at $190,000 a share, she ushered in an era of stallion making in which Devil's Bag and Shareef Dancer would fetch $1 million a share off just five career races. Secretariat's fabulous sweep of the Triple Crown, the first in twenty-five years, set new standards of excellence that influenced the way his two Triple Crown successors, Seattle Slew and Affirmed, were campaigned and managed. Both of those colts were fully tested, brought back to race as four-year-olds by faithful and daring owners who wanted them to prove their quality.

But Secretariat's syndication, his effect on the yearling market, and the gap between expectation and performance, also triggered another way of campaigning and managing race horses. With the stamp of success shifted from the race track to the numbers on the syndication contract, the best horses of the 1980s were accomplishing less and being given far fewer chances to prove their true quality or win admirers.

Now Bob Brennan, who had moved horse and racetrack ownership from the old guard to the public company, had challenged and, at least for a year, untracked the Triple Crown, the institution that had certified Secretariat.

The bidding for the Saratoga barn went up in $1,000 and $5,000 increments. Bob Brennan's representative signalled a bid of $30,000 and Penny Chenery did not answer. Only later, when she found out against whom she had been bidding, did she have any regrets.

"If I had known it was him," she was overheard to say, "I would have kept going."

Bob Brennan pleased the local historic preservationists by announcing that he would have the barn lovingly disassembled and then reconstructed. He displeased another group of preservationists when he added that the barn would be reconstructed at Garden State Park: He thought it would make a nice place to house the Kentucky Derby winner in future years when he came to run in the Jersey Derby instead of the Preakness.